UNCONSTITUTIONAL REGIMES AND THE VALIDITY OF SOVEREIGN DEBT

Unconstitutional Regimes and the Validity of Sovereign Debt

A Legal Perspective

SABINE MICHALOWSKI
University of Essex, UK

Routledge
Taylor & Francis Group

LONDON AND NEW YORK

First published 2007 by Ashgate Publishing

2 Park Square, Milton Park, Abingdon, Oxon OX14 4RN
711 Third Avenue, New York, NY 10017, USA

Routledge is an imprint of the Taylor & Francis Group, an informa business

First issued in paperback 2016

British Library Cataloguing in Publication Data
Michalowski, Sabine
  Unconstitutional regimes and the validity of sovereign debt
  : a legal perspective
  1. Debts, External - Law and legislation - Argentina
  2. Finance, Public - Argentina 3. Jus cogens (International
  law) 4. Repudiation 5. Default (Finance) - Argentina
  6. Argentina - Politics and government - 1955- 7. Argentina
  - Economic policy 8. Argentina - Economic conditions -
  1983-
  I. Title
  343.8'203

Library of Congress Cataloging-in-Publication Data
Michalowski, Sabine.
  Unconstitutional regimes and the validity of sovereign debt : a legal perspective /
by Sabine Michalowski.
     p. cm.
  Includes bibliographical references and index.
  ISBN 978-0-7546-4793-5
  1. Debts, Public -- Law and legislation. 2. Debts, External--Law and legislation. 3.
Debts, Public--Law and legislation--Argentina. 4. Debts, External--Law and
legislation--Argentina. 5. Debt--Argentina--History. 6. Jus cogens (International
law) 7. Debt relief. 8. Debtor and creditor. I. Title.

  K4450.M53 2007
  343'.037--dc22

                                                                          2006100191

ISBN 978-0-7546-4793-5 (hbk)
ISBN 978-1-138-26456-4 (pbk)

Contents

Acknowledgements

First of all, I would like to thank Carlos Juliá, whose book *La Memoria de la Deuda* inspired me to undertake legal research on the issue of Argentina's sovereign debt, and who supported me throughout the writing of the book as a colleague and friend. I would also like to thank Juan Pablo Bohoslavsky, with whom I had many stimulating conversations about various aspects of this book and who provided me with insight into Argentinian law and legal reality. I would further like to express special gratitude to my former colleague Janet Dine for encouraging me to write a chapter on the topic which later formed the basis of this book and for her valuable comments on various chapters of this book. Further thanks go to Andreas Fischer-Lescano, Karen Hulme, Agasha Mugasha and Michael Hantke for their thoughtful comments on draft chapters, Sheldon Leader, Peter Stone and Alejandro Teitelbaum for interesting conversations about some of the relevant issues, and Salvador Bergel, Miguel Angel Espeche Gil, Liliana Costante, Antje Queck, Birgit Friedl and, in particular, Mario Cafiero who provided me with a lot of partly unpublished material. Of course, the opinions expressed and errors made are all mine.

This book required extensive research in Argentina and would not have been possible without the funding received under the AHRC research leave scheme, the funding received by the Research Promotion Fund of the University of Essex, and the support of my colleagues in the Department of Law at the University of Essex. In particular, I would like to thank Sally Painter who encouraged me to apply for this funding and provided valuable assistance throughout the application process.

List of Cases

European cases

German cases

Inter-American cases

International cases

US cases:

Chapter One

Introduction[1]

In the developed world, it is easy to ignore the problem of the sovereign debt of developing countries, or to take no more than a general political interest in the issue when it is portrayed by the media at special occasions, such as the discussions of debt forgiveness in the context of G8 summits.[2] In a debtor country such as Argentina, on the other hand, that is only slowly recovering from a severe economic and financial crisis at the peak of which it defaulted on its debt servicing obligations, one is confronted on a daily basis with the fundamental significance of the problem of sovereign indebtedness and its far-reaching consequences for the social, economic and financial situation and policies.

The debt problem of developing countries touches on many fundamental issues such as concepts of justice; the tension between human rights protection and financial interests; and the relationship between the Developing World and the industrialized North. It is therefore hardly surprising that debt repayment has sparked a highly emotive political and moral debate.[3] From a moral perspective, it could be asked whether it can be justified that a country dedicates resources to the repayment of foreign debts while large parts of the population live below the poverty line and cannot even the fulfil their basic needs, such as food, shelter, health care etc. The moral arguments against debt repayment become even more compelling when taking into account the claim that the international creditors are partly responsible for the debt crisis. In recent years, humanitarian claims for debt relief because of the dramatic adverse impact of debt repayment on the social and economic situation of poor countries gained more and more momentum.[4] From a more political perspective,[5] it is often argued that the debt is unfair; odious; and that, instead of the Developing World being indebted to the North, it is the other way round, as the North owes the Developing World an ecological debt.[6]

---

1   This introduction is partly based on Michalowski (2006), at 303–306.
2   See, for example, the Gleneagles Communiqué issued by the G8 leaders on 8 July 2005 on debt relief for qualifying poor countries, www.g8.gov.uk/servlet/Front?pagename=O penMarket/Xcelerate/ShowPage&c=Page&cid=1119518698846.
3   See, for example, Iguíñiz Echeverría (2001).
4   See, for example, Mitchell (2004). This is, however, often rejected, either because it is argued that the Developing World does not owe any debt, see, for example, Adams (1991), at 194, and/or because the current debt relief plans shift the burden away from the lenders themselves onto the tax payers in the creditor countries, see Adams (1991), at 193; see also Toussaint (2001), at 220–224; Figueredo (2000).
5   See, for example, Juliá (2002), at 215 and 236; Steffan (2001), at 125–128.
6   See, for example, Martínez-Alier (2001); Simms (2006).

Reference to legal principles and concepts is often made in order to support these moral and political claims. From a legal perspective, the Developing World debt is challenged based on principles of international law, as well as those of the domestic law of debtor nations. In this respect, it has been argued that many of the loan agreements are not valid, as they were often entered into by undemocratic regimes and were not used for the benefit of the people of the debtor nations;[7] that the interest rates are usurious;[8] and that the creditors are at least partly responsible for the debt crisis.[9] It was further suggested that conditionalities imposed on debtor nations as a prerequisite of refinancing loans that are needed to avoid defaulting on debt repayment, in particular the requirement to implement structural adjustment programmes (SAPs), adversely affect the protection of social rights in debtor countries, and moreover undermine state sovereignty.[10] However, references to the law largely consist of broad statements, mixed with strong expressions of moral and political convictions of what the law should be, and it often seems as if the law is primarily regarded as a tool that might help to achieve, and give more credence to, political and moral claims.

The international creditors, on the other hand, present the problem primarily from a formalistic legal perspective, when arguing, based on legal concepts such as the fulfilment of contractual obligations, that debts need to be repaid. Indeed, in the specific context of Argentina, the creditors adopt a seemingly objective legalistic attitude when claiming that the debts are contractual obligations that need to be honoured, regardless of the country's economic and social situation. As James Wolfensohn explained in an interview when he was President of the World Bank: 'everyone wants to put money into social purposes and no one more than the (World) Bank, but there needs to be a balance in terms of some responsibilities and obligations which have been undertaken'.[11]

It thus seems as if the legal debate of the problem of debt repayment is characterized, on the one hand, by the allegedly value neutral legalistic approach adopted by the creditors, and, on the other hand, by a moralistic and political approach to the interpretation and application of legal principles. The reality and the ideological and political visions of anti-debt campaigners, on one side, and of creditors trying to get the developing world to repay its debt, on the other, are so far removed from each other that the arguments raised on each side hardly connect. However, in order for the law to add another dimension to the anti-debt-repayment debate, and to provide a tool for rebutting the legal claims of the creditors on legal grounds, a consistent legal framework that favours the arguments against debt repayment over those advanced by the creditors of sovereign debts needs to be developed. This requires to analyse the reasons for non-payment in terms that interact with the world of the creditors, and to phrase the legal challenges in a way that makes it possible to raise them in

---

7   For a discussion see Chapter Three.
8   See, for example, Espeche Gil (2004).
9   See, for example, Lichtenstein (1985); Valdés (1989).
10   For an extensive analysis of SAPs and their consequences see, for example, Woodward (1992); Cheru (1999).
11   23 April 2004, www.businessday.co.za.

court proceedings. Only in this way can the creditors' reference to clear-cut legal rights be reassessed in the light of the legal objections raised by the opponents of debt repayment. And only in this way can a conclusion be drawn as to whether the law really supports the creditors' claims as unconditionally as they want to make us believe, or whether the legal validity of their claims can be challenged successfully.

This is not to suggest that the moral arguments against debt repayment, and the efforts made by anti-debt campaigners to translate them into legal challenges on the basis of which debt repayment was and is questioned, lack significance. On the contrary, it is submitted that the work that has been carried out in this respect is extremely important, as it raises awareness of the underlying issues; demands that the law be in line with concepts of justice; demonstrates which interests it currently favours and serves; and provides useful ideas for further legal research. Indeed, while this book will focus on an academic legal analysis of some of the issues surrounding the debt crisis, the significance of political and moral considerations in the context of debt repayment cannot be ignored. As Noam Chomsky rightly claimed, while it is clear that the developing world debt exists, it is primarily an ideological question who is responsible for this debt and who owes it.[12]

This book is written with the intention of strengthening the arguments against debt repayment by giving them a legal basis, and it aims to challenge the logic according to which creditor claims stand above all other considerations. Recognizing the limits of what can realistically be achieved in one monograph, it will not attempt to address and analyse comprehensively all potential legal arguments according to which debt repayment might be challenged. Instead, the subject of this book is limited to providing a critical evaluation of a very specific issue where moral and legal arguments meet, which is that of the validity of loan agreements that were concluded between creditors and unconstitutional or otherwise illegitimate regimes. This issue is of particular importance, as the heavy and unsustainable debt that developing countries are asked to repay largely originates from periods when they were governed by dictatorial regimes that did not necessarily represent the interests of the people who are now expected to repay this debt. Even though central to the theme of the book, no attempt will be made to define up front and in general what is meant by a debt that is illegitimate, or a regime that is dictatorial, undemocratic, unconstitutional etc., as these definitions, as the book will show, depend on context.

From a legal perspective, to centre the analysis on the question of whether debt taken up by a dictatorial regime validly binds the people of the debtor country might at first sight seem to be focusing on the irrelevant. The issue of invalidity is, if at all, usually raised by debtor states only as a matter of political rhetoric, but not as a serious legal argument against debt repayment. Indeed, it seems as if debtor countries generally accept the binding nature of this debt and that the real issues occupying current legal debate are the legal consequences of the inability of most countries to repay the debt in full. However, it is submitted that what makes a legal analysis of the underlying issues both interesting and necessary is precisely this discrepancy between the arguments of anti-debt campaigners, which to a large extent focus on the invalidity of the debt, and the consistent practice of debtor states and

---

12   *La Nación*, 24 April 2000.

the international financial community unquestioningly to accept the validity of the debt regardless of its origins. A second reason for which a focus on the validity of the original debt might be regarded as misguided is that even if an argument can be made that the original debt was affected by legal flaws, in most cases the originally questionable debts have since been restructured several times, and traded on the secondary markets, so that to challenge the validity of the original debt could be considered to be a moot point. However, it will be asserted that some of the legal arguments based on which the original debt can be regarded as invalid also affect the validity of all acts that took place in regard of this debt, including payment, trading, and restructurings.

The focus of the book on the potential invalidity of the debt means that some legal arguments that received ample academic attention in recent years and which start from the assumption that the debt is valid and seek to explore ways in which the problem of the debtor states' inability to pay might be accommodated, will deliberately remain unaddressed. Thus, discussions such as that of sovereign insolvency;[13] the legalities of unilateral debt restructurings;[14] and the extent to which international law recognizes a defence of economic necessity for states,[15] will not be entered into. Another issue that has recently been at the forefront of public attention, namely debt relief,[16] will also not be examined in the context of this book, as debt relief is largely understood not as a legal concept, or an initiative that would benefit from legal analysis, but instead as a political and humanitarian measure.

Argentina will be used as a case study for the analysis of the legal objections to debt repayment. Not only is Argentina a country in which debt repayment is high on the political and economic agenda, but it is more importantly a country in which the issues of the country's debt were to some extent brought into the domain of the courts. However, while the book takes Argentina as an example, it goes beyond the particular Argentinian case, in that it uses the analysis of Argentinian domestic law in order to evaluate and develop more general legal concepts. The in parts very critical analysis of Argentinian legal and constitutional practice should be understood as an outsider's perspective on how the law could have been used in order to address the problem of the debt that was inherited by the military regime, had there been the political will and leeway to do so, and not as a patronizing demonstration of shortcomings.

Any claims that Argentina's sovereign debt is invalid and should not be repaid, at least not in full, can only be understood, and an analysis of the legal arguments in this respect can only be meaningfully carried out, against the background of how Argentina's sovereign debt came about and increased to an unsustainable level. Chapter Two will therefore provide some background information regarding the history of Argentina's sovereign debt, and the internal and international political and

---

13   For different models see, for example, Krueger (2002b); Raffer (2005).

14   See, for example, Reinisch (1995); García-Hamilton, Olivares-Caminal and Zenarruza (2005); Arora and Olivares-Caminal (2003); Hagan (2005).

15   See, for example, OLG Frankfurt NJW 2003, 268; Reinisch (2003); Pfeiffer (2003); Bothe and Hafner (2003); Tietje (2005); Baars and Böckel (2004), at 460–461.

16   For a critical discussion see, for example, Cheru (2006); Udombana (2005).

economic context in which it was contracted and restructured. The chapter will also reflect on some of the social and political implications of sovereign debt.

The remainder of the book will be dedicated to a legal analysis of the potential invalidity of sovereign debt because of its origins and use. Chapters Three and Four examine possibilities to repudiate such debt under the international law doctrine of odious debts. Chapter Three introduces and critically examines the doctrine of odious debts as it is traditionally understood, that is that debts can be repudiated if they were contracted without the consent of the people, not for the benefit of the people, and the creditors were aware of this. Coming to the conclusion that for many reasons this doctrine would be neither workable nor desirable, Chapter Four then develops an argument that the doctrine of odious debts could be given a different focus by rejecting as invalid loans that contributed to violations of *ius cogens*. At the end of this chapter both the traditional and the *ius cogens* focused doctrines of odious debts are applied to the case of Argentina to demonstrate how they could work in practice and which potential problems they might face.

Chapters Five and Six address constitutional arguments on the basis of which the validity of the debt can be challenged. Chapter Five concentrates on the procedural constitutionality of the debt. Introducing the relevant principles of the Argentinian Constitution, the legal consequences of the fact that the debt was originally contracted by the Argentinian military regime are examined, followed by an assessment of some of the actions taken by the various democratic successor governments with regard to this debt. One important question to be addressed in this context is whether creditors can obtain subjective rights under contractual agreements with *de facto* regimes that cannot be taken away by constitutional successor governments. Moreover, it will be examined how the Argentinian governments should have dealt with the inherited debt upon return to democracy. An argument will be developed that not only was the original debt not contracted by a constitutionally authorized organ, but the recognition, repayment, refinancing and restructuring of this debt by the democratic governments were equally unconstitutional.

In this context, some more limitations of the book need to be pointed out. Even though the discussion of specific debt transactions is limited to the example of Argentina, given the complexity of Argentina's sovereign debt, it is impossible to give a comprehensive overview of all relevant debt operations. Instead, in line with the main focus of the book, the analysis will be narrowed to the legal status of the debt that was contracted by Argentina's military regime in the period of 1976 to 1983, and some restructurings of this original debt that took place over the years. Many questions, for example the consequences of the convertibility regime introduced in the 1990s for Argentina's sovereign debt, will only be mentioned in passing. Furthermore, while the relationship between Argentina and the IMF is highly significant in the context of the country's debt, to do justice to its complexity, a whole book would need to be dedicated to the underlying issues, such as the IMF's responsibility or co-responsibility for Argentina's economic policies that resulted in the worst economic and social crisis in the country's history. It will not even be attempted to address these issues within the constraints of this book.

Having reached the conclusion that parts of Argentina's debt are affected by procedural unconstitutionality, Chapter Six is concerned with questions of substantive constitutionality. It introduces the restrictions imposed by the Argentinian Constitution with regard to the purposes for which public debt can only be taken up, and also Argentinian practice in this respect. The usefulness and desirability of such constitutional limits are assessed by comparing the Argentinian approach with that adopted by the German Constitution, German courts, and the German academic debate. Another reason examined in Chapter Six that could potentially affect the substantive constitutionality of debt related acts and legal instruments would be their incompatibility with the country's obligations to protect economic and social rights, both under international and according to domestic constitutional law.

Chapter Seven assesses the consequences of the unconstitutionality of the debt for the relationship between Argentina and its creditors. The analysis first concentrates on domestic Argentinian law. However, most loan agreements contain waivers of sovereign immunity as well as foreign jurisdiction and choice of law clauses, so that in most cases, the courts of a country other than Argentina will be competent to hear claims for debt repayment, and the applicable law will usually not be domestic Argentinian law. An evaluation of national Argentinian law is therefore only of limited relevance and it is essential to link the analysis of the national law to the international dimension of the problem. After an in-depth analysis of the relevant domestic legal issues, Chapter Seven thus assesses to what extent the unconstitutionality and invalidity of loans can have an impact on debt transactions that are not governed by Argentinian law.

Chapter Eight provides some broader reflections on the legal issues of sovereign debt and examines the potentialities and limits of both international and domestic law in this context.

Chapter Two

Argentina's Debt in its Historical and Political Context

A full historical and political account of the development of Argentina's public foreign debt would exceed the boundaries of this book.[1] Instead, this chapter will provide no more than an introduction to some of the features of Argentina's debt that are of particular importance for the subsequent legal analysis. Therefore, even though the history of Argentina's foreign debt goes back to 1824 when the Argentinian government took up a loan with the London based Baring Brothers Bank,[2] this chapter will concentrate on the time that is of particular relevance for Argentina's still ongoing debt crisis, that is the period that starts with the beginning of the latest military regime in 1976 and continues into present times. However, it should at least be mentioned briefly that before the military coup, the country already had debt problems, though minor in comparison to what was then to come. It is difficult to find reliable statistics, but according to the Annual Reports issued by Argentina's Central Bank, at the end of 1975 the total of Argentina's foreign debt, that is the sum of public and private foreign debt of the country, amounted to 7875 million dollars.[3] During the last months before the military regime took over on 24 March 1976, the country was involved in debt renegotiations with the IMF and creditor banks.[4] The country thus already had a debt problem when the military regime took power. However, between 1976 and 1983 Argentina's debt reached hitherto unknown proportions.

1 The military regime of 1976–1983

Under the military regime, the process of indebting the country took place in different phases. From 1976 to 1979, Argentina's newly contracted foreign debt consisted mainly of public debt, that is a debt taken up by the state itself. For the most part, these loans were not contracted for the purposes of investment into infrastructural, industrial or other developmental projects, the carrying out and success of which could have guaranteed the repayment of said loans.[5] During the relevant period

---

1   For a fuller account see, for example, Galasso (2003). For an English overview of the development of Argentina's sovereign debt see, for example, Dornbusch and de Pablo (1989).

2   Rapoport (2000), at 38; Galasso (2003), at 25–39.

3   Calcagno and Calcagno (1999), at 48; Schvarzer (1983), at 24.

4   Rapoport and Musacchio (2005), at 49; Kanenguiser (2003), at 20.

5   World Bank Memorandum (1985), at 17. See also Hemmer (1990), at 79–80.

the export rate exceeded the import rate, so that the taking up of loans cannot be explained by a need to finance imports.[6] Nor were new loans needed in order to enable the country to service the interest payments on its existing debts.[7] Instead, the incoming money was widely used for the purpose of increasing the federal reserves of the country[8] and was deposited with international banks, frequently the very banks that had loaned the money, but with interest rates below those that the state had to pay for the loans![9] The incoming foreign currency thus deposited exceeded by far the commercial needs of the country at the relevant time.

When looking for explanations as to why the country would take up foreign loans it did not seem to need, several suggestions have been made. Martínez de Hoz, the Secretary of the Economy during the first years of the military regime, explained in his deposition in judicial proceedings that were later brought against him because of his economic policies, that the country initially did not take up international loans because it was in need of the money, but rather because loans were easily available.[10] Other explanations for this financial policy are that the reserves served the purpose of reassuring the financial market of the availability of foreign currency,[11] and that the country needed to accumulate reserves in order to have the funds to set into motion the dramatic changes in the economic policy that were to follow.[12] An immediate consequence of this policy was that, in addition to an increase in the country's foreign debt, the country lost the difference between the interest paid for the loan and the interest received for the deposit, as well as the commission fees involved in both transactions.[13]

The policy of accumulating international reserves was accompanied by a deregulation of foreign investment,[14] and the removal of all restrictions on the movement of foreign capital.[15] In 1978, the *tablita* was introduced, which was a chart that fixed and announced the exchange rate between the US dollar and the Argentinian peso 30 days in advance.[16] This facilitated the attraction of foreign capital, and the fact that interest rates in Argentina were above those at the international

---

6   See expert witness José Dehesa's statement in "Olmos, Alejandro S/denuncia", causa N°14.467, www.cadtm.org/IMG/rtf/sentencia_olmos.rtf; Calcagno and Calcagno (1999), at 65.

7   Calcagno, Calcagno (1999), ibid.

8   Rapoport (2000), at 811; Bradford and Kucinski (1988), at 89–90.

9   See Olmos (2004), at 203–204; Toussaint (2001), at 201.

10   Olmos (2004), at 206.

11   Schvarzer (1983), at 29–30.

12   Ibid., at 29.

13   See the report of expert witnesses Valle and Trocca in "Olmos, Alejandro S/dcia", causa N°14.467, www.cadtm.org/IMG/rtf/sentencia_olmos.rtf .

14   In 1976, see Rapoport (2000), at 789.

15   In 1977, ibid., at 811. This was also a requirement of the Stand-By Arrangement with the IMF in 1976 and 1977, see Cafiero (2005), at 45.

16   Ramos (2002), at 5. According to the World Bank Memorandum (1985) on Argentina, '[t]he new exchange rate policy based on a pre-announced depreciation schedule (*tablita*) of the peso vis-à-vis the US dollar, combined with the opening of the capital account, aimed at dampening inflationary expectations … and fostering economic recovery.' At 212.

level provided further encouragement for the entry of foreign capital.[17] Indeed, high nominal peso interest rates combined with low and prefixed rates of peso devaluation resulted in high yields on foreign currency deposited locally. This policy led to foreign borrowing for the purpose of financial speculation, as investors could invest borrowed foreign capital in Argentina with the expectation of huge gains, and without running the risk of a devaluation of their money.[18] Argentinian enterprises that had access to the foreign capital markets often found it more profitable to take up credits for financial speculation than for investment in productive activities.[19] At the same time, small national companies were no longer able to obtain loans in order to invest in production and growth, as they usually did not have easy access to the international financial market with its low interest rates and would instead have needed to resort to internal credits with extremely high interest rates. One of the effects of the economic system implemented by Martínez de Hoz thus was that of favouring the financial sector over national production.

Galasso describes one of the common mechanisms of taking up debt for the purpose of financial speculation as follows:

> [F]inanciers who had access to the foreign capital markets indebted themselves at reasonable interest rates in the "civilised world" (3 per cent to 4 per cent per year), thereby supplying themselves with dollars which in Argentina they converted into pesos in order to invest them at interest rates of 12 or 14 per cent per month (!), that is 150 per cent or 160 per cent per year. At the end of the investment period, they reconverted the dollars with an extraordinary profit, losing only the devaluation of the peso against the dollar as prescribed in the *'tablita'*. The following step consisted in the departure of these dollars – the initial amount as well as the interests gained – and in immediately taking up new and larger debts, to return to the financial circuit of Buenos Aires and repeat the operation.[20]

Thus, the private sector took up debt to make financial profits and then transfer the proceeds abroad. This meant that the debt financed capital flight, as for every dollar that entered the country a dollar plus the difference between the international and the internal interest rate left the country.[21]

Another form of creating private foreign debt consisted in the so-called self-loans. The way this worked was that borrowers who held assets abroad and in foreign currency were in a position

> to apply for a loan in dollars which they brought to Argentina in order to carry out the speculative game described above. ... In those cases, they are borrowing their own money, which is why these transactions are called self-loans, that is the fund holder, instead of repatriating his assets and subjecting them to any risk in Argentina – such as that it might be declared impossible to retransfer the money abroad, or tax difficulties – prefers to let

---

17   Rapoport (2000), at 811.
18   Ramos (2002), at 5; Dornbusch and de Pablo (1989), at 46.
19   Galasso (2003), at 226.
20   Ibid., at 219.
21   Rapoport (2000), at 811.

the money work as a 'loan', so that when faced with restrictive measures directed towards inhibiting capital flight, he can sustain that he is only repaying a debt,[22]

which was a debt of which they themselves were the creditor. As a consequence of the various policies that invited financial speculation, at the end of 1979, the private foreign debt was twice as high as it had been at the end of 1978 when the *tablita* was introduced.[23]

The massive foreign capital inflows and favourable current account position of 1978–79 were reversed from late 1980, as an expectation of a major corrective devaluation gained ground and international reserves fell to dangerously low levels.[24] Indeed, while the first phase of indebting the country was characterized by a steady increase in the federal reserves, during the second phase a sharp decrease could be noted, and the exit of funds equalled more than 60 per cent of the new debts.[25] From 1980 to 1981, the country suffered a commercial deficit, partly because of the growing demand of imports.[26] More importantly, however, between 1980 and 1982, capital flight increased dramatically, and was estimated to amount to between 16,000 and 22,000 million dollars.[27] To give a demonstration of the dimension of the debt burden, as early as 1982, interest payments alone ate up about three-fifths of the year's export earnings.[28]

These adverse effects of the economic and financial policies adopted by Martínez de Hoz are hardly surprising, as there are obviously limits on how long a system of an overvaluation of the local currency that is sustained by an increase in foreign debt and results in financial speculation and capital flight can be maintained.[29] From December 1979 to March 1981, the state lost 6.2 billion dollars of its reserves, while taking up 7.2 billion of new foreign debt. This debt was mainly taken up by the public sector that needed the currency in order to sustain the overvalued exchange rate and satisfy the currency demands of the private sector.[30] To attract badly needed foreign currency, state owned enterprises, in particular the petrol company YPF and the water and electricity companies, were encouraged to take up foreign debt.[31] Dornbusch and de Pablo explain the link between the economic policies of the military regime and the indebting of public enterprises as follows:

> By 1979–80 the overvaluation had become so extreme that in financial markets there was the view that depreciation was inevitable. The regime of unrestricted capital mobility introduced in late 1976 facilitated this capital flight. Hence, in 1979–80 the Central

---

22   Galasso (2003), at 219–220. See also Rapoport (2000), at 813–814; World Bank Memorandum (1985), at 17.
23   Schvarzer (1983), at 28.
24   World Bank Memorandum (1985), at 2–8.
25   Rapoport (2000), at 812.
26   Ibid., at 811; Schvarzer (1983), at 31–32.
27   For the exact numbers provided in the estimates of various institutions, see Rapoport (2000), at 825.
28   World Bank Memorandum (1985), at 17–19.
29   Schvarzer (1983), at 30. See also Rapoport and Musacchio (2005), at 51.
30   Schvarzer (1983), at 33–34.
31   World Bank Memorandum (1985), at 12 and 51.

Bank and public sector enterprises were forced to borrow massively abroad to obtain foreign exchange which was then sold in support of the exchange rate policy. Private speculators in turn bought the dollars and invested them abroad. With the round trip complete, commercial banks in New York, Zurich and Tokyo had lent to the government the resources to finance capital flight which returned to the same banks as deposits.[32]

In order to make possible the indebting of state owned enterprises, in 1980, Martínez de Hoz issued a Resolution which fixed the margins within which these enterprises could contract foreign debts.[33] The state owned companies were encouraged, if not at times forced, to take up foreign loans and received the borrowed amount in pesos, while the incoming dollars stayed with the Central Bank. However, the enterprises owed the debt in US dollars, without any exchange rate guarantee provided by the state.[34] As a result, these enterprises ended up highly indebted to foreign creditors, not because of their own financial needs, but rather in order to obtain currency that allowed the Central Bank to keep up the illusion of international reserves,[35] and to finance the policies that promoted capital flight.

With regard to private Argentinian companies that had contracted huge foreign debts, the policy was rather different and far more favourable.[36] When they encountered difficulties in servicing their foreign debt, the state introduced in 1981 a system of exchange rate guarantees, according to which the state assumed the risk of a devaluation of the peso.[37] In 1982, the military government assumed the private sector debt by issuing new state bonds.[38] Many different sources suggest that the private sector debt taken on by the Argentinian state was in part a fictitious debt,[39] as portions of the debt had already been repaid by the private debtors without them registering this fact,[40] as it partly consisted of self-loans, and as in some instances Argentinian branches of multinational companies declared the money they received from their foreign parent company as foreign loans. Thus, the Argentinian state not only transformed into public debts the debts of private companies that resulted from regular transactions, thereby freeing them from the risks they had taken in the context of their economic and financial dealings, but furthermore assumed private debt that had been contracted for the purpose of financial speculation and capital flight, and even non-existent debts. The state never reclaimed from the private companies the debts thus repaid on their behalf. All of this not only further increased

---

32   Dornbusch and de Pablo (1989), at 47.
33   Olmos (2004), at 115.
34   Bonelli (2005), at 41.
35   Olmos (2004), at 116–119 and 164; World Bank Memorandum (1985), at 51.
36   For a detailed analysis see Basualdo (2006), at 174–182.
37   World Bank Memorandum (1985), at 67.
38   See also Kanenguiser (2003), at 42.
39   World Bank Memorandum (1985), at 67.
40   Schvarzer (1983) suggests at 36–37 that as much as 50 per cent of the private debt assumed by the state might have been fictitious in this way; and Martínez de Hoz himself surprisingly mentioned the precise figure of 4 billion dollars, quoted by Olmos (2004), at 129.

the already large public foreign debt of the Argentinian State,[41] but moreover meant that the Argentinian people ended up repaying the regular and irregular debts of the Argentinian private sector.

Other irregularities in the taking up of the public debt also need to be noted. In the course of the parliamentary investigation of the foreign debt contracted under the military regime, it was found that the law firm of Guillermo Walter Klein who was the right hand of Martínez de Hoz and in charge of the Department of Economic Planning and Coordination within the Ministry of the Economy, at the same time represented international banks and companies that made loans to and investments in Argentina. His name at times figures on official documents as representative of the state with regard to the same transactions in which he acted as the legal advisor and representative of the foreign contracting party.[42] Thus, in its negotiations and contracts with foreign banks and companies, the Argentinian state was represented by a representative of those self same foreign banks and companies.

It is interesting to note the conclusions reached by Justice Ballestero in the case of *Olmos,* a criminal case brought against Martínez de Hoz and others for their involvement in indebting the country between 1976 and 1983, and in which, *inter alia,* the indebting of the public enterprises was investigated with the assistance of the reports of numerous expert witnesses.[43] According to the court, during the military regime, the most highly responsible Argentinian politicians and economists as well as managers and directors of certain companies and public and private institutions acted with evident arbitrariness and without any scruples to violate the by-laws of the Central Bank. Justice Ballesteros concluded that:

> It is for these reasons that I will send a copy of this decision to the Honourable Congress of the Nation in order for it to adopt, in the respective commissions, the measures which it deems appropriate with regard to the negotiation of the foreign debt of the nation, which, I repeat, crudely increased from the beginning of 1976 by the means of a vulgar and offensive economic policy which put the country onto its knees through the various methods used which were explained throughout this decision, and which tended, *inter alia,* to benefit and support private companies and businesses – national and foreign – to the detriment of state owned companies which ... got poorer every day, all of which was reflected in their value at the moment of privatization. ... In fact, it needs to be remembered that as of 1976 the country was subjected to the will of foreign creditors and that officials of the IMF actively participated in these negotiations.[44]

At the end of the military regime, the country faced an inflation rate of 400 per cent, found itself without international reserves, and with a public foreign debt of 45,000 million dollars which exceeded the country's annual exportations five times.[45] The situation of the country, in itself disastrous, moreover needs to be seen in the context of declining prices for Argentina's exports on the world market, and high interest

---

41   See Schvarzer (1983), at 51–55.
42   Galasso (2003), at 278.
43   See also Toussaint (1999), at 200–201.
44   "Olmos, Alejandro S/denuncia", causa N°14.467, 13 July 2000, Juzgado Nacional en lo Criminal y Correctional Federal, n. 2., JA 2001-I-514.
45   Rapoport (2000), at 905.

rates.[46] The multiplication of Argentina's foreign debt by four and a half during the latest dictatorship that was accompanied by, and some argue intended to facilitate,[47] the opening of the capital market and the financial system to foreign capital, mainly financed capital flight. Indeed, Dornbusch and de Pablo conclude that 'the government has an external debt but the private sector has matching external assets'.[48] According to a World Bank estimate, of 35 billion dollars of loans, 2.5 billion were used to increase the national foreign reserves; 13 billion to service interest payments; 10 billion for unregistered imports, most of which are deemed to have been related to arms purchases; and 19 billion were capital outflow.[49] Among those who benefited most from the taking up of debts were high government officials who transferred funds to their own international bank accounts; those businessmen who engaged in financial speculation and transferred their profits abroad; and the armed forces that used loans to purchase arms.[50] The losers were the export industry; the formerly prosperous nationalized enterprises;[51] and, most importantly, the Argentinian people who had, and still have, to repay these debts which take up a large percentage of the country's GDP.

While it is not possible to explain here the policies of terror exercised by the Argentinian military regime in any detail,[52] it is essential to take into account that the economic and financial policies described above took place in the context of a brutal military regime that governed the country in complete disregard of the human rights of the country's population. Indeed, the regime that pursued the economic and financial policies described above and left the country the legacy of an unpayable foreign debt reigned by the means of terror; prohibited unions and union activities; abolished the right to strike; repressed all political opposition; and under its command an estimated 30,000 people disappeared and many more were detained and tortured. Not only was the Argentinian Constitution with its limitations on the powers of the executive disregarded by the military regime, but under the military dictatorship, there was no democratic control by the people, and no accountability to them. Thus, the military regime was free to carry out its financial and economic policies that benefited foreign creditors and the national elites while having devastating effects for the large majority of the Argentinian people without being subjected to any democratic supervision or faced with an effective political opposition.[53] Indeed, many argue that the brutality of the regime and its economic policies cannot be regarded as two separate features of the latest military dictatorship, but that political oppression and torture were instead two sides of the same coin, in that the latter

---

46   Galasso (2003), at 263.
47   See, for example, Diamond and Naszewski (1985), at 249.
48   Dornbusch and de Pablo (1989), at 47–48.
49   World Bank Memorandum (1985), at 17.
50   Rapoport (2000), at 813.
51   Schvarzer (1983), at 24–30; Ferrer (1982), at 54–60.
52   For a concise overview see, for example, Rapoport (2000), at 738–789. See also *Nunca Más*, the report issued in 1984 by CONADEP, the commission created by the Alfonsín government in order to investigate the crimes committed during the military regime.
53   Ramos (2002), at 4; see also Juliá (2002), at 98.

were necessary means for making possible the economic policies pursued by that regime.[54]

The process of excessive lending and borrowing that took place while the military regime was in power also needs to be seen in the context of the world financial situation.[55] With regard to the motivation of foreign banks to engage in almost unlimited lending operations in the developing world, various explanations are being advanced. The most common explanation is that between 1974 and 1980, the oil crisis led to an extreme liquidity of Western banks where the OPEC countries deposited the dollars they gained from petrol exports. Given the amount of money deposited in their accounts and for which they needed to pay interest, the banks had to find a way of using that money to generate enough income to pay the interests and, obviously, make a profit in the process. As the developed countries found themselves in recession, loans to Developing World governments seemed attractive.[56] Another factor facilitating the excessive lending policies evidenced in those years was the lack of regulation of the international banking system.[57] But how can it be explained that the banks made loans that by far exceeded the developing countries' ability to repay them? During the relevant period, the idea of state insolvency did not seem to exist,[58] so the very fact that the debtors were either sovereign states, or in the case of private debtors the states guaranteed the debts taken up by them, seemed to be sufficient to assure repayment of the money lent.[59] However, as early as the mid-1970s concern with regard to the disastrous consequences of the lending policies that later materialized was expressed in quite a few statements and papers.[60]

That the governments of developing countries, which traditionally did not have easy access to affordable international loans, were happy to accept loans offered to them 'at low cost, with long maturities and without any conditions regarding the destination [of the borrowed money], or guarantees as to their solvency',[61] thereby having large funds at their free disposal, is understandable enough. Even more so when taking into account that many of those governments were, in fact, dictatorships

---

54   This was already pointed out by Walsh in his famous 'Open Letter to the Military Junta', written on the first anniversary of the military coup, at 415; see also, for example, Basualdo (2006), at 126–127; Feinmann (2006), at 90–93.

55   For a more general and concise description of the problems created by lending policies in that era see Frankenberg and Knieper (1984), at 416.

56   Schvarzer (1983), at 9; Calcagno and Calcagno (1999), at 39; Valdez (2004), at 142. For a description of loan policies during that period see, for example, Adams (1991), at 60–64, and 95–99; see also Schvarzer (1983), at 7–10; Congdon (1988), at 112; Toussaint (2001), at 218. But see Payer (1991), at 60–62, who suggests that the OPEC is not to blame for the lending boom. And Buckley (2001) argues that another reason for increased lending to developing countries was that as a consequence of financial reforms in the US, lending within the US was restricted, so that US banks were keen on increasing their overseas operations, at 17–18.

57   Valdez (2004), at 135.

58   Reinisch (1995), at 562.

59   Schvarzer (1983), at 9.

60   Buckley (1999), at 18.

61   Ramos (2002), at 3.

that could use the incoming money for their own purposes, without feeling bound by constitutional restrictions or by concerns for the well-being of their respective countries.

Another explanation might be that short-term gains clouded the vision and led the actors to ignore long-term problems. As Buckley describes the situation that resulted in the debt crisis, the borrowing countries

> chose to consume goods from the developed world and oil from OPEC nations on a deferred payment plan. The banks, with encouragement from their home governments, chose to fund this deferred payment plan. The banks, their home governments and the borrowers all benefited from the plan in the short term. No one gave much attention to the question of repayment.[62]

He points out that the crisis would not have originated if the loans had been used for productive purposes. Looking at the specific case of loans to Latin America, he further argues that the creditors should have been aware of the fact that such a use of the loans was highly unlikely, given the history of Latin American countries[63] and the nature of the regimes with which these loan contracts were being made. The US House Committee on Banking, Finance and Urban Affairs came to the conclusion that the lending banks had been 'opportunistic and imprudent and the regulators almost criminally lax and complacent'.[64]

With the change of the world financial situation and of US fiscal policies in 1979, Argentina, like many other countries, found itself in a critical situation.

> What turned the debt into a crisis was not the absolute level of the debt, but the changing terms of the debt. When the second oil price rise of 1979 occurred, the US Federal Reserve Bank adopted a tight monetary policy which pushed up real interest rates to historically high levels. For debtor countries, this not only made new borrowing more expensive, but also unexpectedly increased the amount of interest they had to pay on their old loans, since much of this commercial borrowing was originally contracted with floating interest rates.[65]

Indeed, given that many loans to developing countries were made on the basis of floating interest rates,[66] the fact that the interest rates were extremely low when the debt was contracted (sometimes the real interest rate was even negative), but they went up from 5.64 per cent in 1977 to 16.77 per cent in 1981, considerably contributed to the fact that the debt burden and the servicing of interests became unsustainable.[67] According to Buckley, 'the dramatic rise in interest rates ... was the direct result of policy decisions in the US and other OECD nations. The developed world, in acting to prevent domestic inflation, imposed a frightful cost on the less

---

62   Buckley (1999), at 12.

63   Ibid., at 21.

64   Quoted after Lichtenstein (1985), at 418.

65   Cheru (1999), in his Report to the Economic and Social Council.

66   Buckley (1999) estimates that in 1982, 70 per cent of Argentina's foreign debt was at floating interest rates, at 22. See also Sarcevic (1986), at 136–137.

67   Buckley (2001), at 22–23; Conesa (2004), at 994; Zafra Espinosa de los Monteros (2001), at 264.

developed world under the very loans the OECD governments had encouraged their banks to make.'[68] The debt crisis that started in the early 1980 also needs to be seen in the context that the dollar exchange rate changed significantly, which increased the debt burden even further, as most of the debt was owed in US currency.[69]

For Argentina, two economists carried out an interesting assessment in order to demonstrate the effects of the interest rate rise on the development of Argentina's foreign debt. They calculated how debt repayment would have differed had the interest rates developed according to the same principles that applied when the debt was first taken up, that is at 1 per cent above the US inflation rate. On the basis of debt repayment made by Argentina, they came to the conclusion that had the interest rate not been increased, and had the difference between the fictitious and the real interest rate been dedicated to the repayment of the capital of the debt, the foreign debt Argentina was faced with at the end of the military regime in 1983 would have been repaid by 1988.[70] Thus, while the debt in itself was excessive, the impossibility to repay the debt was mainly caused by the rise in interest rates.

2 Return to democracy under Alfonsín (1983–1989)

When the democratic government assumed power in December 1983, the country's foreign debt amounted to 63 per cent of the GDP and interest to 8 per cent of the GDP and 69 per cent of the country's annual exports.[71] Given the questionable legitimacy of the military government as such, and of many of the loan operations carried out under that regime, the government of Alfonsín at first took the view that the debt it inherited from the military regime would not be repaid without a thorough investigation into how it had come about and the extent to which the debt was, in fact, legitimate. To that effect, a 180 days moratorium on debt repayment was declared,[72] and in January 1984, a letter was sent to the private creditors, stating that debt repayment would only be made upon submission of documentation proving the existence of the relevant debt.[73] Also, Congress enacted Act 23.062, stating that all administrative acts and provisions of the *de facto* regime lacked legal validity, and, more importantly in the present context, rejected the investment accounts referring to the years of 1976 to 1983 in Act 23.854.[74]

In February 1984, the Senate Investigatory Commission on Illicit Economic Activities was created and vested with the mandate to carry out an investigation of the foreign debt contracted by the military regime. However, the Commission did not have an adequate budget to fulfil its task and its mandate was not prolonged beyond 1985, which meant that there was not enough time to carry out all the investigations that would have been necessary in order to present a conclusive

---

68   Buckley (1999), at 24.
69   See, for example, Brock (1984), at 1043.
70   Calcagno and Calcagno (1999), at 53–55.
71   Machinea and Sommers (1990), at 6.
72   Galasso (2003), at 261; Rapoport (2000), at 906.
73   Kanenguiser (2003), at 51.
74   A power given to Congress by Art.75(8) of the Constitution.

report.[75] In July 1984, the Central Bank set up an investigating commission that had the task of investigating the legitimacy of the external debt of the private sector, but this commission was equally dissolved before it could present any conclusions.[76]

In June 1984, the Argentinian Government submitted a letter of intent to the IMF, stating that the debt Argentina was 'asked to repay had been contracted by the means of arbitrary and authoritarian policies in which the creditors had actively participated and which did not bring any benefits to the Argentinian people,' and that

> the democratic regime found itself in front of a situation in which the country's foreign debt exceeds five times the annual exportations; the monthly inflation rate amounts to 15 to 20 per cent; and the public sector deficit exceeds 16 per cent of the GDP, going together with a reduction of capital, infrastructure, industrial equipments and commercial activities in significant magnitudes.

While stressing that 'Argentina will honour its tradition to fulfil its obligations', the Government at the same time insisted that this should be done 'under the most appropriate conditions to guarantee growth and social peace' and suggested to limit debt servicing to 'the recourses that can be generated through exports without reducing the importations that are necessary for economic growth'.[77]

As pressure of the foreign creditors and the IMF increased,[78] a Stand-By Arrangement with the IMF was concluded at the end of 1984[79] in which the country agreed to the usual IMF conditionalities, in particular a reduction of the fiscal deficit through strictly cutting down on public expenditures.[80] As early as 1984, Argentina started to make payments on interests in arrears.[81] Thus, without carrying out its promise to evaluate the legitimacy of the foreign debt before repaying it, and without waiting at least until the end of the short mandate of the Senate Commission that investigated the legitimacy of the acts that had taken place in the context of contracting the foreign debt, the Alfonsín government decided to go down the route of debt negotiation and debt repayment, the potential illegitimacy of the debt notwithstanding. In 1985, an important part of Argentina's debt was refinanced by the means of Guaranteed Refinancing Agreements. The year 1987 saw a significant renegotiation of Argentina's debt. The bonds issued by the military government in 1982 in the context of the nationalization of the private debt were also refinanced and consolidated.[82]

Alfonsín later justified this policy as follows:

---

75   Juliá (2002), at 175–176.
76   According to Ramos (2002), at 12, this was because the Commission discovered uncomfortable evidence of fraudulent operations in this context.
77   As quoted in Olmos (2004), at 58–59.
78   See Basualdo (2006), at 222; Kanenguiser (2003), at 49–62; Olmos (2004), at 59; Morgan-Foster (2003), at 621. See also Naylor (1994), at 345–346, who argues that the Alfonsín government had its own interests in striking a deal with the IMF and its other creditors.
79   Rapoport (2000), at 908; Machinea and Sommers (1990), at 6–7.
80   Machinea and Sommers (1990), at 8.
81   Ibid.
82   Silva (h) (1992), at 838.

We maintained that we should not pay that which we regarded to be the illegitimate part of the debt because it had originated from irregular credits … but in the concrete exercise of power, things did not turn out this way and only in a very small, in fact irrelevant, number of cases could we effectively prove that we were dealing with this type of loan. It was therefore actually impossible to carry on with a policy of distinguishing between legitimate and illegitimate loans.[83]

This is interesting, given that almost 20 years later, the illegitimacy of many of the loans could be established in the context of the proceedings in *Olmos*.[84] While it is not clear whether the Commission could have determined with any clarity the existence of and responsibilities for concrete illicit acts in the context of Argentina's foreign debt,[85] it is highly possible that at that point in time in many cases such an evaluation could have been made had the Commission finished its investigations. However, even though interrupted, the work of the Commission was the basis for some of the expert witnesses' reports and the judicial decision in the case of *Olmos*.

Why the developing countries, including Argentina, gave in to the pressure to repay debts the origins of which were questioned by the same governments that made the payments, and took up more debts in order to be able to do so, is not easy to answer. One of the standard arguments, the validity of which was doubted by many,[86] was that if a country refused to assume and repay its foreign debt, it would be excluded from the world financial system and cut off from future loans.[87] Given the over-exposure of many Western banks to the risk of sovereign default, the rejection to repay all or part of the foreign debt by one or more of the more important debtor countries, such as Argentina, would have put the survival of some of these banks, and the functioning of the international financial system, at serious risk.[88] It is then difficult to understand why the debtor countries did not use this situation to their advantage and attempt to improve their negotiating positions. In the case of Argentina, the reasons for this are complex, and at least in part go back to a lack of political will to break with the existing financial and economic system, and to a reluctance to alienate the internal and international sectors whose interests would have been severely harmed by such a change of policy.[89] As a consequence, the 1980s, often described as the lost decade, are the era in which Argentina, among many things, lost its main chance to determine the legitimacy of the debt burden inherited from the military regime.

However, to decide to repay the country's foreign debt did not resolve the debt problem. Instead, as the Economic Commission for Latin America (ECLAC), created by the Economic and Social Council of the UN, stated, 'in the four year period of

---

83   In *¿Por qué doctor Alfonsín?* at 169–171, as quoted in Galasso (2003), at 270.
84   "Olmos, Alejandro S/denuncia", causa N°14.467, 13 July 2000, Juzg. Nac. Crim. y Corr. Fed., n. 2., JA 2001-I-514.
85   Juliá (2002), at 177.
86   See, for example, Buckley (1999), at 38–41; Sachs (1989), at 26–28.
87   For a critical appraisal see Krugman (1989), at 316, who suggests that political pressure from creditor countries, particularly the US, might have had a role to play.
88   Buckley (1999), at 25.
89   See, for example, Juliá (2002), at 121.

1978–1981, Latin America received a net transfer of resources ... of 53,000 million dollars ... but in the four year period of 1982–1985, the transfer was negative by 106,300 million dollars. ... However, despite these payments, the debt increased by 30 per cent.'[90] This was partly because, given the high indebtedness and the high interest rates, the annual surplus was insufficient to service the interests, so that new debts had to be taken up in order to be able to repay the debt,[91] which obviously increased the debt burden even more. Moreover, as Jeffrey Sachs explains:

> most 'new money' packages after 1982 have involved considerably less in new loans than was due to the same creditors in interest payments. Thus, when Mexico or Argentina gets a new concerted loan, the check is still written by the country to the creditors, since the new loan only covers a fraction of the interest that is due to the creditors.[92]

In 1984, the then Peruvian President, Alan García, described the situation Argentina had in common with most Latin American countries as follows:

> They lend us fresh money to enable us to satisfy our old debts. And this furthermore under the condition that we subject ourselves to the economic government of the IMF ... Our creditors unilaterally increased the interest rates and also unilaterally closed the markets to our products. Unilaterally, they reduce the prices of raw material.[93]

The logic according to which more debt needs to be taken up to enable a country not to default on its debt servicing did not reduce, but rather increased the debt burden.

Coming back to some specific facts in the context of Argentina's debt management, in 1985, the Austral plan was announced by decree of necessity and emergency with the aim to avoid hyperinflation. The plan involved an adjustment even beyond that which was demanded by the IMF, and consisted of replacing the peso with a new currency, the austral; a freezing of prices and salaries; a reduction of interest rates; a devaluation with subsequent freezing of the exchange rate; and strict fiscal and monetary policies.[94] This economic programme found the approval of the IMF and served as the basis for a debt rescheduling and for the provision of fresh loans in order to finance the outstanding and current debt servicing.[95] It also allowed for the same mechanisms of financial speculation that already took place under the auspices of Martínez de Hoz, as excessively high interest rates and free capital flow made it possible to obtain exponential profits on investments in very short periods of time.[96]

In mid-1988, the Argentinian economy was in a critical state. As an attempt to redress this, the Primavera plan was introduced.[97] However, this plan did not prove particularly successful, and at the beginning of 1989, a large run on foreign currency

---

90   Quoted by Galasso (2003), at 265–266.
91   Rapoport (2000), at 908.
92   Sachs (1989), at 26.
93   As quoted by Galasso (2003), at 265.
94   Dornbusch and de Pablo (1989), at 106–107.
95   Ibid., at 107.
96   See *Clarín*, 9 February 1986, quoted in Galasso (2003), at 271.
97   Rapoport (2000), at 922.

combined with a massive capital flight took place.[98] When Alfonsín handed over power to Menem in 1989, the country was suffering hyperinflation and during his time in office the foreign debt had increased by 44 per cent to a total of 65,300 million dollars.[99]

3 The Menem era

The debt saga continued and worsened during the decade of the Menem government. In November 1989, Menem reached a Stand-By Arrangement with the IMF according to which Argentina agreed to privatize some of its public enterprises, such as the telecommunications company ENTel, and the Argentinian airlines.[100] Privatization was promoted as a way to help resolve the debt crisis. Public enterprises were sold in part for cash, but were also in part swapped for debt, that is the foreign creditors could recuperate their money by acquiring shares in the newly privatized companies. Given that the market value of the debt had dropped to about 15 per cent of its nominal value, that the state nevertheless accepted them as payment at 100 per cent of their nominal value,[101] and that many of the companies were furthermore sold at undervalued prices,[102] the deal could not have been much better for the creditors. In many cases, the very same companies that had benefited from the 'nationalization' of the private debt bought back this debt when the price of the bonds was low, and then exchanged them for shares in newly privatized companies. Thus, the former debtors who were bailed out by the state turned into creditors and then benefited from the privatization of state owned enterprises that became necessary to service the debt they had, in part, been responsible for.[103]

In December 1992, the Brady Plan was agreed[104] which involved the restructuring of 23,000 million dollars of capital debt, and 8,600 million dollars of interest. The creditors could choose between two options: the first option consisted of exchanging the old debt for a bond with a cut of 35 per cent, the bond being paid after 30 years in one single payment, with interest of 0.81 per cent above Libor. The second option was a bond, also repayable after 30 years, with an increasing interest rate of 4 per cent for the first few years and 6 per cent from the seventh year onwards.[105] For the participating creditor banks, this massive restructuring operation meant freeing themselves from the risk of Argentina's insolvency. For Argentina, it meant that the creditors were no longer a number of easily identifiable international banks, but

---

98   Ibid., at 924–925.
99   Kanenguiser (2003), at 79.
100 Cafiero (2005), at 47; Kanenguiser (2003), at 85.
101 Bonelli (2005), at 96.
102 Kulfas and Schorr (2003), at 19–20; for a critical analysis of the privatization strategy see Galasso (2003), at 305–331; also Rapoport (2000), at 969.
103 Galasso (2003), at 248.
104 For an economic analysis of the Brady Plan see Basualdo (2006), at 346–354.
105 Calcagno and Calcagno (1999), at 56; Galasso (2003), at 295.

instead a multitude of anonymous bondholders.[106] Furthermore, to restructure all of the foreign debt in the form of Brady bonds, without distinguishing between legitimate and illegitimate debt, might be seen as a recognition of this debt, or as a waiver of any rights to invoke the illegitimacy of the debt. Undoubtedly, whatever the legal position of the debt, the fact that the debt was now in the hands of new and diversified creditors made it far more difficult to establish a link between the newly assumed debt and the original potentially illegitimate debt. Most importantly for an evaluation of the costliness of the Brady Plan for Argentina, the exchange of debt for Brady bonds was performed on the basis of a 100 per cent value of the old debt, whereas its market value at the time of the restructuring was only 18 per cent. The nominal value of the 20,900 million dollars of restructured debt was thus no more than 3,762 million, so that a debt 'reduction' of 2,550 million dollars left the country with a debt of 18,350 million dollars,[107] a calculation which makes the Brady Plan look detrimental instead of beneficial for the country. In addition, the Brady bonds were backed by a US Treasury bond which was financed via credits taken up with IFIs.[108] Thus, in actual fact, between 1992 and 1993, the debt increased by 6.8 per cent due to the costs of the Brady Plan.[109] Buckley therefore seems to be right when stating that:

> When in September 1992 Nicolas Brady announced to the annual meeting of the IMF and the World Bank that while problems remained the crisis was, for the most part, over, this was, from the perspective of the international financial community, an accurate observation. From the perspective of the debtor nations nothing could have been less accurate.[110]

What was often presented as an act of debt relief for the debtor states in reality turned out to be a way for the banks to reduce their exposure in the developing countries.

In 1991, the Menem government introduced the system of convertibility between dollar and peso, that is the peso was pegged to the dollar at a value of one to one. The statute introducing this policy (Act 23.928), prohibited the issuing of money that was not backed 100 per cent by available reserves.[111] At first, this new system had a positive effect on the economy.[112] However, in order to finance and sustain such a system, the country needed a steady inflow of dollars, and foreign investment was not sufficient to provide these funds. The overvaluation of the peso had the effect of making imports cheap, while at the same time adversely affecting the competitiveness

---

106 Galasso (2003), at 295; Kulfas and Schorr (2003), at 21. In 1989, the creditors of Argentina's foreign debt were international banks (61.1 per cent), IFIs (around 20 per cent), and only about 10 per cent of the debt was owed to individual bondholders, see Galasso (2003), at 293.
107 Galasso (2003), at 295.
108 Kulfas and Schorr (2003), at 23.
109 Ibid.
110 Buckley (1999), at 41–42.
111 Rapoport (2000), at 977.
112 Ibid., at 980.

of Argentinian products on the international market.[113] The government increasingly had to resort to foreign loans in order to satisfy the demand for dollars.[114]

Just as during the latest military dictatorship, under Menem both the public and private foreign debt of the country increased significantly, and the incoming money was not used to increase productivity, but rather to finance the growing public deficit, financial speculation and capital flight.[115] One effect of the foreign public and private debt was an increasing capital flow out of the country, in the form of interest and debt repayment. This trend was further exacerbated by the internationalization of companies which transferred their profits abroad. In 1998 alone an estimated 100,000 million dollars left the country.[116] Another important factor leading to Argentina's fiscal crisis was the privatization of the social security system[117] which was strongly supported, if not requested, by the IMF as part of the structural adjustment measures expected from the country.

Galasso describes Argentina's situation at that time as follows:

> Argentina lives to pay the service of its debt. The state budget does not consist in planning the annual expenditures and resources directed towards improving the situation of its inhabitants, their quality of life in the areas of health care, education, food, housing etc. … It only exists in order to adapt expenditures and resources to the servicing of the foreign debt, and to estimate how much of [the debt] could be renegotiated with new loans.[118]

At the IMF's Annual Meeting in 1998, the Menem government was presented as a success story. Not only did the IMF's Managing Director characterize Argentina's experience under Menem as exemplary, but he went as far as saying that 'Argentina has a story to tell the world: a story which is about the importance of fiscal discipline, of structural change, and of monetary policy rigorously maintained.'[119] This is particularly amazing when taking into account that only 3 years later Argentina suffered the most serious financial crisis of the country's history, which to a large extent was the logical consequence of the policies adopted by the Menem regime with the IMF's approval.[120]

When Menem handed over the government to De la Rúa in 1999, the country's public foreign debt amounted to 85,000 million dollars,[121] the provincial public foreign debt to 22,000 million dollars, and the private foreign debt was estimated at somewhere between 40,000 and 56,000 million dollars.[122]

---

113 Ibid., at 1002–1003.
114 Kulfas and Schorr (2003), at 33–34.
115 Rapoport and Musacchio (2005), at 53.
116 Rapoport (2000), at 1010.
117 Stiglitz (2006), at 167.
118 Galasso (2003), at 323.
119 IMF's Independent Evaluation Office's Report (2004), at 12.
120 See, for example, ibid., at 26–27 with regard to the IMF's failure to carry out an adequate debt sustainability assessment.
121 Rapoport (2000), at 1007.
122 Galasso (2003), at 331.

4 The explosion of the financial crisis under De la Rúa[123]

At the beginning of the year 2000, the new Argentinian government concluded a Stand-By-Arrangement with the IMF, aimed at strengthening international confidence in the financial stability of the country.[124] In December 2000, the De la Rúa Government achieved an agreement which in Argentina was called the *blindaje* (shield), according to which the IMF, the IDB, the World Bank, some local banks and pension funds, and the Spanish government granted a credit of 32,700 million dollars.[125] This money was intended to guarantee the payment of the country's obligations that became due in 2001, and to recreate trust in the country.[126]

After Cavallo took over as Secretary of the Economy, in July 2001 Congress enacted the so called Zero Deficit Act (ley 25.453), the aim of which was to achieve a balanced budget. According to the underlying policy, every month the effective tax income would be used first to service the interests of the debt, and the remaining balance would then be used for other public expenditures.[127] The Act empowered the executive to reduce, *inter alia*, pensions and the salaries of public employees if public spending exceeded the state's activa. The executive made use of this empowerment in August 2001 and reduced, retrospectively as of 1 July 2001, both salaries and pensions by 13 per cent.[128] In August 2001, the Inviolability of Bank Deposits Act (Act 25.466) was enacted in order to increase the trust in the financial system.

Also in summer 2001, Cavallo initiated the *megacanje* (mega-swap), which was a voluntary restructuring of the country's debt by swapping it for new bonds which postponed the maturity of the debt, but increased its stock.[129] According to Michael Mussa who was then the IMF's chief economist, while the mega-swap would save the country 12,000 million dollars of debt repayment between 2001 and 2005, this came at the cost of additional debts of 66,000 million dollars as of 2006.[130] Indeed, it seems as if the main purpose behind the *megacanje* was not to resolve or lessen the debt burden, but instead merely to buy time and postpone the default.[131] In the course of this operation, the Argentinian state paid 90 million dollars of fees to Wall Street firms.[132] The *megacanje* has been called one of 'the most infamous deals that Wall Street ever peddled to a government'.[133] In the course of criminal proceedings

---

123 For an analysis of some of the debt related policies during this period see Lischinsky (2003).
124 IMF's Independent Evaluation Office's Report (2004), at 39.
125 Galasso (2003), at 342.
126 Kulfas and Schorr (2003), at 45.
127 Ibid., at 46; Kanenguiser (2003), at 173.
128 Decreto 1.060/01.
129 Kulfas and Schorr (2003), at 46–47; Galasso (2003), at 344; IMF's Independent Evaluation Office's Report (2004), at 90; for a critical discussion of the *megacanje* see also Blustein (2005), at 125–132.
130 Mussa (2002), at 65–66.
131 IMF's Independent Evaluation Office's Report (2004), at 64–65.
132 Blustein (2005), at 125.
133 Ibid. For an analysis of the many irregularities which allegedly took place in the context of the *megacanje* see, for example, Cafiero and Llorens (2002), at 122–138.

against Cavallo, De la Rúa and the American banker David Mulford for their role in the *megacanje*, Justice Ballesteros concluded that:

> Having demonstrated the senselessness of the swap ... as well as that it was clearly foreseeable that the country would eventually fall into default and that the little time that was bought increased enormously and unjustifiably the public debt, it is possible to sustain, with the certainty that this procedural stage requires, that the accused operated with absolute awareness that they acted to the detriment of the national interests.[134]

Closely linked to the debt problem was the question of the sustainability of the convertibility between dollar and peso. While it became more and more obvious that the regime could only be maintained at the cost of taking up more debt, and while it seemed inevitable that the peso at some point would have to be devalued or the economy dollarized, the government, and in particular Cavallo under whose leadership the convertibility had first been introduced in 1991, was not willing to take this step.[135]

In August, the IMF debated whether or not to augment its programme with Argentina and approve an additional loan of 8,000 million dollars which would partly be used to finance the mega-swap[136] and partly to augment the country's reserves. Although the chance of success of the programme was estimated at no more than 20 to 30 per cent, and even though a clear majority of those present at a selected senior staff meeting at which the question was discussed, were of the opinion that 'the additional few billion dollars would not make a difference, but would be more likely to disappear in capital flight, leaving Argentina more indebted to the IMF,'[137] others suggested that 'the augmentation would buy time (4 to 5 months at most) and ensure that the [Argentinian] authorities, not the IMF, took responsibility for the critical decisions needed (that is a change in the exchange rate regime and debt restructuring)'.[138] The loan was approved 'in order to buy the authorities (and the international community) time to put together a solution that would be both less disorderly and less costly than an immediate collapse of the regime.'[139]

However, while a disbursement of 5,000 million dollars was made in September 2001 to increase the country's reserves, already by mid-November the reserves were

---

134 See "Cavallo Domingo Felipe y otros s/ abuso de autoridad y violación de los deberes de funcionario público", 28 September 2006. Both the first instance court (in 2003) and the Court of Appeal (on 20 May 2004) declared the criminal charges against Cavallo *et altera* to be without merit ("CAVALLO, Domingo F. y otros s/falta de mérito"). However, based on new evidence regarding the detrimental nature of the *megacanje* for the country and the *mens rea* of the accused, on 28 September 2006 Justice Ballestero revised his earlier decision and was satisfied that a *prima facie* case against Cavallo, De la Rúa and the American banker David Mulford justified the continuance with criminal proceedings against them.

135 See, for example, Godio (2002), at 31–50; Kanenguiser (2003), at 166.

136 IMF's Independent Evaluation Office's Report (2004), at 54; Bluestein (2005), at 153–154.

137 IMF's Independent Evaluation Office's Report (2004), at 53.

138 Ibid.

139 Ibid., at 54.

down to exactly where they had been before the payment was made. It has been suggested that a large part of this money was in fact used in order to finance capital flight, as individuals and companies exchanged their pesos for dollars, still at an exchange rate of one to one, to then transfer the money out of the country before the feared devaluation would take place. Thus, the IMF loan mainly enabled some to rescue their money, while increasing the foreign debt of the state by this latest loan.[140] Between January and December 2001, capital flight was estimated to amount to about 13,000 million dollars,[141] and it was mainly international companies that transferred money abroad.[142]

While many of the big players thus had the possibility of transferring dollars abroad,[143] on 1 December 2001, the Government enacted Decree 1570/2001, which introduced the so-called *corralito*,[144] limiting cash withdrawals by individuals to 250 pesos or 250 dollars per person per week. Thus, the ordinary Argentinian citizen could no longer freely dispose of their savings and bank deposits. This led to political uprisings which, on 20 December 2001, resulted in police repression of a demonstration against the government, leaving 5 demonstrators dead, and provoked the resignation of President De la Rúa.[145]

5 Crisis management under Duhalde

On 23 December 2001, Rodríguez Saá announced the default of Argentina's foreign debt, but when Duhalde took over as President at the beginning of January 2002, he declared that only those bonds that had not been restructured would be in default.[146] On 6 January 2002, the Public Emergency and Reform of the Monetary System Act (Act 25.561) was enacted. This Act declared the public emergency in social, economic, administrative, financial and monetary matters and delegated far-reaching powers to the executive to proceed with the reorganization of the financial and banking system. The Act suspended the applicability of the provisions of the Inviolability of Bank Deposits Act, but emphasized that the federal executive would take measures aiming at the preservation of the capital of savings accounts, including deposits that were made in foreign currency, by restructuring the original obligations in a manner compatible with the evolution of the solvency of the financial system.

---

140 Bluestein (2005), at 171; see also Bonelli (2005), at 215–217. The IMF's Independent Evaluation Office's Report (2004) comes to the conclusion that IMF policies adopted in the course of the year 2001 'allowed the government to carry out a series of desperate and unorthodox measures to "gamble for redemption"', thereby allowing the crisis to drag on, at 64–65. See also the critical analysis of IMF policies in Argentina by Krueger (2002).
141 Galasso (2003), at 345.
142 Bonelli (2005), at 215–216.
143 For an analysis of capital flight during the final year of the system of convertibility see Basualdo (2006), at 369–380.
144 The literal translation of *corralito* is playpen.
145 See, for example, Godio (2002), at 121–148.
146 Kulfas and Schorr (2003), at 49.

Finally, on 3 February, based on the empowering provision contained in the Public Emergency and Reform of the Monetary System Act and on its generic constitutional powers to enact emergency legislation under limited conditions,[147] the Argentinian Government enacted Decree 214/2002 which, *inter alia*, declared the *pesification*, that is the conversion into pesos, of all bank accounts held in US dollars, at a conversion rate of 1,40 pesos for 1 US dollar.[148] All debts with banks taken out in dollars were converted into debts in pesos at a conversion rate of one peso for one dollar. Creditors of bank deposits of up to $30,000 were given the opportunity to opt for a Treasury bond to compensate for the devaluation of their accounts. The banks received compensation for the asymmetrical *pesification* of debts and obligations, a measure which significantly increased the public debt in 2002.[149]

Even though the IMF had, according to its own reports, contributed to Argentina's crisis, this fact did not lead the IMF to reduce its claims against the country. Instead, during the negotiations with the Duhalde government of a Stand-By Arrangement to refinance Argentina's debts, which the government felt was essential in order to avoid Argentina's financial isolation and being cut off from World Bank and IDB loans,[150] the IMF imposed policy measures as prerequisites of the agreement.[151] These requirements partly expressly favoured the interests of the country's creditors.[152] The IMF moreover complained that Argentina took policy decisions such as the lifting of the *corralito* without prior consultation with the IMF,[153] and that court decisions questioning the constitutionality of the *corralito* and the *pesification* caused legal uncertainty and made any agreement with the country difficult.[154] During that period, the political costs and consequences of depending on the IMF became particularly obvious.

6 The Kirchner administration from 2003 to present times

Under the Kirchner administration, both the debt problem and the country's relationship with the IMF continued to play an important role in the political arena. In September 2003, the Argentinian government reached a Stand-By Arrangement with the IMF whereby the IMF agreed to refinance Argentina's debt with the IMF, subject to certain performance criteria which included progress in restructuring

---

147 See Art 99 (3) of the Constitution.
148 At that time, dollars could be bought for about two pesos for one dollar, but the exchange rate went up very quickly, and within 2 months more than three pesos needed to be paid for one dollar.
149 See, for example, Elespe (2005a), at 11.
150 See Amadeo (2003), at 55.
151 For a detailed account of the negotiations between the Argentinian government and the IMF see Amadeo (2003); see also, for example, IMF Country Report 03/226.
152 For example by insisting on changes to insolvency law, see IMF Country Report 03/226, at 24.
153 Ibid., at 13.
154 Ibid., at 11.

the country's debt.[155] However, in August 2004, the IMF delayed its review of Argentina's compliance with the terms of the Arrangement, and the disbursement of money to Argentina according to the Arrangement. The reasons for this were issues around the pending debt restructuring, and that the renegotiation of the contracts of privatized public services providers did not proceed as the IMF demanded.[156] Instead of negotiating these issues with the IMF, Argentina chose to repay the IMF with its own funds when payments became due.

Given the financial impossibility of servicing all of its foreign debt, in September 2003 the Argentinian Government submitted to the Annual Meeting of the IMF and the World Bank in Dubai a proposal that suggested a restructuring of the country's foreign debt other than with IFIs. The proposal, which included a cut of 75 per cent in the capital of the debt, was at the time accepted by the IMF on the basis that the IMF itself, together with the other IFIs, would receive preferential creditor status, meaning that the Argentinian debt with the IFIs would be repaid in full, including interest. However, the IMF as well as the G7 Governments and the creditors concerned later put a lot of pressure on the Argentinian Government to improve this offer.[157]

After long and painful negotiations, the restructuring was accepted by 76 per cent of the bondholders. According to official figures, this debt restructuring resulted in a reduction of Argentina's sovereign debt from 191,000 million dollars at the end of 2004 to 125,000 by mid-2005, and in longer maturities of the debts, and an increased amount of debt in the local currency.[158] Even leaving aside the high costs of this debt restructuring in terms of future interest payments,[159] the country is still left with an enormous public debt, and for the coming years, 3 per cent of the GDP is designated for debt servicing.[160] Another problem still unresolved in this context is that of the hold-out creditors, that is those bondholders who did not accept the restructuring of their debt, and now resort to the courts, mainly in the US, in order to obtain repayment in full.[161]

In December 2005, President Kirchner declared the intention to repay in full and in one payment all of the country's outstanding debt with the IMF, which amounted to about 9,000 million dollars, and payment was made in January 2006. This measure was taken even though most of the debt had not matured at that time, and despite the President's discourse of blaming the IMF for many of the country's problems. The government justified this payment as the only way in which the country could regain its sovereignty and rid itself of the supervision, pressure and conditionalities of the IMF.[162] However, while this measure was widely celebrated as debt cancellation, it was regarded by others as no more than an act of replacing the creditor, as in order to be able to pay the debt with the IMF, the country needed to borrow the money from

---

155   SEC Prospectus (2005), at 16.
156   Ibid., at 17.
157   See, for example, *Clarín*, 22 April 2004.
158   Rapoport and Musacchio (2005), at 57; Hocsman (2005), at 60.
159   For a critical discussion see, for example, Giuliano (2006).
160   See also Rapoport and Musacchio (2005), at 57–58.
161   See, for example, *CVI v Argentina*, 443 F3d 214 (2nd Cir NY 2006).
162   See, for example, *Página* 12, 16 and 18 December 2005.

the Central Bank. Thus, the public foreign debt with the IMF has turned into a public internal debt with the Central Bank.[163]

7 Social implications

Since the early 1980s, Argentina's debt repayment obligations exceeded by far the country's economic possibilities. This means that ever since the return to democracy, policy choices needed to be made in order to decide which of the conflicting demands should be prioritized: the contractual obligations towards the creditors, which would involve dedicating a high percentage of the GDP to debt servicing; or the social obligations towards the people of the country. Despite the importance of the rights that are at issue when people lack food, housing, essential medication, and do not have the opportunity to make a living, rights which are protected both by international treaties[164] and the Argentinian Constitution,[165] the country's foreign indebtedness meant that the country was never entirely free to determine its policies in this respect without being subjected to strong pressure by its creditors. The creditors' logic was explained quite graphically by James Wolfensohn, when he was President of the World Bank. In reply to the question of whether Argentina should increase its budgetary surplus in order to be able to dedicate more money to debt repayment, instead of prioritizing social expenditures, he replied:

> at some point, as an individual, you can't just go on not paying your credit cards, and not paying your bank, and not paying your mortgage and saying well, what I really want to do is to educate my kids. ... Well, of course you want to educate your kids, but at a certain moment the rules are that if you want to keep playing the game you do have some other obligations and that is the issue with countries.[166]

---

163   See, for example, the open letter sent to President Kirchner by a number of MPs, http://64.233.187.104/search?q=cache:GRIj9hFZfvcJ:www.lafogata.org/05arg/arg12/ arg_22-3.htm+CARTA+DOCUMENTO+al+Presidente+de+la+Naci%C3%B3n+N%C 3%A9stor+Kirchner+y+a+los+legisladores+nacionales&hl=es&gl=ar&ct=clnk&cd=1.

164   The UN Declaration of Human Rights (UDHR), for example, grants the individual the right to social security and the realization of 'the economic, social and cultural rights indispensable for his dignity and the free development of his personality' (Article 22); the right to an adequate standard of living, 'including food, clothing, housing and medical care and necessary social services', as well as the right to social benefits in cases of need (Article 25); and the right to education (Article 26). Comparable rights can be found in the Convention on the Rights of the Child (CRC) which protects, for example, the right to health (Article 24): the right to social security (Article 25); the right to an adequate standard of living (Article 27); and the right to education (Article 28). And the International Covenant on Economic, Social and Cultural Rights (ICESCR) guarantees the right to social security (Article 9); to social protection (Article 10); to an adequate standard of living and to food (Article 11); to the highest attainable standard of health (Article 12); and to education (Article 13).

165   Article 75(22) of the Argentinian Constitution gives certain international treaties, including the ICESCR, the ICCPR, the UDHR, and the CRC, constitutional rank.

166   23 April 2004, www.businessday.co.za.

The dependency of debtor countries on negotiating debt reschedulings etc. puts the IMF, the World Bank, and the Governments of the G7 States in the position to influence the economic policies of these countries, which usually involves that the fulfilment of obligations towards creditors be regarded as a matter of prime concern. Beyond insisting on debt repayment, the IMF made debt renegotiations and restructuring subject to conditionalities, such as the implementation of structural adjustment programmes (SAPs), and also insisted on the adoption of policies that favour foreign investors in Argentina, for example the owners of privatized public service providers.[167] The logic of structural adjustment programmes[168] is based on the idea that in order to achieve economic recovery and fiscal stability, a country needs to cut down on government spending and expenditures, including reductions in public service salaries, social programmes, and the provision of health and education. They also usually favour the privatization of public service provision. According to the IMF, while these measures might have the short-term effect of creating severe social hardship, they are the only means to ensure long-term growth and prosperity. However, even if one were to accept that this was really the purpose behind the imposition of SAPs,[169] it seems as if the short term adverse consequences materialized, the beneficial long-term prognosis turned out to be mistaken.[170] After many years of implementing IMF supervised adjustment strategies, in 2001 Argentina found itself in a severe crisis, as the consequence of which unemployment figures rocketed,[171] savings and pensions were devalued, poverty rates reached an unprecedented level, and the social protection of large sectors of the Argentinian society dropped worryingly.[172]

It cannot be ignored that there is no agreement as to whether and to what extent external factors contributed or even caused this downfall. Indeed, many voices can be heard contending that Argentina's crisis and the resulting deterioration of the social situation of large parts of the population were mainly caused by internal factors, such as corruption, ungovernability, or the lack of will to fully implement

---

167 For example when insisting on legislation allowing for an increase of the charges for their services, see Amadeo (2003), at 151.

168 For an extensive analysis of structural adjustment programmes and their consequences see, for example, Woodward (1992). See also Oloka-Onyango (1995), at 21–29.

169 Many challenge this and suggest that the main reason behind SAPs is to influence economic and financial policies in developing countries in favour of the interests of Northern countries and multinational companies; see, for example, Cheru (1999); Juliá (2002), at 28.

170 For a critical comment see, for example, Figueredo (2000), at para. 1.

171 See Morello (2002), at 839–840.

172 The public health system, for example, almost collapsed, see *Estado de los hospitales públicos del país* (Situation of the public hospitals in the country), an Annexe to the Report on Health in Argentina, presented by the influential Centre of Legal and Social Studies (CELS) to the Inter-American Commission on Human Rights, which gives an impressive overview of the disastrous situation of many hospitals in which even the most basic equipment, such as needles, anaesthetics etc., were missing, at www.cels.org.ar. For statistics on health; social security; unemployment; poverty rates etc. see the web page of the National Institute of Statistics and Censuses, www.indec.gov.ar.

the adjustment programmes suggested by the IMF.[173] However, there is nevertheless now widespread agreement that the one-fits-all adjustment policy imposed by the IMF has an adverse impact on the dire social rights situation in debtor countries,[174] including Argentina.[175] While there can be no doubt that factors inherent in the political culture of Argentina significantly contributed to the desolate situation of the country,[176] it is equally clear that the current crisis in Argentina cannot be considered without placing it in the context of the debt crisis.[177]

The UN High Commission on Human Rights emphasized in 1999 that 'The serious problem of the foreign debt burden remains one of the most critical factors adversely affecting economic, social, scientific and technical development and living standards in many developing countries, with serious effects of a social nature.' Furthermore, it pointed out that 'structural adjustment policies have serious implications for the ability of the developing countries to abide by the Declaration on the Right to Development and to formulate national development policies that aim to improve the economic, social and cultural rights of their citizens.'[178] For the specific case of Argentina, Lozada explained the direct and indirect links between debt and social rights as follows:

> Debt servicing occupies a highly significant place in the national budget and thus displaces other payments dedicated to an autonomous development and the creation of genuine and not only precarious employment; health; education; and security. Not only this, debt repayment also requires external assistance from and causes dependence on international credit institutions and the Northern countries that dominate them. Such a dependency causes the obligation to follow to the letter the 'adjustment' policies of these organisations, in particular the IMF.[179]

While no studies exist which demonstrate in any detail how exactly debt repayment affects the enjoyment and promotion of economic and social rights in debtor countries, it is submitted that the very fact that large amounts of money are transferred from the developing to the developed countries, while the people in many of the former live in poverty and lack even basic social protection, speaks for itself. Indeed:

---

173 See, for example, Asp (2003), at 384; Mussa (2002), at 112–113. The IMF's Independent Evaluation Office's Report (2004), while admitting some faults committed by the IMF, nevertheless mainly blames Argentina's policy choices, for example at 31.

174 See Cheru (1999), who demonstrates the connection between neo-liberal policies and the social rights situation more globally. Also Adams (1991), at 90.

175 The UN Committee on Economic, Social and Cultural Rights remarked in its Report on Argentina (1999) that 'the implementation of the structural adjustment programs has hampered the enjoyment of economic, social and cultural rights, in particular by the disadvantaged groups in society', at para. 258, and recommended that 'the State party, when negotiating with international financial institutions, take into account its Covenant obligations to respect, protect and fulfil all the rights enshrined in the Covenant', at para. 276. See also Mudho (2003).

176 See, for example, Ferrer (2003), at 141–147; and Mussa (2002), at 13–26.

177 See, for example, Stiglitz (2002), at 69; and Rapoport (2002).

178 UN Commission on Human Rights, Resolution 1999/22, 23 April 1999.

179 Lozada (2002), at 117.

It is perfectly clear that the majority of the countries of the South can only continue to pay their foreign debt at the cost of increasing and deepening poverty; reducing to a minimum the provision of essential goods; increasing the number of cases in which the basic necessities are not satisfied; and encouraging the consummation and deterioration of natural resources.[180]

Thus, the debt burden adversely affects the protection of economic and social rights not only because of the diversion of money from social purposes to debt servicing, but also because of the structural adjustment programmes that are imposed on debtor countries in exchange not for debt relief, but rather usually debt rescheduling which either postpones the maturity of certain debt, or consists of new credits with which parts of the maturing debt can be cancelled, and which obviously add to the debt burden of the country.

8 Concluding remarks

This very brief and selective overview of the history of Argentina's sovereign debt over the past 30 years can unfortunately only give a very sketchy introduction to the political, economic and social complexities surrounding the debt problem. What becomes obvious, though, is that Argentina's sovereign debt increased significantly under the last military regime; that many of the loan transactions undertaken at the time reek of irregularities; that not only the policies of the Argentinian authorities, but also the lending practices of the international banks were irresponsible; that the debt burden grew exponentially because of a rise in interest rates; that after the return to democracy the debt was never audited to determine to what extent it was, in fact, legitimate; that ever since, the country had to take up new debt in order to service its debt; and that despite debt servicing and constant debt restructurings, Argentina is today still faced with a huge internal and foreign public debt. Thus, the debt policies of a military regime that governed without any democratic participation or control decisively shaped the future of the country, as it not only left it with an unsustainable debt, but through this indebtedness has moreover influenced and conditioned the economic, financial and social policies of the democratic governments ever since.

---

180 Pazmiño Freire and Kumin (2001), at 158.

Chapter Three

The Doctrine of Odious Debts

Among the legal theories upon which anti-debt campaigners rely as providing a potential legal argument against debt repayment,[1] the doctrine of odious debts is probably the most popular. In its traditional version, the doctrine of odious debts is mostly summarized as follows: a sovereign debt is odious and can be repudiated if (1) it was contracted without the consent of the people of the country that is said to owe the debt; (2) it was not contracted for the benefit of the people of that country; and (3) the creditors were aware of the odious nature of the debt. The doctrine accepts the basic assumption of *pacta sunt servanda*, but lobbies for exceptions in cases in which, based on moral rather than legal reasons, it is felt that on the balance, the risk of the loan should lie with the creditor, not with the people of the debtor state. It is not concerned with the economic unsustainability of the sovereign debt of developing countries, but instead focuses on the circumstances under which the debt was contracted. The underlying idea is that it would not be fair to expect the people of a country to repay a debt that was not only contracted without their control, but that was, to the knowledge of the creditor, taken up for a purpose or used in a way that was not in the interests of the people.[2] Thus, the doctrine aims to provide a mechanism according to which a sovereign debt can be repudiated and does not need to be repaid, even if the contracts are otherwise valid.

The discussion of the odious debts doctrine first surfaced in the 1920s,[3] but it has gained a lot of popularity in recent years, particularly in the context of the debate about the Iraqi debt, where it seems to have been relied upon not only by anti-debt campaigners,[4] but also by the US Government. John Snow, US Secretary of the Treasury, for example, stated in an interview that 'the people of Iraq shouldn't be saddled with those debts incurred through the regime of the dictator who is now gone'.[5] However, when the moral principles on which it is based are subjected to legal analysis, the seemingly straightforward doctrine raises many complex legal issues, from the fundamental question of whether or not international law does, in fact, recognize the doctrine of odious debts, to the exact scope of the doctrine and the subtleties of its application.

---

1   For an ample collection of publications arguing in favour of the repudiation of parts of the debt of developing countries based on the doctrine of odious debts see, for example, www.odiousdebts.org.
2   See Sack (1927), at 157.
3   Ibid., at 157–181.
4   See, for example, Kaiser and Queck (2004); Adams (2004).
5   Interview on 10 April 2003 in 'Your world with Neil Cavuto', www.foxnews.com/printer_friendly_story/0,3566,83939,00.html. For an analysis see Toussaint (2006).

1 Does international law recognize the doctrine of odious debts?

Whether or not international law recognizes the doctrine of odious debts is controversial. Thus, an analysis of the extent to which the doctrine of odious debts might be used by a debtor state in order to refuse debt repayment needs to start with an examination of the status of this doctrine in international law. To this effect, the different sources of international law, that is treaties, international customary law and the general principles of international law, as well as judicial decisions and legal doctrine[6] will be examined in order to evaluate whether they provide evidence for a recognition of the doctrine of odious debts as a rule of international law.

1.1 State practice

Several historical events are usually mentioned as evidence of the existence of state practice according to which debts that are regarded as odious can be repudiated, and as a basis for the conclusion that the doctrine of odious debts forms part of international customary law.[7] The repudiation by the US of Cuba's debts with Spain is often quoted as one of the most significant examples of the repudiation of a country's debts based on their odious nature.[8] At the end of the Spanish-American War of 1898 in which the US supported Cuba's fight for independence from Spain, Spain claimed that Cuba was obliged to repay loans that the Spanish state had taken out to finance its operations in Cuba and which Spain had secured with Cuban revenues. The Spanish argument was that:

> It would be contrary to the most elementary notions of justice and inconsistent with the dictates of the universal conscience of mankind for a sovereign to lose all his rights over a territory and the inhabitants thereof, and despite this to continue bound by the obligations he had contracted exclusively for their regime and government.[9]

Thus, Spain presented the loans in question as loans entered into for Cuba, and argued that as a consequence of losing its rights over Cuba, it should no longer be bound to repay these loans. However, the US alleged that large parts of the loans in question had been used in order to finance Spain's colonial policies in Central America, and the suppression of the insurrection in Cuba against Spanish dominance. In the light of this, the American Commissioner at the Paris Conference at which peace negotiations between the US and Spain took place argued forcefully that:

> From no point of view can the debts above described be considered as local debts of Cuba or debts incurred for the benefit of Cuba. In no sense are they obligations properly chargeable to that island. They are the debts created by the government of Spain, for its own purposes and through its own agents, in whose creation Cuba had no voice. From the moral point of view, the proposal to impose these debts upon Cuba is equally untenable

---

6   See Art 38(1) of the Statute of the ICJ.
7   A good overview of incidents in which debt was repudiated in the international, as well as in the national setting, can be found in King (2003), at 21–34 and 40–42.
8   See, for example, Sack (1927), at 159; King (2003), at 25.
9   Moore (1906), at 353.

... The burden of the so-called 'Cuban debt', imposed upon the people of Cuba without their consent and by force of arms, was one of the principal wrongs for the termination of which the struggles for Cuban independence were undertaken ... The debt was contracted by Spain for national purposes, which in some cases were alien and in others actually adverse to the interest of Cuba.[10]

Thus, the American Commissioner based the repudiation of Cuba's debt on the considerations that it was not incurred with Cuba's consent, and that the debt was not beneficial for the Cuban people. His statement does not provide a detailed legal analysis of the doctrine of odious debts, and seems to have been based mainly on moral, rather than on legal considerations.[11] It is in line with the then predominant view in the Anglo-Saxon world that successor states were not bound by law to assume the debts of their predecessor, but instead had no more than a moral obligation to do so, and that the winning power was free to define this moral position according to its own free will.[12] While it is nevertheless by many regarded as a clear expression of the doctrine of odious debts,[13] another possible interpretation of this statement would accordingly be to view the repudiation of these debts as mainly reflecting the balance of power at the relevant time.[14]

Among other examples frequently cited as applications of the odious debts doctrine are: Mexico's rejection in 1867 to assume the debts contracted by Austria in order to strengthen its power over Mexico;[15] the refusal of Britain in 1902 to assume the debts that the Boer Republics had contracted to finance their war against Britain;[16] and the repudiation of Polish debts to Germany in the Treaty of Versailles of 1919.[17]

In the Working Paper on the odious debts doctrine prepared by the Centre for International Sustainable Development Law (CISDL), Jeff King ends his overview of state practice with regard to odious debts with a paragraph headed 'recent state practice in the Balkans'. There, he suggests that the apportionment of the debts of the former Yugoslavia that was based on the principle of equitable distribution 'can be related in principle to the "public benefit" aspect of the odious debt doctrine'.[18] However, it is submitted that there is a fundamental difference between the principle of equitable distribution and the principle of odious debts. The former is based on principles of fairness between the various successor states and starts from the

10   Ibid., at 358–359.
11   See, for example, Foorman and Jehle (1982), at 23; Feilchenfeld (1931), at 340.
12   Hoeflich (1982), at 55–56.
13   See, for example, Frankenberg and Knieper (1984), at 431.
14   See Kaiser and Queck (2004), at 7.
15   For a discussion see Sack (1927), at 19–20 and 158; King (2003), at 24.
16   For a discussion see Hoeflich (1982), at 59; King (2003), at 26.
17   Article 255(2): In the case of Poland that portion of the debt which, in the opinion of the Reparation Commission, is attributable to the measures taken by the German and Prussian Governments for the German colonization of Poland shall be excluded from the apportionment to be made under Article 254. For a discussion see Feilchenfeld (1931), at 450–453; Sack (1927), at 159–160.
18   King (2003), at 28–29.

assumption that a valid debt exists that needs to be assumed. The assessment of the benefits that the various successor states received accordingly mainly serves the purpose of deciding how to achieve a fair distribution of this debt. The doctrine of odious debts, on the other hand, is concerned with the question of repudiating a debt because of its nature and purpose, and this repudiation would be directed towards the creditor. It is thus submitted that the state practice in the Balkans cannot be viewed as an example in which states recognized and implemented the doctrine of odious debts. To the contrary, it seems more convincing to regard it as evidence of a state practice according to which in cases of state succession debts are usually assumed by the successor states.[19]

The debates surrounding debt cancellation for Iraq revived the discussion of the doctrine of odious debts. However, the interim Iraqi Government did not invoke that Iraq's debts should be repudiated as odious,[20] and the decision to grant Iraq substantial debt reduction was reached as part of a Paris Club deal[21] and through bilateral agreements with creditor countries which do not form part of the Paris Club,[22] without reference to considerations related to those underlying the doctrine of odious debts.[23] The case of the cancellation of parts of Iraq's debt can therefore not be regarded as evidence of a state practice that recognizes the doctrine of odious debts as a principle of international law.

Another example sometimes mentioned, not so much as one of state practice, but nevertheless as a case of the recognition of the odious debts doctrine by an important state organ, is that of the British House of Commons International Development Committee which is said to have suggested a rejection of Rwanda's debts as odious.[24] However, it is submitted that the text of the report does not support this conclusion. In the executive summary to the report, before suggesting the cancellation of Rwanda's debt that was incurred by the previous regime, the Committee argues that: 'the international community failed to act when the genocide took place in Rwanda in 1994. It now has a responsibility to do everything possible to prevent such events occurring. Debt relief can make a significant contribution.' Seen in this context, it seems more convincing to interpret the recommendation as based on humanitarian considerations than on the doctrine of odious debts. This interpretation is further supported by the fact that in the text of the report, the recommendation of debt cancellation is made in the context of the economic unsustainability of Rwanda's

---

19   See Ipsen (2004), at 354; Anderson (2005), at 430.

20   See Gelpern (2005), at 406.

21   www.clubdeparis.org/en/press_release/page_detail_commupresse.php?FICHIER=com
11011125170.

22   Toussaint (2006).

23   See also Alexander (2004). However, the Economic and Financial Committee of the Iraqi National Assembly made a recommendation to repudiate the debt with the Paris Club as odious, instead of negotiating a debt reduction. See *Recommendation of the Economic and Financial Committee (EFC) to the Iraqi National Assembly (INA), the Interim Iraqi Government and to the Iraqi People on the External Odious Debts (OD) and Reparations inherited from the tyrannical Saddam Regime*, www.jubileeiraq.org/blog/Iraqi%20National%20Assembly%20resolution%20on%20debt.doc.

24   Hanlon (2006), at 113.

debt, as it is preceded by the statement that 'We are concerned that debt relief for Rwanda must be provided as rapidly as possible, in order to make a real contribution to Rwanda's economic recovery.'[25] The statement on odious debts can be found in para. 10 of the introduction, where it says that: 'David Woodward, a development consultant, reminded us in evidence that in some cases the responsibility for unproductive use of loans lay with previous rather than current debtor governments. For example, the bulk of Rwanda's external debt was incurred by the genocidal regime which preceded the current administration.' The next sentence brings in some statistical data, and the paragraph then ends with the statement that 'some argue that loans were used by the genocidal regime to purchase weapons and that the current administration and, ultimately, the people of Rwanda, should not have to repay these "odious debts."' Thus, the Committee merely noted that this opinion exists, without itself accepting or rejecting this view.[26]

As there do not seem to be any recent cases in which a state repudiated a debt as odious,[27] although this could have been done on numerous occasions, for example with regard to the debts of former colonies after gaining independence, or the debts of the former Eastern block countries, it is difficult to say with much conviction that state practice exists from which it could be inferred that the doctrine of odious debts is recognized as a rule of customary international law.

1.2 Case law

With regard to case law, the one and only decision[28] that lends some support to the doctrine of odious debts is the arbitral decision in the so-called *Tinoco* case, which arose between Costa Rica and Great Britain.[29] In that case, the British Government brought two claims against the Costa Rican government that succeeded the Tinoco

---

25   House of Commons Select Committee on Development, Session 1997/98, Third Report: Debt Relief, at para. 56.

26   Hanlon's interpretation has, however, for example been accepted by Jochnik (1999), at 140–141.

27   But see *Jackson v People's Republic of China*, 794 F2d 1490 (11th C. 1986), at 1495, where China rejected liability for bonds issued by the Imperial Chinese Government in 1911 *inter alia* on the basis that these debts were odious.

28   Abrahams (2000) suggests at 46 that the British decision in *West Rand Central Gold Mining Company, Limited v R* [1905] 2 KB 391 is also based on the doctrine of odious debts, but it is submitted that this is a misinterpretation of that decision. Lord Alverstone CJ rather held at 402 that '[w]hen making peace the conquering Sovereign can make any conditions he thinks fit respecting the financial obligations of the conquered country, and it is entirely at his option to what extent he will adopt them. It is a case in which the only law is that of military force'. He continued at 403 that 'it was suggested that a distinction might be drawn between obligations incurred for the purpose of waging war with the conquering country and those incurred for general State expenditure. What municipal tribunal could determine, according to the laws of evidence to be observed by that tribunal, how particular sums had been expended, whether borrowed before or during the war?'

29   *Great Britain v Costa Rica* (1923), Reports of International Arbitral Awards, Vol. 1, 371.

regime, only one of which, that the Government of Costa Rica and the Banco Internacional de Costa Rica were indebted to the Royal Bank of Canada because of transactions performed by the Tinoco regime, is relevant to the discussion of the concept of odious debts.[30] This claim was based on the fact that in July 1919, a cheque for 1,000,000 colones, to be payable in provisional bills of 1,000 colones, drawn by the Minister of the Treasury against the Banco Internacional de Costa Rica, was deposited in the government's account with the Royal Bank of Canada. The cheque was presented to the Banco Internacional de Costa Rica, which delivered in payment thereof to the Royal Bank one thousand 1,000 colones bills. A day later, the Minister of the Treasury wrote a note to the Royal Bank, certifying that for the colones bills held by the Royal Bank, 'this Ministry will pay interest at the rate of 10 per cent per annum on the amount of the deposit that is utilized and ... before September 15 next, the notes of this deposit will be replaced by current issues.'[31] Thereafter, the Tinoco Government drew against this account, and the Royal Bank honoured the cheques. Based on these facts, Great Britain argued that the Costa Rican Government and the Banco Internacional de Costa Rica must recognize the validity of the 1,000 colones notes still held by the Royal Bank and honour their obligation to the Royal Bank following from these transactions.

The Government of Costa Rica denied the validity of the claim on the basis that the restored Costa Rican Government had passed the Law of Nullities. That law invalidated all contracts between the executive power and private persons made during the time of the Tinoco Government, and also annulled all transactions on which the bank transfer was based.[32] William Taft, US Supreme Court Chief Justice and the sole arbitrator in that case, first of all established that despite the fact that it had come into power by a military putsch, the Tinoco regime was a *de facto* regime during most of the time of its government which lasted from January 1917 to September 1919, as Tinoco governed the country with the acquiescence of the people, and his regime was recognized by a number of foreign nations. However:

> It is evident from the exhibits that in the spring of 1919 the popularity of the Tinoco regime had disappeared and that the political and military movement to end that regime was gaining strength ... The sinking credit of the Tinoco government and the expenses of the maintenance of the army raised in its defense, had produced a stress in its finances which led to the legislation authorizing the issue of the fifteen millions of colones. The emergency was illustrated in the use of the very irregular form of the notes of issue by the Banco Internacional ... It became perfectly clear from mob violence and disturbances in June, and the evidences of the unpopularity of the Tinoco regime, that it was in a critical condition ... The present claim of the Bank rests in its payment of ... $100,000 to Federico Tinoco, "for expenses of representation of the Chief of State in his approaching trip abroad," and $100,000 to Jose Joaquin Tinoco, as Minister of Costa Rica to Italy, for four years' salary and expenses of the Legation ... in Italy, to which post the latter had been appointed by his brother. The Royal Bank cannot here claim the benefit of the

---

30 For a discussion of the other part of the claim see Chapter Seven, 2, infra.

31 *Great Britain v Costa Rica* (1923), Reports of International Arbitral Awards, Vol. 1, at 389.

32 For the rather complex facts underlying the claim of the bank see ibid., at 375.

presumptions which might obtain in favour of a bank receiving a deposit in regular course of business and paying it out in the usual way ... The whole transaction here was full of irregularities. There was no authority of law, in the first place for making the Royal Bank the depositary of a revolving credit fund. ... The thousand dollar colones bills were most informal and did not comply with the requirements of law as to their form, their signature, or their registration. The case of the Royal Bank depends not on the mere form of the transaction but upon the good faith of the bank in the payment of money for the real use of the Costa Rican Government under the Tinoco regime. It must make out its case of actual furnishing of money to the government for its legitimate use. It has not done so. The bank knew that this money was to be used by the retiring president ... for his personal support after he had taken refuge in a foreign country. It could not hold his own government for the money paid to him for this purpose. The case of the money paid to his brother ... is much the same ... To pay salaries for four years in advance is a most unusual and absurd course of business. All the circumstances should have advised the Royal Bank that this second draft, too, was for personal and not for legitimate government purposes. It must have known that Jose Joaquin Tinoco in the fall of his brother's government, which was pending, could not expect to represent the Costa Rican Government as its Minister to Italy for four years, that the reasons given for the payment were a mere pretence and that it was only, as in the case of his brother Federico, an abstraction of the money from the public treasury to support a refugee abroad.[33]

With regard to the remaining deposit, the judge decided that it was not important to establish the exact nature of the arrangements made in this respect as:

Whatever it was, it is so closely connected with this payment for obviously personal and unlawful uses of the Tinoco brothers that in the absence of any explanation on behalf of the Royal Bank, it cannot now be made the basis of a claim that it was for any legitimate governmental use of the Tinoco government.[34]

Many commentators of the decision allege that it is based on the doctrine of odious debts, or principles close to it.[35] It has, for example, been suggested that Taft's holding stands for the principle that 'contracts made by recognized governments may be held unenforceable under international law because they contravene the legal requirements for the creation of a valid public debt, one such requirement being that they be in the public interest'.[36] From this interpretation it is only a small step to regarding the *Tinoco* decision as a recognition and application of the doctrine of odious debts.[37] Others argue that the reason for which Taft accepted Costa Rica's unilateral repudiation of the debt had nothing to do with the odious nature of the debt, but that he rather focused on the obvious irregularities of the transaction.[38] However, while it is true that Taft did not expressly refer to the doctrine of odious debts, it is not entirely accurate to claim that he did not reject the debt on the basis

33 Ibid., at 393–394.
34 Ibid., at 394.
35 See, for example, Anderson (2005), at 410; Kaiser and Queck (2004), at 8.
36 King (2003), at 42.
37 See, for example, Abrahams (2000), at 48; King (2003), at 42; Christoph Paulus (2005a), at 85.
38 Gelpern (2005), at 411.

of arguments that are closely related to that doctrine.[39] Indeed, his decision seems to be based on a combination of factors, these being that the debt in question had been incurred for personal and not for legitimate government purposes; that the transactions were full of irregularities; that they were made when the popularity of the regime had already faded away and its fall was imminent; and that the bank must have been aware of these facts. Thus, the purpose of the loan and the fact that it was not taken up for the benefit of the people of Costa Rica; the fact that the regime no longer had the support of the people; and the awareness of the Royal Bank of these facts, were important factors for the outcome of the case, and these considerations closely resemble the three elements of the odious debts doctrine. However, the decision does not provide a detailed and principled legal analysis of the issue of odious debts. Instead, it seems to be based on a very narrow factual setting and on what Taft regarded as a fair outcome under the given circumstances, and he did not justify his conclusion with reference to well-defined principles of international law. It is then questionable to what extent this isolated decision provides evidence of the recognition of the doctrine of odious debts as a rule of international law.

At first sight, the *Jarvis* case[40] might also be regarded as an application of principles close to the doctrine of odious debts. There, the American-Venezuelan Commission regarded a debt as unenforceable, even though a loan that was made to Páez, a former president of Venezuela, to support an unsuccessful revolution against the existing Venezuelan government, was 14 years later assumed in the form of new government bonds when Páez briefly took power in Venezuela. The Commission opined that:

> Differences of opinion may possibly exist as to the political ethics which would justify a temporary ruler in paying his personal debts with national obligations; but more certainly none can exist as to the legal proposition that a subsequent contract made in aid and furtherance of the execution of one infected with illegality partakes of its nature, rests upon an illegal consideration, and is equally in violation of the law. The opportune service rendered by Jarvis in 1949 in violation of law created no legal obligation on the part of Páez, much less on the part of the Government of Venezuela. And a past consideration which did not raise an obligation at the time it was furnished will support no promise whatever.[41]

While the first part of the statement, which refers to personal debts of a temporary ruler, resembles some of the considerations on which the doctrine of odious debts is based, it is submitted that the decision in the *Jarvis* case largely depended on the fact that the original loan was seen to violate US law, and that the underlying agreement was accordingly held to be illegal. Thus, the outcome relied on the legal invalidity of the contract, not on circumstances that exceptionally justified its repudiation.

---

39   But see Mancina (2004), who argues just that, at 1248.
40   *US on behalf of Jarvis v Venezuela*, US and Venezuelan Commission, Report of Robert C. Morris before the United States and Venezuelan Claims Commission 1904, 301.
41   Ibid., at 305.

1.3 Academic recognition of the doctrine

As an academic doctrine, the principle of odious debts was first formulated by Alexander Sack, a professor of international law, whose writings on the issue are still one of the main points of reference for the contemporary discussion of odious debts. His contention was that:

> When a despotic regime contracts a debt, not for the needs or in the interests of the state, but rather to strengthen itself, to suppress a popular insurrection etc., this debt is odious for the people of the entire state. This debt does not bind the nation; it is a debt of the regime, a personal debt contracted by the ruler, and consequently it falls with the demise of the regime. The reason why these "odious" debts cannot attach to the territory of the state is that they do not fulfil one of the conditions determining the *lawfulness* of State debts: *that State debts must be incurred, and the proceeds used, for the needs and in the interests of the state.* ...

> "Odious" debts, contracted and used, for purposes which, *to the lenders' knowledge*, are contrary to the needs and interests of the nation, are not binding on the nation – when it succeeds in overthrowing the government that contracted them – unless the debt is within the limits of real advantages that these debts might have afforded ... The lenders have committed a hostile act against the people, they cannot expect a nation, which has freed itself of a despotic regime, to assume these "odious" debts, which are the personal debts of the ruler.[42]

Various points therefore come together in order to make a debt odious, although it is not entirely clear to what extent they are all essential for qualifying a debt as odious: the regime that took up the debt was despotic; the debt was not incurred for the needs and use of the state, but rather that of the regime; it did not confer a real benefit on the state; and the creditors were aware of this. If the debt can then be regarded as odious, it follows that it is not a state debt, but instead a personal debt of the regime. This is interesting, as it seems to suggest that Sack's focus was not on the invalidity of the loan, but instead on who would be bound by it. Sack was mainly concerned with the purposes for which the debt was incurred, and with the lenders' awareness of these purposes, but less so with the lack of consent of the people, which is usually regarded as another prerequisite for regarding a debt as odious. Another important issue emphasized by Sack was that:

> the very question of the "odious" nature of this or that debt will only arise *exceptionally*, when it appears, *absolutely indisputably*, that these debts are really "odious", not only in the eyes of the new government of the whole or part of the territory of the former state, but also in the opinion of competent and impartial representatives of the family of nations.

> Political and economic doctrines are too diverse and contradictory ... for the attitude of the new government towards this or that debt contracted by its predecessor to be sufficient when the question of the "odious" nature of this debt is determined.[43]

---

42   Sack (1927), at 157. The translation follows very closely that in Frankenberg and Knieper (1984), at 428–429.

43   Sack (1927), at 162.

Thus, he wanted his theory to be applied only to exceptional and clear cases in which the odious nature of the debt could be determined objectively. According to him, a debt that was properly contracted by a regular government can nevertheless be odious if the new government can prove to an international tribunal:

> a) that the purposes in the light of which the old government had contracted the debt in question were "odious" and openly contrary to the interests of the people ...
>
> b) that the creditors, at the moment when the loan was issued, were aware of its "odious" destination. ...
>
> These two points established, it is for the creditors who dispute the claim to prove that the funds made available through these loans were *in fact* used for purposes that were not "odious" and harmful to the people ... but instead for general or special needs of that state that were not of an "odious" nature.[44]

Sack distinguished the situation of a loan that was not contracted in a regular way, that is by a regular government and according to the correct procedure. In that case, the creditors need to prove from the outset that the state was, in fact, enriched by the loan.[45] This is interesting, as it shows that the doctrine of odious debts as envisaged by Sack was meant to apply exclusively to cases in which a loan agreement would otherwise be valid, that is, contracted by a competent organ according to the relevant procedural norms. Where this was not the case, the creditors would be reduced to claims for unjust enrichment against the debtor, that is the people of the new state, but could not raise claims based on a valid contract.

Since Sack's writings in 1927, only a few legal scholars continued the academic discussion of the odious debts doctrine. Probably the most important analysis in this respect was that submitted by Feilchenfeld in 1931. Feilchenfeld was of the opinion that the doctrine of 'imposed and odious debts' had not become rules of law.[46] He further argued that the 'international financial law', which according to Sack governed the fate of sovereign debts in the context of state succession and of which the doctrine of odious debts was but one part, was not, in fact, a recognized source of international law, given the lack of a general practice accompanied by a recognition of these principles as rules of law.[47] With regard to the legal status of the doctrine, he came to the conclusion that:

> there is an increasing tendency to admit that, while no strict rules of law exist, there are certain principles of equity which should apply, and which provide that in all cases of state succession some allocation or distribution of debts should take place. No agreement has, however, been reached on the question what these principles of equity are, and what effects they should have on the details of financial settlements.[48]

---

44   Ibid., at 163.
45   Ibid, at 30. Jèze (1922), at 302, seems to share this assumption.
46   Feilchenfeld (1931), at 558.
47   Ibid., at 591–598.
48   Ibid., at 575.

However, Feilchenfeld analysed in some detail how such a doctrine could work were it to be recognized by the international community.[49]

Looking at other academic writers, O'Connell acknowledged the existence of the principle of odious debts, but suggested a lack of unanimity as to the exact scope and limits of the doctrine, and was himself critical of it, given its highly political nature.[50] Hyde accepted that there might be an exception to the principle that a successor state should take on the debts of its predecessor,

> if a debt were incurred for purposes essentially hostile to the interests of the territory transferred, as manifested by the opposition of a majority of the inhabitants or of the local authorities thereof to the creation of the fiscal obligation, or by the employment of the funds so obtained to hold in subjection those inhabitants, or to repress their endeavour to bring about the change of sovereignty actually resulting.[51]

It is interesting to note that while the doctrine of odious debts is not given academic consideration by legal academics in the UK, German public international law scholars generally tend to accept that the doctrine of odious debts forms part of customary international law, and explain the doctrine by stating that it would be unreasonable to expect a successor state to assume such debts.[52] The doctrine also gave rise to academic publications in the US.[53] Overall, however, it needs to be noted that there is no unanimity as to whether the doctrine of odious debts does[54] or does not[55] and should[56] or should not[57] form part of international law.

---

49 Ibid., at 701–716.
50 O'Connell (1956), at 187–189.
51 Hyde (1947), at 404; see also Wood (1986), at para. 4.10(3).
52 Bothe, Brink, Kirchner and Stockmayer (1988), at 38; Leyendecker (1988), at 181; Frankenberg and Knieper (1984); Ipsen (2004), at 355–356; Verdross and Simma (1984), at 629; Folz (2000), at 609.
53 See, for example, Mark Thompson (1996); Okeke (2001); Acquaviva (2002); Vreedenburgh (2004); Mancina (2004); Gelpern (2005); Chander (2004); Anderson (2005); Kremer and Jayachandran (2002).
54 See, for example, Frankenberg, Knieper (1984), at 429; Fischer-Lescano (2003), at 233–239; Mark Thompson (1996), at 500–501; Okeke (2001), at 1202–1203; Acquaviva (2002), at 187–188 and 213.
55 Vreedenburgh (2004) at 589; Mancina (2004), at 1252–1253; Gelpern (2005), at 406.
56 Anderson (2005), at 439–441; Fischer-Lescano (2003), at 233–239; Frankenberg, Knieper (1984); Rasmussen (2004), at 1177; Chander (2004), at 927; authors in favour of a prospective application of the doctrine are Kremer and Jayachandran (2002); Gelpern (2005), at 412–413; authors who mention the existence of the doctrine in passing and approve of it without further analysis or discussion are, for example, Williams and Harris (2001), at 406.
57 Foorman and Jehle (1982), at 22; Mancina (2004), at 1255–1262; Beemelmans (1997), at 115.

1.4 General principles of international law

The extensive report on the doctrine of odious debts submitted by CISDL suggests that the doctrine can to some extent find a legal basis in general principles of international law, such as unjust enrichment, abuse of rights, and obligations arising from agency.[58] In respect of unjust enrichment, it is difficult to see how it could form the basis of a repudiation of debt repayment. The principles of unjust enrichment usually govern situations in which someone has obtained a benefit but no legal ground justifies that the person who received the benefit keep it. Thus, the underlying principles might become interesting in the context of odious debt type scenarios, for example when deciding whether money already paid on those loans needs to be reimbursed by the creditors. However, this is a question that only arises once the primary question, that is that of the invalidity of the loan agreements, has been determined.[59] The principle of unjust enrichment might therefore be important for but cannot form the basis of a repudiation of debt repayment.

With regard to the issue of abuse of rights, Frankenberg and Knieper suggest that: 'Odious debts are excepted from the obligation of fulfilment not because they are considered an excessive burden for the successor, but rather because they are contracted under abuse of rights. The abuse is constituted in a purpose which contradicts the interest of the attributable subject (the population)'.[60] As the CISDL report acknowledges, it is neither clear that 'abuse of rights' is in fact recognized as a general principle of international law, nor how exactly such a principle is to be defined.[61] Reference to this principle can then do little to assist in providing a legal basis for the doctrine of odious debts.

1.5 The position of the International Law Commission

In the course of the drafting of the Vienna Convention on the Succession of States in respect of State Property, Archives and Debts (1983), Special Rapporteur Bedjaoui suggested in his report the inclusion in the Convention of two articles expressly referring to the issue of odious debts. The first draft article defined odious debts as follows:

> For the purposes of the present articles, "odious debts" means: (a) all debts contracted by the predecessor State with a view to attaining objectives contrary to the major interests of the successor State or of the transferred territory; (b) all debts contracted by the predecessor State with an aim and for a purpose not in conformity with international law

---

58   King (2003), at 34–39.
59   King himself, ibid., mentions this as a 'deficiency' of the application of the principles of unjust enrichment in this context.
60   Frankenberg and Knieper (1984), at 428.
61   King (2003), at 35. For an overview of the discussion on the recognition of the doctrine of abuse of rights in international law, see Brownlie (2003), at 430.

and, in particular, the principles of international law embodied in the Charter of the United Nations.[62]

He then suggested a second article that would clarify that 'odious debts contracted by the predecessor State are not transferable to the successor State'.[63] The ILC did not include these two articles in the final draft of the Convention. However, this was not an expression of opposition against a recognition of the doctrine of odious debts.[64] Instead, the ILC: 'recognized the importance of the issues raised in connection with the question of "odious" debts, but was of the opinion ... that the rules formulated for each type of succession of States might well settle the issues raised by the question and might dispose of the need to draft general provisions on it.'[65] Thus, the ILC was clearly of the view that the concept of odious debts should form part of the rules governing state succession in debts,[66] but did not think that specific provisions dealing with the issue were called for. However, the Convention has not come into force, so that it does not provide a source of international law, and some of its provisions were expressly rejected by the developed countries.[67] It is then not clear to what extent the assumptions of the ILC in this area are an expression of customary international law. Furthermore, the applicability of the Convention would be limited to relations between States, and not cover treaties or other legal relationships between States and private creditors.

1.6 Conclusions as to the recognition of the doctrine under international law

Whether or not the aforementioned instances of state practice, the *Tinoco* decision and the writings of Sack and some other academics are sufficient to support the claim that the doctrine of odious debts has found recognition in international law is controversial.[68] Given the lack of recent state practice to that effect, and indeed the more or less consistent approach by successor states to assume the debts of their predecessors in recent times, it is submitted that the doctrine of odious debts as a principle of international law stands on rather weak ground.[69] It might be true that the reluctance of successor governments to reject the repayment of debts that could qualify as odious was in many cases the result of enormous economic and political pressure exercised by the creditors who usually made it perfectly clear that such a move would mean international isolation and that the state be cut off from future

---

62   Bedjaoui (1977), at para. 173. While the definition under (a) closely resembles the definition of the odious debts doctrine thus far applied in the context of this chapter, the definition in (b) goes beyond this and will be discussed in Chapter Four.
63   Bedjaoui (1977), at para. 173.
64   However, see Mancina (2004), at 1250.
65   Report of the International Law Commission on the work of its thirty-third session (4 May – 24 July 1980, Document A/36/10, (1981) 2 YB ILC, part 2, at 79.
66   See also Verdross and Simma (1984), at 629–630; Ipsen (2004), at 356.
67   See Ipsen (2004), at 347–348.
68   See, in this respect, supra notes 53 and 54.
69   See also Christoph Paulus (2005a), at 86.

lending.[70] While one could argue that a doctrine that forms part of international law will not cease to do so if it is falling into disuse due to pressure exercised over those who would have the right to rely on this doctrine,[71] this argument stands and falls with the question of whether the doctrine did, at some point, form part of international law, and the result of the preceding analysis suggests that this is rather questionable.

However, the debates around debt cancellation for Iraq gave the doctrine of odious debts a new boost. Anti debt campaigners who asserted that Iraq's debt is odious and therefore does not need to be repaid[72] were joined by a rather unlikely ally, namely the US government.[73] Moreover, in June 2003, a bill, the Iraqi Freedom From Debt Act, was introduced in the US House of Representatives,[74] calling for the cancellation of Iraq's debt, given that based on 'international precedent, debts incurred by dictatorships for the purposes of oppressing their people or for personal purpose may be considered "odious"' (Sec.2(3)). This applied to the debt of Iraq, as 'a significant amount of Iraq's outstanding loans were taken out at the behest of Baath Party leadership and rather than being used for the benefit or the well-being of the Iraqi people were used for building lavish palaces, secret police, prisons, and illegal weapons programs' (Sec.2(2)). However, given the reality of the debt reduction for Iraq, it has already been argued above that the case of the cancellation of parts of Iraq's debt cannot be regarded as evidence that the doctrine of odious debts is a recognized principle of international law.

The conclusion that the existence of a doctrine of odious debts as a rule of international law is not clearly established does not mean that it is therefore obsolete to analyse the content and potential use of such a doctrine. Instead, from an academic perspective it is nevertheless interesting to examine whether its future recognition should be promoted[75] as a basis for the repudiation of the debt of developing countries.

70　In the context of Argentina's attempt to repudiate parts of its debt after the end of the latest military regime, see, for example, Kanenguiser (2003), at 49–62; Olmos (2004), at 59; Morgan-Foster (2003), at 621.

71　ICJ, *Military Activities in and against Nicaragua (Nicaragua v US)*, (1986) ICJ Rep 14, at para. 186; Ipsen (2004), at 229.

72　See, for example, Adams (2004); Kaiser and Queck (2004).

73　See note 5.

74　H.R. 2482, 16 June, 2003.

75　This was also the suggestion made by Feilchenfeld (1931), who argued at 701 that no sufficiently coherent international practice based on the recognition of legal rules existed that could justify regarding the doctrine of odious debts as a legal principle, and that 'a debt may be legal even when there are no apparent reasons for its creation or when existing reasons appear unjust. It is possible, however, to investigate the justice of a debt independently from its legality, and equally possible to investigate the grounds which in future legislation should or should not justify the existence of a debt.'

2 The doctrine of odious debts and regime change

Even if the doctrine of odious debts is, or were to be, recognized under international law, an essential question concerning its applicability to large parts of the Developing World debt is whether it only applies to the case of state succession,[76] or whether it could equally be relied on in cases of a mere government change, but state continuity.[77] If the former were the case, large parts of the debt of developing countries would be excluded from the application of this doctrine, as in many cases, democratic regimes were left with large debt burdens by their undemocratic predecessors, but no state succession took place. Only if the doctrine were also applicable to the case of government succession could these countries potentially qualify for an application of the doctrine of odious debts.

Sack focused his analysis on the case of state succession. However, whether this means that he thought that cases of regime change should be excluded from the scope of application of the doctrine is not clear. More recently, the view that the doctrine of odious debts is limited to cases of state succession seems to have been endorsed by the Iran-United States Claims Tribunal. When commenting on Iran's claim that part of the debts owed by Iran to the US were odious, the Tribunal felt that it was unnecessary 'to take any stance in the doctrinal debate on the concept of "odious debts" in international law', as 'said concept belongs to the realm of the law of State succession ... The revolutionary changes in Iran fall under the heading of State continuity, not State succession.'[78] Accordingly, the Tribunal was of the opinion that the issues it had to decide fell outside of the scope of the potential application of the doctrine of odious debts.[79] Equally, in the German academic legal discussion, among those who regard the doctrine of odious debts as part of international law, there is a widespread rejection of its extension to cases of regime change, as it is argued that unlike in the case of state succession, there is no state practice that supports the application of the odious debt doctrine in the case of regime change.[80]

However, to restrict the odious debts doctrine to cases of state succession is somewhat artificial. First of all, the distinction between state and regime succession is not always clear-cut, as for example the controversial discussion of whether the Russian Revolution belonged to the realm of state succession or whether it was a

---

76 See, for example, Delaume (1967), at 315–316; Baars and Böckel (2004), at 459, n.175; Wälde (1987), at 124; Wood (1986), at 4.10(2), who seems to make this point in the context of succession in debt, generally, not with particular regard to the question of odious debts.

77 Nitti (1931), who argued in favour of a principle that is very similar to the odious debts doctrine, specifically envisaged cases of regime change, rather than state succession, at 754–755.

78 *US v Iran*, Case No. B36, Award No. 574-B36-2, 1996, at para. 54.

79 See also Christoph Paulus (2005a), Buchheit, Gulati and Thompson (2006), at 19, n.60.

80 See, for example Bothe, Brink, Kirchner and Stockmayer (1988), at 38; Leyendecker (1988), at 193.

mere case of regime change shows.[81] More importantly, it is questionable whether in respect of succession in debts the cases of state succession and regime change are sufficiently different to justify applying the doctrine of odious debts to one but not to the other. In favour of making a distinction, it has been argued that these two scenarios are entirely different: In the case of state succession, the problem that needs to be resolved is to what extent and on what legal grounds the successor state is under an obligation to assume the debts of its predecessor's debts. In the case of a mere regime change, on the other hand, the debtor, that is the state represented by the former regime, keeps in existence, so that a legal basis would be needed to justify the repudiation of the debt by the successor government.[82] While this distinction between the two situations certainly exists, it is not at all clear that it follows that the doctrine of odious debts should therefore be restricted to cases of state succession. From a formalistic perspective, if anything, a recourse to the principle of odious debts is more obvious in the case of regime change than in the case of state succession, exactly because in cases of state continuity but government change, the debtor remains in existence. The change of government usually does not affect the debtor-creditor relationship, so that these are the cases where a legal justification in the form of the odious debts doctrine would be needed if the new regime does not want to assume the debt. On the other hand, whether or not international law recognizes a legal principle according to which successor states need to honour the debts of their predecessors is controversial.[83] Therefore, it may be that a successor state can repudiate debts simply on the grounds that it is under no obligation to honour them, while this option as such is not open to successor governments, and repudiation could in that case only be justified by reference to principles that exceptionally relieve the new government from this obligation, for example because the debts were odious.

Leaving aside formalistic arguments, it is submitted that the test for the exclusion or inclusion of cases of regime change into the ambit of the doctrine of odious debts should depend on whether the considerations based on which the doctrine of odious debts is accepted in cases of state succession equally apply to cases of regime change. If the reasons for developing a legal principle that makes it possible that debts can exceptionally be repudiated as odious are considerations of equity, fairness, justice and reasonableness which demand that the people of a country should not be required to repay debts that were contracted without their consent and without benefiting them, it is difficult to justify that these principles should only apply to cases of state succession.[84] To do so would mean to distinguish between the case of a dictator who contracted odious debts but at the end of his regime a new state emerged, and the case of the very same dictator if he were succeeded by a democratic regime.[85] From

---

81   See Foorman and Jehle (1982), at 10 and 20; for a general argument in this context see Fischer-Lescano (2003), at 232–233; for the discussion of whether the change in South Africa from Apartheid to a democratic state was a case of state succession or regime change, see Abrahams (2000), at 55–56.

82   Leyendecker (1988), at 193; Bothe, Brink, Kirchner and Stockmayer (1988), at 38–39.

83   Brownlie (2003), at 625. Buchheit, Gulati and Thompson (2006) argue that it does, at 3–5.

84   Frankenberg and Knieper (1984), at 427.

85   Gelpern (2005), at 411; King (2003), at 47; Fischer-Lescano (2003), at 233.

the point of view of the people, the debt is as unbeneficial in the latter case as in the former. And why the risk that the creditors who knowingly lent money to such a dictator for odious purposes need to assume should differ in the two scenarios is equally inexplicable. Therefore, as Feilchenfeld argued:

> if the opinion prevails that certain burdens should not fall upon the population of a debtor state, protection should be given, even if there has been neither annexation nor dismemberment; for unless such protection is generally admitted, it is illogical to advocate it in the case of state succession, which in itself affords no reason why the burdens of the population of a debtor state should be alleviated.[86]

This was also the opinion of Taft in the *Tinoco* decision, as that was clearly a case of debt repudiation after a regime change, and not after state succession.[87] It nevertheless needs to be noted that there is much less support for the assumption that a doctrine of odious debts that justifies the repudiation of debts in the case of regime change is a recognized principle of international law, than is the case with regard to state succession.[88]

3 How can it be determined whether a debt is odious?

It was already explained that most promoters of the odious debts doctrine assert that three requirements need to be met in order for a debt to be regarded as odious, which are that: (1) it was contracted without the consent of the people of the country that is said to owe the debt; (2) it was not contracted for the benefit of the people of that country; and (3) the creditors were aware of the odious nature of the debt.

3.1 Absence of consent

While it seems convincing to question that the people of a country should be responsible for repaying debts that were contracted without their consent, the issue of how to determine whether or not the people have consented to the taking up of a loan is rather complex. In a representative democracy, it can be said that the democratically elected government has the general consent of the people to govern the country. On the other hand, where a government takes power without being elected or otherwise having the backing of the people, it governs the country without the consent of the people, and there will, in principle, not be consent with regard to specific acts, such as the taking up of loans.[89] However, this already raises several difficult issues, such as that of the extent to which the consent of the people and democratic representation can be equated. What, for example, is the situation where

---

86 Feilchenfeld (1931), at 716. See also Christoph Paulus (2005a), at 93.
87 See also Fischer-Lescano (2003), at 233.
88 Fischer-Lescano (2003), for example, argues at 230 that the doctrine of odious debts is a principle of customary public international law, but only in the case of state succession, not in cases of regime change, but he nevertheless suggests at 232–233 that the doctrine should be extended to the situation of regime change.
89 Kaiser and Queck (2004), at 8; King (2003), at 42.

a government did not come into power by the means of democratic elections, but instead was instated after a successful revolution with widespread approval of the population? Or where no system of democratic representation exists, but where the people nevertheless largely approve of the government?

It has been suggested that even in countries which are ruled by undemocratic regimes, it might be possible to demonstrate the consent of the people, for example in the form of widespread popular approval of the government itself, or of a particular transaction or a project.[90] Here, it is of course problematic how to assess whether or not the population of a country governed by a dictator or military regime largely approved of that regime, or of a particular loan project, and how to determine in the absence of periodic democratic elections whether this consent is still present at any given time at which a loan is contracted. In the *Tinoco* case, Taft US CJ placed importance on the fact that while for several months the Tinoco regime had governed the country with the acquiescence of the people, this changed during the final months of his government, evidenced by armed uprisings etc. This seems to suggests that what would count is the actual situation in a country at a given time, but it is submitted that this might be difficult to assess and to monitor. Similar problems arise when trying to determine whether there was widespread opposition to a government or a particular loan transaction in a democratic country. Given the immense difficulties in ascertaining the actual opinion of the people, if this is what would need to be ascertained in order to decide whether or not a loan was taken up with the consent of the people, the doctrine of odious debts would be completely unworkable.[91]

The impracticability of determining whether there was actual consent or lack thereof in any given case could to some extent be overcome by the use of rebuttable presumptions. It could, for example, be presumed that in undemocratic regimes where the government itself is not legitimized by the consent of the people, governmental acts will also not enjoy the people's consent, a presumption which could be rebutted if, exceptionally, actual consent can be clearly established in a given case. In the context of democratically elected governments, on the other hand, it could be presumed that the government acts with the people's consent, and consent to loans taken up by such democratic governments could thus be presumed to have the consent of the people, unless it can exceptionally be demonstrated that such consent was lacking in a particular context.[92]

However, in the context of democratic regimes, it might be questioned whether the general consent granted by the means of elections necessarily equals consent to specific loan contracts. For example in a democratic country whose constitution sets out specific requirements for the constitutionality of contracting public debts, presumably the people can only be said to have consented to the taking up of loans within the constraints of the constitutional framework. It could then be said that if a loan taken up by a democratic regime does not comply with constitutional

---

90   King (2003).
91   See also Feilchenfeld (1931), at 704.
92   This seems to be in line with the approach suggested by Feilchenfeld, ibid.

requirements, the loan was contracted without the consent of the people,[93] or at least that the presumption of consent should no longer apply. Thus, where a constitution setting out formal requirements for democratic representation is in place, it could be said that the existence of consent of the people to governmental acts depends on compliance with constitutional standards, such as that a loan is contracted or approved by the constitutionally competent organ, and that it is taken up for purposes that are in compliance with constitutional authorizations or principles. However, while these considerations are important in the context of the validity of a loan agreement under national law, it is submitted that the formal validity of the state act should not have a bearing on the issue of whether or not a debt is odious,[94] as the doctrine of odious debts is based on equitable, not on formalistic legal considerations.

The preceding analysis demonstrates that even if one were to apply a presumption in favour of consent in democracies, and against the existence of consent in undemocratic states, to determine the existence or lack of consent is not always straightforward. The close link of these issues to fundamental but controversial questions of how to define democracy or the lack thereof complicates matters further.[95] Thus, even if one were to exclude the debts incurred by democratic regimes altogether from the scope of application of the doctrine of odious debts, the question of how to distinguish clearly between democratic and undemocratic regimes would remain.

A potential way to overcome the problems with the consent requirement would be simply to dispose of it. Sack did not seem to have had a separate requirement of lack of consent in mind when developing the doctrine of odious debts. When examining the main situation for which the doctrine of odious debts was originally developed, that is the case of state succession, it is difficult to see what role the consent requirement could play. The reason why successor states are widely regarded as obliged to assume the debts of the former state seems to be that it is regarded as just that a state that benefits from loans that were contracted by its predecessor should repay them.[96] However, the people of the successor state as the demos of the new nation will not normally have consented to a debt incurred by the former state. Accordingly, what seems to be essential is the extent to which the people of the successor state benefit from the loan, not whether or not consent was present or absent when the loan was agreed.[97] It is then submitted that the consent requirement is somewhat superfluous, at least as long as it is regarded as entirely separate from the question of benefit, a point to come back to in the next section.

---

93   Kaiser and Queck (2004), at 8.

94   See also Bedjaoui (1977), at para. 123, in a slightly different context.

95   Kremer and Jayachandran (2002) suggest at 31 that consent of the people could be equated with free and fair elections, using criteria similar to those used by non-profit organizations like the Centre for Democracy which observes elections.

96   Williams and Harris (2001), at 408; Reina (2004), at 588–589; O'Connell (1951), at 205–206.

97   For an overview of the various theories on state succession with regard to debt, see, for example, Foorman and Jehle (1982), at 11–14; Hoeflich (1982), at 42–47.

3.2 Absence of benefit

While the preceding discussion has shown that the 'absence of consent' requirement of the odious debts doctrine is not easy to establish, it will soon become obvious that to determine the presence or absence of benefits of a loan to the people of a country is even more difficult. Indeed, it is enormously contentious according to which criteria it can be assessed whether or not a specific loan was beneficial to the people of a country. As early as 1947, Hyde pointed out the need for a general agreement on how to apply the benefit test and argued that while to arrive at such an accord would be difficult:

> The advantages derivable from an adequate response to this requirement, through the enhancement of the credit of borrowing States, and the safeguarding of the equities of prospective creditors, might be fully commensurate with the burden established by such an achievement.[98]

However, it remains to be seen whether it is really possible to achieve Hyde's laudable goal. Of course, there is no lack of opinions as to when debts should be regarded as unbeneficial, but as is to be expected, these opinions vary hugely depending on the political convictions and affinities of the person, organization or institution expressing them. A seemingly easy and uncontroversial case seems to be that of evaluating the debts of Iraq. The US Iraqi Freedom From Debt Bill argues that the building of 'lavish palaces, secret police, prisons, and illegal weapons programs' are not for the benefit of the people' (sec.2(2)), and that the same applies to debts 'incurred by dictatorships for the purposes of oppressing their people or for personal purpose' (sec.2(3)). A report on the odiousness of Iraq's debts produced by members of Erlassjahr, a German based anti-debt campaigning organization, suggests a comparable analysis in order to ascertain if and to what extent Iraq's debts benefited the Iraqi people: Where a credit was used 'directly or indirectly to maintain or extend the machinery of repression', including maintaining the Iraqi army and the Republican Guards, these loans did not only not benefit the population, but they rather 'directly impaired its interests by paving the way for repression and a war of aggression'.[99] The same is said to be true for credits that were used 'to maintain the lifestyle of the President and his personal entourage'.[100]

Moving from the case of Iraq to more general considerations on how to determine whether debts are beneficial to the people of a country, the CISDL working paper on the doctrine of odious debts proposes a distinction between loans that are contracted for specific purposes, and those that are not. The report suggests that '[w]hen a loan is contracted for a specific purpose, its classification as contrary to the populations' interests is a relatively simple task', as:

> agreements concluded for the following reasons are presumptively not in the interests of the population: personal enrichment; purchase of arms to suppress popular uprisings;

---

98   Hyde (1947), at 413–414.
99   Kaiser and Queck (2004), at 17.
100   Ibid.

purchase of arms to fight imperial wars that are not supported by the population; strengthening of domestic institutions whose main purpose is to maintain a dictatorial state; investment in infrastructure that benefits a discretely defined minority who enjoy a pre-existing position of advantage.[101]

With regard to loans used for improving the general infrastructure of a country, or for social programmes, the suggestion is that such projects should be deemed to be beneficial to the people, regardless of the democratic or undemocratic nature of a government.[102] This, however, with the important caveat that infrastructure such as roads etc. might be used for military, rather than civil purposes, in which case it should be open to the people of that state to rebut the presumption that loans financing such projects had been of benefit to them.[103]

When it comes to the even more difficult question of how to determine the benefit of loans that are taken up for the general purpose of increasing a government's budget, King argues, on the one hand, that it would be appropriate to presume that such loans are not beneficial to the population.[104] On the other hand, he suggests that:

> the national budget must then be assessed for the year upon which the funds were received and expenditures classified according to oppressive, neutral and beneficial disbursements; amounts paid in support of directly oppressive institutions (eg state security agencies, state run media, prisons for political prisoners, police hardware, political campaigns etc.), may be deemed entirely not in the interests of the population.[105]

Some go further than this and assert that loans to a dictator for general budgetary reasons should always be regarded as 'funds that served to support an illegitimate and odious regime, and must thus be viewed as basically illegitimate', whatever the specific use that was ultimately made of the funds.[106]

It is submitted that the distinctions suggested between the various types of loans, that is loans for specific as opposed to loans for general purposes, are not as obvious and meaningful as they appear to be at first sight. In this context, it might be worth considering that a loan that was granted and used for specific purposes which are largely accepted as beneficial, might have the unbeneficial consequence of freeing up funds that can then be used for unbeneficial purposes, such as army expenses etc., so that there would then be an indirect connection between the loan and the unbeneficial measures.[107] Patricia Adams' argument in the context of the Iraqi debt that: 'Surely, not every loan and credit to Iraq was odious; doubtless, some loans and parts of loans were intended for, and were used for, legitimate governmental purposes and in the interests of the public; indeed, some of the most offensive expenditures

---

101 King (2003), at 44.
102 Ibid., at 46, Kaiser and Queck (2004), at 17.
103 Ibid.
104 King (2003), at 44.
105 Ibid., at 45. Even if this were achievable in an audit of a country's debt, the question would remain of how to deal with the requirement of creditor awareness with regard to such a complex analysis of a state's budget and expenditures.
106 Kaiser and Queck (2004), at 18; see also Adams (2004).
107 Feilchenfeld (1931), at 707.

may have been financed from Iraq's oil revenues,'[108] shows the problem very clearly. If the doctrine of odious debts were restricted to those debts that were not used for legitimate government purposes, then money can be lent to dictators, and the people burdened with a repayment obligation, for those expenditures that are regarded as legitimate by the international community, as long as the oppression itself is financed by other sources. Even if it could be determined, which in real life will almost never be the case, that a loan for beneficial purposes did not have any indirect unbeneficial consequences in the form of freeing up funds for non-beneficial purposes, it needs to be considered that any loan granted to a government might have a stabilizing effect in that it potentially enables the undemocratic regime to consolidate its position.[109] Indeed, even such beneficial acts as pumping some money into social programmes could have the effect of containing social protests and prolonging the survival of the undemocratic regime.[110] Thus, it is difficult, if not impossible, to say with any certainty that there can be such a thing as an entirely or at least predominantly beneficial use of funds by an oppressive regime.

Nevertheless. it seems as if the discussion of these issues is largely based on the assumption that it is relatively clear-cut how to define what are beneficial or unbeneficial uses of funds by an undemocratic regime, and that one can draft something resembling a blacklist of purposes which will not benefit the people of countries governed by undemocratic regimes. With regard to debts incurred for the objectives thus blacklisted, no further analysis of whether a specific loan benefited the people seems to be necessary, as long as it can be established that the regime itself is undemocratic. However, it might be questioned whether this position is helpful, as it could, for example, be said that prisons, government buildings and palaces are lasting assets that survive the undemocratic regime and might then give some benefit to the population.[111] Also, whether or not it can be sustained in a general manner that the prison system of an undemocratic state, or its army, will not hold at least some benefits to the people is questionable.[112] In this respect, when discussing the Spain-US controversy over the Cuban debt, O'Connell pointed out that it is not 'always justifiable to argue that money raised for the legitimate maintenance of law and order

---

108   Adams (2004), at 9.
109   See also Pogge (2005), at 115. Hanlon (2006) makes a comparable point when arguing at 118 that because of fungibility, where dictatorial governments contract loans for legitimate purposes, they might be enabled to attract hard currency which can then be used for purposes for which loans could not have been contracted, for example to buy arms where an embargo is in place.
110   See also Buchheit, Gulati, Thompson (2006), at 25–26 with further references to the moral and political debate regarding the more fundamental question of whether it can ever be beneficial to conclude contracts with or grant aid to odious regimes.
111   See also Chander (2004), at 926. However, others have argued that 'the entire amount be annulled where the proceeds support an actively oppressive institution, even though some of the infrastructure may be inherited, this may be viewed as an equitable concession; otherwise the creditor would profit from its own wrongdoing.' See King (2003), at 46.
112   See also Christoph Paulus (2005a), at 94.

and the suppression of revolution, is essentially contrary to the true interests of the territory; on this topic politics assume dominance over legal analysis.'[113]

Indeed, it is easy to foresee ferocious ideological battles over the question of the benefits of certain debts. For example, it is not at all clear that everybody would agree with King's suggestion that state run media are a directly oppressive institution. And Lothian rightly points out that the rejection of repaying certain debts is sometimes mainly based on ideological objections to the economic policies in pursuance of which the government contracted them.[114] Here, it becomes evident that the question of the beneficial nature of loans cannot be addressed without first determining whose prerogative it is to answer this question. Sack, the father of the odious debts doctrine, was of the opinion that the odious, and thus presumably also the unbeneficial, nature of a specific debt should not be decided by the new government, but must instead be determined by 'competent and impartial representatives of the family of nations'.[115] This is a pragmatic view that tries to balance the interests of stability of the financial market with the interests of debtor countries, favouring the former in all but extreme cases in which widespread agreement on the moral claim of the debtor state can be achieved. While this might be the only possibility for the doctrine of odious debts ever to find international recognition, it shows one of the fundamental shortcomings of the doctrine, as it imposes on the people of a newly democratic state an objective, international view on which investments of the former dictator they should regard as beneficial with the consequence that they are obliged to repay the foreign loans taken up to finance them.

However, it is a fundamental premise of democratic systems that it is the people themselves who should determine what is beneficial to them. If this is accepted, the argument that the odious debts doctrine should not be recognized because it facilitates the repudiation of debts for political or economic disagreement with the policies of the successor government loses some force. Even if it is true that what a successor government really challenges when rejecting debt repayment are the economic policies of its predecessor, it is submitted that this is just as legitimate as, if not more legitimate than questioning specific projects financed by loans, given that such policies potentially influence the future of the country even more adversely and irreversibly. If it is the people who decide what is beneficial to them, this must include which economic policies they want to follow, and the doctrine of odious debts should take this into account. In a similar way, but in the specific context of decolonization, the ILC suggested with regard to debts taken up for investment in infrastructure that:

---

113 O'Connell (1956), at 189. When he continues by stating that 'for this reason the only exact test of whether or not a debt is odious is the extent to which it is unbeneficial to the population of the territory it burdens', one is left to wonder how he thought that these benefits can and should be determined.

114 Lothian (1995), at 440; but see Kremer and Jayachandran (2002), who argue at 27 that loans taken up by non-democratic regimes should be regarded as unbeneficial and odious, regardless of whether they are used for purposes of repression or for the personal enrichment of the rulers, if the regime pursues 'bad economic policies'.

115 Sack (1927), at 162.

even if the successor State retained some "trace" of the investment, in the form, for example, of public works infrastructures, such infrastructures might be obsolete or unusable in the context of decolonization, with the new orientation of the economy or the new planning priorities decided upon by the newly independent State.[116]

However, while such an approach seems to provide the best way to give adequate weight to the sovereign will of the people, such a far-reaching concept of odious debts was not envisaged by Sack and is not likely to find approval as a principle of international law,[117] given the controversial nature of the odious debts doctrine even in its objective version.

It is submitted that any attempt to arrive at an agreement on how to distinguish objectively between beneficial and unbeneficial debts is bound to cause insuperable problems. As the preceding summary of the discussion surrounding the question of the beneficial or unbeneficial nature of debts demonstrates, the issue cannot be easily separated from that of the features of the regime in question. In many countries, large amounts of money go into financing government buildings, the secret police, prisons, weapons programmes, the army etc., and there does not seem to be widespread belief that to dedicate money to those purposes is illegitimate as a matter of principle. Consequently, it seems as if the view that such expenses are unbeneficial to the people when incurred by the regime of Saddam Hussein or other dictatorial regimes does not simply rely on the objective of the loans as such, but is instead based on a combination of two factors: the purposes of the use of the money, and the undemocratic nature of the regime. Can the problem of how to determine whether a debt is or is not beneficial then be overcome by focusing on the nature of the regime itself, and by arguing that loans taken up by a dictatorial regime are always unbeneficial to the people, as living under such a regime is, as such, not beneficial to them? Alternatively, should a presumption in favour of the unbeneficial nature of all debts incurred by a non-democratic regime be applied, which can be rebutted if the beneficial character of the loan can exceptionally be demonstrated?

The problem here is that when shifting the focus of the discussion from the unbeneficial nature of a specific loan to the undemocratic nature of a borrowing regime, agreement would have to be reached as to which regimes will or will not count as democratic. While in many cases, the assessment of whether a country is or is not democratic might be uncontroversial, such an evaluation will not always be straightforward, particularly bearing in mind that no universally accepted agreement on the definition of democracy has yet been reached within the international community.[118] It is then difficult to see how a democracy requirement can be turned into the main yardstick for an evaluation of whether or not regimes are odious and should therefore be excluded from taking up loans.[119] Indeed, before international consensus on this question can be reached, the democracy assessment would largely

---

116 Report of the International Law Commission on the work of its thirty-third session (4 May–24 July 1980, Document A/36/10, (1981) 2 YB ILC, part 2, at 103.

117 It is, for example, rejected by Buchheit, Gulati and Thompson (2006), at 28.

118 For an overview of the discussion with further references see Ipsen (2004), at 428–430; Cassese (2005), at 395; Franck (1992); and the contributions in Fox and Roth (2000).

119 See also Buchheit, Gulati and Thompson (2006), at 27.

depend on the political makeup of the body entrusted with this decision, and the economic and political interests it represents. Such an approach would give lenders, or an international institution, the power to judge the legitimate or democratic nature of regimes as such. It thus merely creates different problems, but does not provide a way to depoliticise the odious debts doctrine, or to make it more workable. However, to the extent that agreement on the notion of democracy might emerge, and a minimum standard beyond which a regime would be regarded as illegitimate at the international level become more clearly defined,[120] this approach might provide an opportunity to avoid the battles over how to define the beneficial nature of individual loans.

What can be seen so far is that there is no easy way to determine whether or not a specific loan benefits the people of a country that is governed by a dictatorship. The main problems here are those of how to determine what is beneficial in such a situation and, even more importantly, who decides. Whether or not the judgment focuses on the benefits of specific loan agreements, or on the nature of a regime, it is submitted that the objective approach suggested by Sack requires an agreement on highly political issues which will not only be difficult to reach, but which, if it needs to be reached at the international level, will inevitably be a compromise position which reflects existing power structures and is therefore not likely to give a lot of weight to the view of the people who are affected by the outcome of such a decision.

The discussion surrounding the issue of unbeneficial debts has not stopped at debts incurred by undemocratic regimes. In respect of the sovereign debt of democratic countries, it has been suggested that there should be a strong presumption that democratic regimes spend the funds they borrow for the benefit of the people, which can only in very exceptional circumstances be rebutted by the people of the debtor state, for example in the case of government corruption, or where money was borrowed for the private enrichment of individuals, instead of for public purposes.[121] However, it is doubtful whether it is appropriate to deal with such cases by extending the odious debts doctrine to democratic countries. In democratic societies, it is the people who decide what does and does not benefit them, and this is done, depending on the specific constitutional framework, in the form of constitutional or other legal provisions which define the political and economic system of the state. Thus, once a system is regarded as democratic, the questions of consent and of benefits cannot be separated, because it is the people who define benefits, and no one else, and they do it prospectively, not retrospectively. To allow a future government to question this, or to set up some international mechanism that decides on behalf of all nations world-wide which expenses are beneficial to the people, would undermine

---

120 In fact, Cassese (2005) argues that a minimum standard that requires '*representative* governance based on *regular, free and fair elections*, and accountable to the electorate; *respect for human rights*; *rule of law*' is already accepted by the international community, at 395. See also Franck (2000) and Fox (2000), at 90. But see the critical analysis by Roth (2000).

121 Feilchenfeld (1931), at 710.

this sovereignty.[122] Instead of dealing with loans that involve corruption or personal enrichment of the leaders of democratic states by regarding them as unbeneficial to the people, these cases instead should be, and usually are, dealt with through constitutional, administrative, contract and criminal law principles.

3.3 Creditor awareness of the odious nature of the debt

The idea of creditor responsibility forms an important part of the doctrine of odious debts, as it is thought that creditors who loan money to regimes in awareness of the fact that it will be used for purposes that are unbeneficial to the people, thereby commit a hostile act against the people and cannot expect them to repay such loans.[123] Thus, the doctrine to some extent aims at punishing lenders for their lending policies, and it has further been argued that it is only fair to impose the risk of the odious use of a loan on the lender if the lender was aware of this use.[124] Moreover, to the extent that the doctrine intends to influence lending policies, its purpose can only be achieved if the creditors are aware of the factors that would render the debt odious.[125] One of the questions arising in this context is that of the standard of awareness to be required from the creditors before a debt can be repudiated as odious. Sack referred to 'knowledge',[126] without clarifying whether this would require actual knowledge, or whether reckless ignorance might be sufficient. Others attempted to define the meaning of awareness by suggesting that it includes actual knowledge, wilfully shutting one's eyes to the obvious, and wilfully or recklessly failing to make such inquiries as an honest and reasonable person would make.[127] This, of course, raises the question of the extent to which the creditors are, in fact, under a responsibility to make inquiries, and what exactly they should inquire about.

Given that the criteria according to which it can be determined whether there was consent of the people, and whether a loan was used in a manner beneficial to them, are vague and disputed, presumably the creditors can only in very clear and uncontroversial cases be expected to have had actual awareness of the odious nature of a debt. With regard to their duty to make inquiries into the use of the loans by a regime, or the existence or absence of the people's consent, it should be borne in mind that if one wanted to impose on creditors a duty to make some democracy or consent assessment in each case of a loan agreement with a state, and to assess the beneficial nature of the purpose for which the loan is taken up, this would give creditors a political watchdog role.[128] It is submitted that the appropriateness of

---

122   See also Kremer and Jayachandran (2002), at 26–27. However, with regard to doubts that the sovereignty argument is helpful given the existing inequality of power between debtor and creditor nations, see Knieper (1988), at 452–453.

123   A similar consideration is present in Taft's decision in *Tinoco, Great Britain v Costa Rica* (1923), Reports of International Arbitral Awards, Vol. 1, 371.

124   Christoph Paulus (2005a), at 93.

125   See ibid., at 92–93.

126   Sack (1927), at 157.

127   King (2003), at 46; see also Kaiser and Queck (2004), at 8; Christoph Paulus (2005a), at 95.

128   And make loans much more expensive, see Paulus, ibid., at 89–90.

entrusting individual lenders, for example private banks, or foreign governments, with, or imposing upon them, such a highly political task is rather questionable.[129]

3.4 Burden of proof

With regard to the rather important question of who has the burden of proof in respect of the prerequisites of the doctrine, according to Sack it is the responsibility of the debtor state to show that a debt was contracted for purposes contrary to the interests of the people and that the creditors, at the moment when the loan was issued, were aware of this.[130] For those who in addition require the lack of the people's consent to the loan, the debtor moreover has the burden to show that the people did not consent to the taking up of the loan.[131] Once the debtor state has demonstrated this, 'it is for the creditors who dispute the claim to prove that the funds made available through these loans were *in fact* used for purposes that were not "odious" and harmful to the people ... but instead for general or special needs of that state that were not of an "odious" nature.'[132]

When discussing the possibilities of a doctrine closely resembling that of odious debts, Feilchenfeld made the thoughtful observation that:

> [i]t should be realized that some of the tests involved are so vague, and so likely to occasion difficulties in the matter of evidence, that their application would make denial of protection [of the creditor] very improbable if the burden of proof is upon the debtor state, or make legal protection in the field of public debts too uncertain if the burden of proof is upon the creditor.[133]

4 Odiousness of restructured debts and of debts traded on the secondary markets

Even if it could be established that the debts of a country had originally been odious, in many cases the debts contracted by undemocratic regimes are no longer owed to the original creditors in their original form, but were instead rescheduled and restructured by democratic governments. Large parts of the debt of developing countries are moreover being traded on the secondary markets. It then needs to be considered if the odious debts doctrine could have a place, and how it could operate, within this reality. The most comprehensive examination of the surrounding issues can be found in the CISDL working paper on odious debts, where Thomas identifies many of the potential problems that an application of the odious debts doctrine to

---

129 See also Leyendecker (1988), at 199–203.
130 Sack (1927), at 163.
131 See, for example, Chander (2004), at 923.
132 Sack (1927), at 163.
133 Feilchenfeld (1931), at 714–715.

restructured debts[134] and debts traded on the secondary market[135] might raise, and tentatively suggests some highly technical legal arguments to overcome them.

It should be remembered, though, that the odious debts doctrine is not based on legalistic principles, but instead on the predominantly moral consideration that under certain circumstances a debt can be repudiated even though the underlying contract might be valid. A new state or regime is presumably not only free to reject such debts, but could also decide to accept them.[136] It is then submitted that a debt that was originally odious but was subsequently restructured, or traded on the secondary market with the consent of the successor government, cannot later be repudiated. This is not based on estoppel,[137] but instead on the consideration that if a democratic successor government decides to recognize an odious debt instead of repudiating it, the exceptional situation which gave rise to the applicability of the odious debts doctrine no longer persists. The people represented by their government exercised a choice with regard to this debt that needs to be respected, unless it was not the expression of the free decision of the democratic government, but instead caused by duress,[138] an argument that would raise difficult issues of sovereignty.

5 Mechanisms to implement the doctrine of odious debts

Sack, the 'inventor' of the odious debts doctrine, was of the opinion that in order to avoid arbitrariness on the part of debtor states who might be tempted to try to rid themselves of onerous debts by repudiating them as odious if that were easily possible, no unilateral repudiation of odious debts by debtor states should be allowed. Instead, the application of the odious debts doctrine should be the exclusive domain of an independent international tribunal.[139] Others suggest that the same purpose could be achieved by settling the issue by the means of a multilateral agreement, that is a convention or international treaty, or through an ad hoc multilateral procedure.[140] With regard to debt cancellation for Iraq, for example, a proposal was made 'to institute an international arbitration tribunal composed of neutral jurists, representatives of Iraq, and representatives of the creditors'.[141] Other suggestions are to establish an international institution dealing specifically with questions of odious debts, which could, for example, consist of jurists who serve long terms and can therefore be expected to be independent, or of 'well-respected individuals like former heads of

---

134 Thomas (2003), at 95–97.

135 Ibid., at 97–99.

136 Whether or not the same freedom exists under national law will be examined in Chapters Five to Seven at the example of Argentina.

137 An issue considered by Thomas (2003) both with regard to the restructuring of the original debt, and with regard to debt traded on the secondary markets, at 97 and 99, respectively.

138 See Thomas (2003), at 99.

139 Sack (1927), at 163.

140 See also Kaiser and Queck (2004), at 9.

141 See Anderson (2005), at 437–438 with further references.

state of debtor countries ... international lawyers and human rights scholars'.[142] The proposal to entrust an international commission under UN supervision with this task has been countered by stating that UN involvement might not be appropriate, as many of the UN members could themselves be regarded as regimes that do not represent the interests of their people, while others made these odious loans, so that it is difficult to justify that the UN has the legitimacy to decide which debts are or are not odious.[143]

Many difficulties can be foreseen with regard to an approach which invites an international institution or an ad hoc international tribunal especially created for that purpose to make an *ex post facto* assessment of the odiousness of certain debts the repayment of which a government rejects. Even if the problem of political bias could be overcome by a careful choice of those sitting on such bodies, the preceding analysis clearly demonstrates that the criteria according to which such an institution would have to audit a country's debt are not only vague, but moreover so controversial and political that agreement on them seems very difficult to reach. Thus, there are no clear standards at which an international institution could orientate its assessment of the odiousness of certain debts, a fact that would not only make the exercise of its task very difficult, but would also put the legitimacy of its decisions into question.

To overcome the problem of its potential bias, it has been suggested that instead of allowing the international body to evaluate the legitimate or illegitimate nature of certain debts retrospectively, it should only have the power to make assessments for the future, that is, assess in advance whether or not future loans to a particular regime will be legitimate.[144] The promoters of this view suggest that the task of the international institution should be to focus on the legitimacy of regimes, rather than on that of specific loans.[145] It is not really clear why an international body could be trusted to be less biased when making *ex ante* statements about the legitimacy of foreign governments as such, than when making an *ex post facto* assessment of specific loans, given that in both cases, a highly political decision needs to be made. If anything, not the probability of bias, but rather the reasons for bias might differ. In the case of an *ex post facto* assessment the bias might come either from compassion with the plight of the people of a debtor nation that is facing huge foreign debt and whose population is poverty-stricken,[146] or from taking the side of the creditors who might face substantial losses if debts are not repaid which, if it happens on a large scale, might endanger the stability of the world financial system. In the case of an *ex ante* assessment, on the other hand, bias could stem from political sympathies or antipathies, but also from economic and political interests, so that, for example, countries might be put on the 'blacklist' because their regimes, though democratically elected, are regarded as politically suspect, to make sure that the country is financially isolated. Alternatively, a country might not be blacklisted,

---

142 Kremer and Jayachandran (2002), at 31–32, but they envisage the role of this institution to be exclusively prospective.
143 Akacem and Miller (2006), at 5.
144 Kremer and Jayachandran (2002), at 29–30; see also Gelpern (2005), at 413, who pronounces herself to be in favour of their approach.
145 Kremer and Jayachandran (2002), at 29.
146 Ibid., at 21–22.

despite a regime's obvious undemocratic nature, as would probably have been the case with Iraq when the country was the ally of powerful Western nations when it was at war with Iran.[147] Indeed, it has been pointed out that the politicized nature of international institutions makes it next to impossible to receive unbiased and non-political assessments of the democratic nature of certain governments.[148]

While it might be possible to avoid some of these problems by conferring on the international body the task of making an *ex ante* evaluation of the odiousness of particular loans, rather than of governments, an international body would then still have to judge whether or not particular loans are beneficial to the people of a country, which would raise the same difficulties that have been extensively discussed above. The practicability of requiring such an assessment prior to the making of loan agreements is also very questionable.

6 Common objections to the doctrine of odious debts

6.1 Drying up of funds for developing countries

One of the main standard arguments against the doctrine of odious debts is pragmatic rather than legal, and that is that if creditors had to fear that the loans they grant to governments might, at a later point, be declared odious and therefore do not need to be repaid, they will be more reluctant to lend money to governments in the future,[149] thereby making it more expensive and difficult, if not in some cases impossible, for governments of developing countries in need of funds to have access to the international financial market.[150] As the argument goes, by refusing to assume the debt of its predecessors, new regimes would harm their reputation in the international financial market and cut themselves off from all future financial credits.[151] This might in part explain why debtor countries that inherit a substantial debt burden from their predecessors do not normally repudiate these debts as odious, as the political and economic costs of doing so are regarded as too high.[152]

Leaving aside the soundness of carrying on with borrowing policies that in the past had such devastating consequences that the debt problem has become one of the main problems of developing countries, it can be questioned whether the recognition of the odious debts doctrine would really discourage future lending in general,[153] or only future odious lending. If the latter was the case, it is hard to see why that would be a negative consequence that militates against the recognition of the odious

---

147   Buchheit, Gulati and Thompson (2006), at 28. See also Gelpern (2005), at 412.
148   Buchheit, Gulati and Thompson (2006), at 28; Adams (2004).
149   See, for example, Akacem and Miller (2006), at 6.
150   See, for example, Kremer and Jayachandran (2002), at 21; Norwegian Ministry of Foreign Affairs (2004), at 20.
151   Gelpern (2005), at 407; see also Anderson (2005), at 407.
152   For a discussion see also Christoph Paulus (2005a), at 89–91.
153   For an interesting discussion of the likelihood of adverse consequences, though in the context of default, see Buckley (2005), at 355–357.

debts doctrine.[154] Indeed, it seems as if one of the main purposes behind the doctrine of odious debts is to discourage burdening the population of a country with debts contracted by undemocratic regimes in order to oppress the people, and/or for the rulers' own personal enrichment or that of certain elites close to them.[155] If the recognition and application of the doctrine of odious debts had the effect of changing lending policies, it would thus achieve one of its purposes.

It is, however, submitted that such an accomplishment would only be possible if clear standards existed according to which it can be defined whether or not a debt is odious, as lenders will otherwise not be able to adjust their lending policies.[156] Thus, one of the main problems of the doctrine of odious debts so far identified, that is the vagueness of the criteria of lack of consent, and lack of benefit to the people, not only makes the application of the doctrine extremely difficult, but moreover sheds doubts on the probability that it could achieve its goal of changing lending practices. As long as this problem is not overcome, and it is submitted that the preceding analysis demonstrates the unlikelihood of this happening, the doctrine, if endorsed with all its ambiguities, might have the effect of discouraging lending to sovereign states in the developing world altogether, not just odious lending.

6.2 Complexity of the procedure

Another problem with the doctrine of odious debts is that even if an international institution dealing with the issue of odious debts were to be put in place, the process of determining whether or not a debt is, in fact, odious and can therefore be repudiated would take years, so that a debt restructuring which leads to a significant debt reduction might be more quickly achievable and also provide the debtor state with a more beneficial way of dealing with the debt problem.[157] However, as for example the recent example of Argentina shows,[158] debt restructuring is not necessarily a straightforward and quick way of resolving the debt problem of a country. More importantly, debt restructuring and debt repudiation are different issues, the former being based on the financial inability of a debtor country to service all its debts, the latter focusing on the purpose for which the loan was contracted, and on creditor responsibility in this respect. The two situations may overlap, but are nevertheless different. It is, for example, possible that a country would not qualify for debt restructuring, as it might have the financial resources to repay its debt in full, but refuses to do so because of the odious nature of the debt. In the case of a debt restructuring, usually all creditors of a certain type of debt will face cuts in their claims, whereas in the case of a repudiation of a debt as odious, a creditor who had some responsibility in making a loan that was not beneficial to the people of a country has to face the consequences of this act. Accordingly, debt restructuring

---

154 Thomas (2003), at 94.
155 Sack (1927), at 157. See also Hanlon (2006), at 109–110.
156 Gelpern (2005), at 412.
157 Ibid., at 407 and 410.
158 For an overview of Argentina's latest debt-restructuring efforts see, for example, García-Hamilton Jr., Olivares-Caminal and Zenarruza (2005).

should not be regarded as an alternative to repudiating a debt as odious, but instead as a mechanism which might be useful in certain circumstances, but which aims at resolving issues that are entirely different from those with which the doctrine of odious debts is concerned.

7 Conclusion

Given the uncertain status of the doctrine of odious debts in international law in the case of state succession, and even more so with regard to regime changes, the main purpose of the preceding analysis of the doctrine of odious debts was to come to a conclusion as to whether or not its recognition as a principle of international law would be desirable. However, the analysis identified many shortcomings of the doctrine, one of its main weaknesses being that it is very difficult to give it a clear enough content to make it workable at least at a basic level.[159]

More fundamental considerations should be added. The doctrine of odious debts is designed to find an equitable balance between the interests of the people burdened by a dictator with a debt which was unbeneficial, if not detrimental, to their interests, on the one hand, and those of the creditors who want to be repaid for the loans they made, on the other.[160] The starting point of the doctrine is the rule that contracts are binding and need to be honoured (*pacta sunt servanda*); that the rights of the creditors should normally prevail and even survive a case of state succession; and that the people of a country can repudiate unbeneficial debts only under exceptional circumstances and with the approval of an international body. The doctrine as commonly advanced thus does not question the general validity of loan transactions that were concluded with dictatorial regimes.[161] However, it is not at all evident that contracts entered into by dictators on behalf of the country will always create legally binding obligations for the country. Indeed, Sack distinguished between regular and irregular despotic regimes, although it does not become clear according to which criteria the distinction is to be made. Where a loan was not contracted by a regular government and according to the correct procedure, he seems to have assumed that the creditors were limited to recovery according to the principles of unjust enrichment.[162] The odious debts doctrine, on the other hand, would only apply to those cases in which a debt was properly contracted by a regular government, but nevertheless odious.[163] This distinction between contracts that validly bind the country, and those that do not, is important in law, but largely overlooked by discussions of the doctrine of odious debts. If a contract is invalid, for example because the dictator did not have the power validly to indebt the country, or where the contract was void because of

---

159 For a suggestion to borrow criteria from the UNIDROIT Principles of International Commercial Contracts and develop case groups in order to specify the content of the doctrine of odious debts see Christoph Paulus (2005a), at 95–99.

160 Sack (1927), at 163.

161 Buchheit, Gulati and Thompson (2006) make the same observation with regard to war debts, at 11.

162 Ibid, at 30.

163 Ibid.

other irregularities, *pacta sunt servanda* cannot apply, and a reliance on the odious debts doctrine would be unnecessary.[164] To ignore this means to extend the odious debts doctrine, and with it the need to justify the repudiation of a debt, to cases in which there is no binding contract.

The underlying perception of how to achieve a fair and equitable balance through an odious debts doctrine consequently seems to be that the people of a debtor state should only be relieved of repaying a loan if they not only did not have a say in the taking up of the loan, but if it was moreover made for unbeneficial purposes, and the creditors were aware of this. As the beneficial or unbeneficial nature of the loans will not be decided by the people, but instead by an international body, the people of the debtor country would consequently be bound by loans made to undemocratic regimes in full awareness of the odious use of the money, as long as these loans are later regarded by an international body as having benefited the people. The doctrine furthermore results in the people being expected to repay unbeneficial loans taken up by undemocratic regimes, as long as the creditors were not aware of these factors.[165] This might be justified if the primary purpose of the doctrine were to influence lending practices and to punish lenders for making odious loans.[166] If, on the other hand, the purpose behind the odious debts doctrine is primarily that the people of a country should not be burdened with unbeneficial loans taken up by dictators, it is not so clear that the people, not the creditors, should carry the risk of the misuse of funds where the creditors were not aware of the odious nature of the loan. After all, it is the creditors, not the people, who have control over who they lend money to. It is then not obvious that it is more acceptable that the people, rather than the creditors, should be put in the position to reclaim the misspent money from the rulers.[167] As it stands, the doctrine starts from a bias towards creditor interests and it is rather surprising that it is regarded so favourably by anti-debt campaigners.

It might be worth introducing some considerations raised by Nitti who developed a theory that shows quite a few similarities with the odious debts doctrine, but gave it a different focus. Just like Sack, he was of the opinion that a distinction between regime debts and state debts was necessary, but he distinguished the two according to slightly different criteria:[168]

> In a country where all manifestations of freedom are suppressed, where Parliament was abolished; where no local liberties, or freedom of the press, the right of association etc. exist, the government contracts loans in order to consolidate its regime of violence. This is the situation of all European dictatorships that emerged after the [First World] war. The capitalists who provide them with money know that they lend to factual (*de facto*) and not legal (*de iure*) governments; that they lend to governments who abolished the constitutions, and they therefore do not ignore the risks to which they expose themselves. When these governments are defeated and freedom is restored ... do those who succeed have to pay loans that were made to fight that what has now triumphed? ...

---

164 See also Christoph Paulus (2005a), at 87–88.
165 See also Buchheit, Gulati and Thompson (2006), at 16.
166 Christoph Paulus (2005a), at 92–93.
167 But see Christoph Paulus (2005b), at 59.
168 For yet another definition of regime debts see Jèze (1922), at 302–305.

This is why state debts need to be separated from regime debts. While the former need to be paid, the latter do not have any legal or moral basis.[169] ... In these cases, the capitalists run the risk of all those who lend to an illegal regime under which the will of the people cannot manifest itself, but [the people] can ... tomorrow legitimately revoke that which was done today outside the law.[170]

Thus, Nitti focuses on questioning the validity of agreements with *de facto* regimes. For him, the only relevant criterion to differentiate between odious and non-odious debts would be whether or not the regime that contracted the debts was a *de facto* or a *de iure* government.[171] His doctrine does not link the validity of the loan with the specific use of the money, but instead seems to include all loans that were made to such a regime. Whether or not loans need to be repaid by the people of a debtor country would then depend on the definition of *de facto* as opposed to *de iure* regimes. Given that whether or not a regime governs a country *de facto* or *de iure* depends in this context on the national law of the relevant state, such an argument can only work to the extent that a country that is governed by a dictator has a Constitution according to which this government is, in fact, illegitimate. If that is the case, the loan agreements might already be invalid according to the national law of the country, as in many cases dictators will not have the authority to bind the country validly.[172]

However, the recognition in international law of a doctrine of odious debts thus defined would have the advantage to clarify that the invalidity of the relevant loans could then be invoked against foreign creditors under international law, whether or not the loan is governed by the domestic law of the debtor country. However, to the extent to which *de facto* regimes can validly represent their countries under international law,[173] it might be difficult to achieve a recognition of this approach as a principle of international law. Moreover, it is not clear that the distinction between *de facto* and *de iure* regimes is entirely satisfactory from the moral perspective on which the odious debts doctrine is based, as it might not make much difference to the people whether or not they are governed by a lawful or an unlawful dictator. Another problem that would need to be resolved in this context would be at what point in time and by what means a *de facto* might turn into a *de iure* regime. Can, for example, a dictator who comes into power by unlawful means and then changes the law, at some point be regarded as governing the country *de iure*?

In terms of a conclusion, it is submitted that the odious debts doctrine as it is usually understood and promoted is not only not a principle that is firmly established in international law, but it has moreover many insufficiencies as a means to address the debt problem. This is mainly because of the vagueness of its criteria, but also

---

169 Nitti (1931), at 754.

170 Ibid., at 755.

171 He for example regarded the government of the Russian Tsar as immoral but lawful, with the consequence that loans taken up by that regime were state, not regime debts, ibid., at 754.

172 King's suggestion, (2003) at 36, to justify the doctrine of odious debts based on the principle of agency points in a similar direction.

173 See, for example, Brownlie (2003), at 89–101; and Ipsen (2004), at 272–275.

because of the ideological connotations of the doctrine which cause problems of sovereignty and political bias and raise many concerns as to the implementation of the doctrine. Moreover, although it is based on the idea that odious debts do not need to be repaid, the doctrine mainly seems to be regarded as providing a defence against claims for debt repayment, which means that it would not help the debtor states to reclaim payments that were already made. Overall, from a legal perspective, the doctrine of odious debts in its traditional form has so many weaknesses that it does not provide a useful tool with which debt repayment can be successfully challenged.

This is not to say that campaigns in favour of a recognition and application of the doctrine are therefore in vain. Instead, it is submitted that the arguments invoked in favour of the odiousness of large parts of the debt of developing countries are important in order to raise awareness of the fact that many of the loans which contributed to the debt problem of the developing world stem from morally and legally questionable operations. On 2 October 2006 Norway unilaterally cancelled $80 million of debt of 5 developing countries[174] for reasons that resemble the doctrine of illegitimate debt[175] which is closely related to the doctrine of odious debts.[176] Norway recognized that the loans had benefited Norwegian interests, but not the developmental needs of the borrowing countries. They should accordingly never have been made and Norway cancelled this debt in recognition of its responsibility for these lending policies. However, the Norwegian approach is clearly focused on development policies, and is sceptical towards a doctrine of illegitimate debt, due to 'extremely difficult *delimitation problems*' and 'the fact that the *practical implications* of legitimacy-based debt forgiveness are extremely problematic'.[177] However, the Ministry of Foreign Affairs argued that 'this does not necessarily mean that the debate on "illegitimate debt" is a blind alley. Firstly, the debate itself may result in loans not being granted for countries and regimes which, on moral grounds, *should not* receive them.'[178] Even though the odious debts doctrine is questionable as a legal tool, it could thus have an important political impact, in that it might convince creditors to cancel a debt, or debtor governments to rethink whether or not to repay it.

---

174 www.jubileedebtcampaign.org.uk/?lid=2423.
175 See Hanlon (2002).
176 For a critical analysis of this doctrine see Bohoslavsky (2006a).
177 Norwegian Ministry of Foreign Affairs (2004), at 19.
178 Ibid., at 21.

Chapter Four

Redefining the Doctrine of Odious Debts

1 Introduction

As already noted above, in his report to the ILC on a draft of the Vienna Convention on Succession of States in respect of State Property, Archives and Debts (1983), Special Rapporteur Bedjaoui suggested a twofold definition of odious debts. According to a draft article to the Convention suggested by him, odious debts would comprise '(a) all debts contracted by the predecessor State with a view to attaining objectives contrary to the major interests of the successor State or of the transferred territory', a definition which is very close to the doctrine of odious debts discussed in the previous chapter. However, Bedjaoui proposed that a second group of debts be regarded as odious, namely 'all debts contracted by the predecessor State with an aim and for a purpose not in conformity with international law and, in particular, the principles of international law embodied in the Charter of the United Nations'.[1] These two concepts of odious debts differ with regard to their content, as the former, the traditional version of odious debts, focuses on the interests of the successor state, while the latter concentrates on conformity with international law. From this follows a different focus on who would be harmed by the odious nature of the debt. In the first scenario, it is the people of the debtor state, whereas in the second scenario it is the international community.[2]

This shift in focus could resolve one of the problems of the doctrine of odious debts as traditionally defined, which is that while it is the people of the debtor state who need to be harmed by the burden of having to repay an unbeneficial debt which they did not agree to assume, it is an international institution that will define the beneficial or unbeneficial nature of the debt. If the focus moves to a violation of international law principles, the decision of an international body would then not be one of controlling whether the act of a state or government pursued undemocratic or unbeneficial purposes with regard to its people, something it is submitted only the people themselves could judge, but instead whether the policy was in violation of international law principles. To perform such an evaluation seems to fall much more comfortably within the competence of international bodies and it does not add restrictions on the sovereignty of the debtor state that go beyond those already in place in the form of binding international law principles.[3]

---

1   Bedjaoui (1977), at 70.

2   Ibid., at para. 129.

3   For a discussion of the interplay between international law and state sovereignty see, for example, Ipsen (2004), at 40.

One of the interesting features of this approach is that the violation of international law does not have to affect the people of the predecessor state in order for the doctrine of odious debts to apply, given that what counts is whether the debts are harmful to the international community, not that they are harmful to the predecessor state. Therefore, a debt would be odious, and would not have to be repaid, if it was contracted 'in order to purchase arms that were used to flout human rights through genocide, racial discrimination or apartheid',[4] or 'to finance a policy of subjugating a people and colonizing its territory, or, in general, any policy contrary to the right of the peoples to self-determination,'[5] regardless of whether these policies were directed against the people of the predecessor state, as the international community would be just as offended by these loans if such acts had been directed against other states or peoples. This would have the rather bizarre side effect that a government could then, with the backing of its people, borrow money in order to suppress or attack the people of another country, or a minority within the country, without having to repay the loan, which might encourage such borrowings. However, if creditors knew that they would not be repaid when making such loans it is very likely that they would stop lending money for those purposes. Furthermore, the country's act would at the same time trigger responsibility under international law,[6] so that the country would have to face the consequences of the unlawful acts for which the loans were used.

Even though, as already noted above, the reference to odious debts suggested by Bedjaoui was not included in the Vienna Convention on Succession of States in respect of State Property, Archives and Debts (1983), it seems as if a doctrine of odious debts with an international law focus finds some support in Article 33 of the final text of the Convention, which recognizes as state debts only those that arose 'in conformity with international law'.[7] Thus, under the Convention, if a loan agreement violates international law, the obligations arising there from do not have to be assumed by the people of the successor state. It is not entirely clear whether this means that in such cases the underlying loan contract is regarded as invalid or unenforceable. An argument in favour of unenforceability was already made by Feilchenfeld, long before the Convention was drafted. He argued that while a loan agreement that violates international law may nevertheless be valid, 'at least an equitable argument might be advanced that international law ought not to lend its protection for the maintenance of rights, the creation of which it disapproved'.[8] Thus, whether or not the loan contract is, in principle, valid, if it violates international law, the underlying obligation would not have to be assumed by the successor state, and the creditors could not succeed in international tribunals when claiming the repayment of such debts.[9]

---

4   Bedjaoui (1977), at 134.
5   Ibid., at para. 135.
6   For details regarding the system of international responsibility of states see, for example, Crawford and Olleson (2003), at 446–470.
7   22 ILM (1983), at 322; see also Ipsen (2004), at 356; Leyendecker (1988), at 182.
8   Feilchenfeld (1931), at 699.
9   While with regard to claims for debt repayment, it is not essential whether or not the odiousness of the debt results in invalidity or unenforceability, the distinction would be

Though interesting, the approach that debts are odious if they were contracted 'with an aim and for a purpose not in conformity with international law and, in particular, the principles of international law embodied in the Charter of the United Nations'[10] does not provide any specifics concerning the question of how to determine which debt is not 'in conformity with international law' and is therefore odious.

2 Odiousness of debts because of a violation of *ius cogens*

Here, some of the principles contained in the Vienna Convention on the Law of Treaties (1969) might be instructive. With regard to the issue of what is required in order for a treaty between states to be invalid, the Convention adopts a very restrictive approach, opting for the validity of treaties in all but the most extreme cases of violations of international law principles. Article 53 states in this respect that:

> A treaty is void if, at the time of its conclusion, it conflicts with a peremptory norm of general international law. For the purposes of the present Convention, a peremptory norm of general international law is a norm accepted and recognized by the international community of States as a whole as a norm from which no derogation is permitted and which can be modified only by a subsequent norm of general international law having the same character.

The fact that the violation of *ius cogens* results in the nullity of the treaty *ab initio* suggests that in cases of *ius cogens* violations, the principle of *pacta sunt servanda* does not become operative, as a binding treaty was never created.[11] If this were to be applied to loan transactions, if debts are odious because of a *ius cogens* violation, creditors could not rely on *pacta sunt servanda*, as there would not be a binding contract on which claims for repayment could be based, and against which the debtors' claims of odiousness would have to be balanced.

2.1 Content and scope of ius cogens[12]

The Vienna Convention on the Law of Treaties does not apply to the legal relations between states and private parties. However, while many controversies still surround the concept of *ius cogens*, ranging from its very recognition to questions of its content and its consequences,[13] the principle that a violation of *ius cogens* invalidates

---

important in order to determine whether or not the parties can claim restitution of that which was already paid.

10   Bedjaoui (1977), at 70.

11   However, it is not clear how nullity *ab initio* can be squared with the restrictive procedure according to which a *ius cogens* violation of a treaty can only be invoked.

12   For an analysis of the concept of *ius cogens* and an overview of its historic development see Ford (1994).

13   For a discussion see, for example, Sinclair (1984), at 203–215; Ipsen (2004), at 186–193.

treaties arguably forms part of international customary law.[14] This means that while the Vienna Convention on the Law of Treaties codifies the principle of *ius cogens* in the particular context of treaties concluded between states,[15] and delineates the mechanisms according to which the invalidity can be invoked, the principle as such exists beyond the Vienna Convention. Thus, treaties between states that have not signed the Vienna Convention would also be invalid if they violated *ius cogens*, although this consequence would not follow from Article 53 of the Convention, but instead arise from customary international law.[16] Unlike other norms of customary international law, *ius cogens* norms bind even those states that never accepted, and maybe even object to them.[17]

Whether *ius cogens* is recognized by customary international law beyond the particular case of treaties is not so clear. When discussing the concept of *ius cogens* during their work towards the text of the Vienna Convention on the Law of Treaties, ILC members suggested that peremptory norms were not exclusively derived from legal rules, but also from 'considerations of morals and of international good order'.[18] The justification for a recognition of substantive limits to international treaties was based on the conviction that there were certain rules of law and moral principles which in civilized societies could not be disregarded or modified by agreements.[19] The same idea is sometimes formulated by equating *ius cogens* with those norms that form the international *ordre public*.[20] If *ius cogens* norms are then based on universally accepted legal or moral principles that are so significant that states cannot opt out of them, it could be argued that it does not make sense to limit the applicability of *ius cogens* to state actions in the realm of treaties between states.[21] Instead, given their particular quality and their increased worthiness of international protection, *ius cogens* norms should be universally applicable.[22] States could then

---

14   See, for example, *Barcelona Traction, Light and Power Company* (*Belgium v Spain*), 1970 ICJ 3, at 303 per Judge Ammoun. This concept also underlies US cases brought under the Alien Tort Claims Act (ATCA); see, for example, *Siderman de Blake v Republic of Argentina*, 965 F2d 699 (9th Cir 1992), at 714–715; *Presbyterian Church of Sudan v Talisman Energy, Inc.*, 244 FSupp2d 289 (SDNY, 2003), at 305; *Doe v UNOCAL*, 395 F3d 932 (9th Cir 2002), at 945. But see Czapliński (2006), who questions at 86 that the principle of *ius cogens* formed part of international customary law prior to the coming into force of the Vienna Convention on the Law of Treaties.

15   This was also the position of the International Law Commission, see Reports of the Commission to the General Assembly, (1966) YILC, Volume II, at 247.

16   See, for example, Cassese (2003), at 204–205; Parker and Neylon (1989), at 444.

17   See, for example, Ford (1994), at 152.

18   Fitzmaurice (1958), at 40–41.

19   De Luna (1966), at para. 31.

20   Fischer-Lescano (2003), at 236; Chowdhury and de Waart (1992), at p.7, n.4 with further references. For an overview of the difference in terminology in this context see Tavernier (2006), at 1.

21   For an extension of the concept of *ius cogens* to unilateral acts of the state see, for example, Andreas Paulus (2005), at 311. See also Article 26 of UN General Assembly Resolution 56/83 of 2002 on *Responsibility of States for Internationally Wrongful Acts*.

22   Ipsen (2004), at 190; see also Brownlie (2003), at 490; Ford (1994), at 153–154; Rozakis (1976), quoting Suy, at 17. However, Rozakis himself is rather critical of this,

equally not contract out of the obligation to comply with *ius cogens* by entering into private contracts that are in conflict with *ius cogens* norms,[23] for example by concluding a contract regarding slave labour. This seems logical, because if a norm is 'accepted and recognized by the international community of States as a whole as a norm from which no derogation is permitted', then the protection of the interests of private parties in the validity of contracts that violate such norms cannot be more important than protecting the international community, and the victims in the particular case, against their violation. Where debt agreements violate *ius cogens* norms, this could accordingly affect the contractual obligations of the debtor state with the private party and result in the invalidity of the loan.[24]

Before analysing the implications of this, it needs to be determined which norms can be regarded as peremptory norms of international law.[25] Here, the Vienna Convention on the Law of Treaties does not provide any guidance, as it merely stipulates the general definition of *ius cogens*, but does not offer a list of provisions that might qualify as *ius cogens* norms. The current consensus on which norms form part of *ius cogens* seems to include the outlawing of wars of aggression and crimes against humanity, the prohibition of torture,[26] and the right to self-determination.[27] Whether the protection of all fundamental human rights forms part of *ius cogens* is, on the other hand, rather controversial.[28] The European Court of First Instance expressed itself in favour of this view, when referring to:

---

see 18–19. For a critical view see further De Wet (2004). The European Court of First Instance equally seems to have understood the concept this way when deciding that it could examine the compatibility of UN Security Council Resolutions with '*jus cogens*, understood as a body of higher rules of public international law binding on all subjects of international law, including the bodies of the United Nations, and from which no derogation is possible', *Ahmed Ali Yusuf and Al Barakaat International Foundation v Council of the European Union and Commission of the European Communities*, Case T-306/01 (21 September 2005), at para. 277.

23 See Harris (2004), at 856; Fischer-Lescano (2003), at 236.

24 For a discussion of an odious debts doctrine based on *ius cogens* violations see also Fischer-Lescano (2003); and Queck (2004).

25 For a general overview of *ius cogens* norms and jurisprudence see, for example, Tams (2005), at 139–145; Ford (1994), at 163–168.

26 See, for example, Brownlie (2003), at 489; *Prosecutor v Furundzija* (Case No: IT-95-17/1-T), paras 155–157. See also some of the US decisions in the context of litigation under the ATCA, in particular *Siderman de Blake v Republic of Argentina*, 965 F2d 699 (9th Cir 1992), at 714. For a more extensive suggestion of norms that pertain to *ius cogens* see Parker and Neylon (1989), at 428–442.

27 *Legal consequences for states of the continued presence of South Africa in Namibia (South West Africa) notwithstanding Security Council Resolution 276* (1970), 1971 ICJ 16, at 98–90 per Judge Ammoun (Separate opinion); Gros Espiell, E/CN4/Sub2/405/rev1 (1980), at para 12; Cassese (2005), at 65; Parker and Neylon (1989), at 440–441; Chowdury, de Waart (1992), at 7. See also ILC Report A/56/10 (2001), at 208 and 283–284 with further references.

28 For an overview of the discussion see Parker and Neylon (1989), at 441–442 with further references. See also Andreas Paulus, (2005) at 306. The statement in *Barcelona Traction, Light and Power Company (Belgium v Spain)*, 1970 ICJ 3 at 301 (and see also

the superior rules of international law falling within the ambit of *jus cogens* ... , in particular, the mandatory provisions concerning the universal protection of human rights, from which neither the Member States nor the bodies of the United Nations may derogate because they constitute 'intransgressible principles of international customary law'.[29]

While it is not entirely clear how to define which norms do and do not form part of *ius cogens*,[30] at least a minimum catalogue seems to be largely uncontroversial.[31]

The Vienna Convention on the Law of Treaties stipulates that a treaty is only void *ab initio* if it violates a norm that is recognized as part of *ius cogens* at the time when the treaty is concluded. For an analogy with the norms of the Convention, this brings in the additional problem that it not only needs to be established what the norms of *ius cogens* are, but furthermore at what point in time they were recognized as such.[32] If norms obtain the status of *ius cogens* when a contract is already in existence, in analogy with Article 64 of the Vienna Convention on the Law of Treaties this should void the contract from the time at which the new *ius cogens* norm emerges. Thus, to the extent to which principles that could be relevant in the context of the debt of developing countries, such as the right to development, might in the future be recognized as part of *ius cogens*, loan agreements violating these principle could be regarded as void from the moment at which such a new *ius cogens* norm has clearly found recognition.

2.2 Establishing a link between a loan contract and a ius cogens violation

The main problem of an odious debts doctrine based on a violation of *ius cogens* is the rather fundamental issue of how to determine that a loan agreement violates *ius cogens*. The decisive question would be what link between the loan and the *ius cogens* violation would need to exist in order to justify such a finding. Article 53 of the Vienna Convention seems to call for a direct link between the treaty and the *ius cogens* violation in that it demands that the treaty itself conflicts with a peremptory norm of general international law. One of the examples suggested by the International Law Commission during the debates that preceded the final text of the Convention was that of 'a treaty contemplating or conniving at the commission of acts, such as

---

304) that suggests with reference to provisions that have *erga omnes* effect, that 'Such obligations derive, for example, in contemporary international law, from the outlawing of acts of aggression, and of genocide, as also from the principles and rules concerning the basic rights of the human person, including protection from slavery and racial discrimination', is sometimes quoted as supporting the view that fundamental human rights norms form part of *ius cogens*. See, for example, Cassese (2005), at 65–66; see also 'Simón, Julio Héctor y otros s/ privación ilegítima de la libertad, etc. –causa No. 17.768', Argentinian Supreme Court (14 June 2005), at para. 13 per Justice Boggiano.

29   *Ahmed Ali Yusuf and Al Barakaat International Foundation v Council of the European Union and Commission of the European Communities*, Case T-306/01 (21 September 2005), at para 282.

30   For a critical analysis with extensive reference to case-law see Tavernier (2006), and also Kadelbach (2006).

31   See also Kadelbach (2006), at 28.

32   See, for example, Andreas Paulus (2005), at 304; De Wet (2004), at 118.

trade in slaves, piracy or genocide, in the suppression of which every state is called upon to co-operate.'[33] Another frequently used example of a treaty which violates *ius cogens* is one in which two states agree to start a war of aggression against a third state.[34] As such treaties do not themselves amount to the prohibited behaviour, that is genocide, a war of aggression etc., it seems to be sufficient for a violation of Article 53 that the content of the treaty is not in conformity with *ius cogens*.

This is comparable to Bedjaoui's suggestion that a debt could be odious if the debtor state contracted it 'with an aim and for a purpose not in conformity with international law'.[35] He seems to have had in mind a direct link between the loan and the violation of international law in that the debt should only be regarded as odious if the loan was contracted in order to facilitate the violation of international law principles. According to him, this might, for example, be the case where debt was contracted 'with the intention of using the funds to violate treaty obligations'.[36] Thus, where two parties agree a loan in order to enable the borrower to obtain equipment to carry out torture, it could be said that already the loan agreement itself violates *ius cogens* in the form of the prohibition of torture. Relevant for establishing the link between the loan and a violation of international law that justifies defining debts as odious would accordingly be the intention of the parties to the loan and the purpose for which the loan is contracted.

One of the problems here is that the loan agreements themselves will in most cases be neutral with regard to *ius cogens* violations, unless it can exceptionally be determined that the loan contract included the agreement on a purpose which amounts to a violation of *ius cogens*, such as in the above example of a loan that was contracted for the purchase of torture equipment. However, cases of loan agreements that expressly stipulate a purpose that is in conflict with *ius cogens* norms will be rare. What will in many cases be much easier to demonstrate is that governments use the loans obtained in order to commit violations of *ius cogens* norms, for example where they use the incoming money in order to purchase arms with which they commit crimes against humanity within their own country, or acts of aggression towards the people of other countries. However, when focusing on the use of the borrowed money it becomes more difficult to establish a direct link between the loan and the *ius cogens* violation, or at least a sufficiently close link that would justify regarding the loan contract itself as void.

In this respect, it has been argued that an analogy with Article 53 of the Vienna Convention on the Law of Treaties suggests that the law does not protect financial transactions which aid the violation of *ius cogens*, and that as a general rule, debts are odious and the underlying contracts void, if they assist a despotic regime in violating *ius cogens* provisions.[37] In order to test the desirability and workability of this broad definition of odious debts, criteria would have to be developed according to which it can be determined what counts as assistance with *ius cogens* violations

---

33   Wetzel and Rauschning (1978), at 37.
34   See, for example, Sinclair (1984), at 209.
35   Bedjaoui (1977), at 70.
36   Ibid, at para. 133; see also Menon (1992), at 163.
37   Fischer-Lescano (2003), at 235.

that would result in the invalidity of a loan agreement. Several scenarios come to mind from which criteria for such an assessment might be borrowed: the discussion of complicity and aiding and abetting in the context of international criminal proceedings; the analysis of the same issues in the context of claims brought in the US under the Alien Tort Claims Act (ATCA) against multinational companies for human rights violations; and the ILC's approach to state responsibility.[38]

2.2.1 *Criteria applied in international criminal proceedings*

The most comprehensive discussion of the question of aiding and abetting *ius cogens* violations in the context of international criminal law can be found in the *Furundzija* decision of the ICTY,[39] where it was determined that aiding and abetting is, for example, present where a person facilitates a crime by giving 'additional confidence to his companions;'[40] or where a person provides the means for the commission of a crime.[41] The tribunal referred to the holding in the *Zyklon B* case according to which the accused's complicity depended on 'whether there was any evidence that he was in a position either to influence the transfer of gas to Auschwitz or to prevent it. If he were not in such a position, no knowledge of the use to which the gas was put could make him guilty'.[42] In the light of these definitions, the tribunal opined that unless the accomplice's doing had a substantial effect on the principal act, knowledge of the use of the goods supplied by them would not in itself be sufficient to amount to aiding and abetting.[43] Overall, the tribunal concluded that:

> The assistance given by an accomplice need not be tangible and can consist of moral support in certain circumstances. ... [T]he acts of the accomplice need [not] bear a casual relationship to, or be a condition *sine qua non* for, those of the principal. ... [T]he relationship between the acts of the accomplice and of the principal must be such that the acts of the accomplice make a significant difference to the commission of the criminal act by the principal.[44]

With regard to torture, the tribunal stated that 'to be guilty of torture as an aider or abettor, the accused must assist in some way which has a substantial effect on the perpetration of the crime and with knowledge that torture is taking place'.[45] For the criminal liability of bankers for loans it would then presumably have to be established that they had knowledge of the use and that the loan moreover made a significant contribution to the commission of the offence by the borrowing regime.

---

38   For a detailed analysis of such claims under the ATCA see Joseph (2004), at 23–61.
39   *Prosecutor v Furundzija* (Case No: IT-95-17/1-T), at paras 190–235.
40   Ibid., at para. 202.
41   Ibid., at para 216, with reference to Article 25(3)(c) of the Rome Statute for an International Criminal Court.
42   *Trial of Bruno Tesch and Two Others*, (1946) MLR Volume 1, 93 (British Military Court).
43   *Prosecutor v Furundzija* (Case No: IT-95-17/1-T), at para 223.
44   Ibid., at paras 232–233.
45   Ibid., at para. 257.

The only cases of bankers who faced trials under international criminal law related to their professional activities seem to be those of Emil Puhl and Karl Rasche who were tried by the Nuremberg Tribunal. Puhl had been Deputy President of the German Central Bank during the Third Reich and played an active role 'in arranging for the receipt, classification, deposit, conversion and disposal of properties taken by the SS from victims exterminated in concentration camps'. *Inter alia*, he had been actively involved in organizing the recasting of the gold originating from the gold teeth and crowns of concentration camp inmates so that it could be resold. According to the tribunal, his role in these transactions was 'not that of mere messenger or businessman. He went beyond the ordinary range of his duties to give directions that the matter be handled secretly by the appropriate departments of the bank'.[46] Rasche, who had been the chairman of Dresdner Bank, on the other hand, was acquitted with regard to the charge of knowingly loaning 'large sums of money to various SS enterprises which employed large numbers of inmates of concentration camps, and also to Reich enterprises and agencies engaged in the so-called resettlement programs'. This was because:

> The real question is, is it a crime to make a loan, knowing or having good reason to believe that the borrower will use the funds in financing enterprises which are employed in using labour in violation of either national or international law? Does [Rasche] stand in any different position than one who sells supplies or raw materials to a builder building a house, knowing that the structure will be used for an unlawful purpose? A bank sells money or credit in the same manner as the merchandiser of any other commodity. It does not become a partner in enterprise, and the interest charged is merely the gross profit, which the bank realizes from the transaction, out of which it must deduct its business costs, and from which it hopes to realize a net profit. Loans or sale of commodities to be used in an unlawful enterprise may well be condemned from a moral standpoint and reflect no credit on the part of the lender or seller in either case, but the transaction can hardly be said to be a crime. Our duty is to try and punish those guilty of violating international law, and we are not prepared to state that such loans constitute a violation of that law, nor has our attention been drawn to any ruling to the contrary.[47]

Thus, the Tribunal very clearly indicated that it did not see any basis for finding that there was a violation of international law resulting in criminal responsibility where money was lent for unlawful purposes, including in such extreme cases as collaborating with agencies of Nazi Germany or enterprises resorting to forced labour.

---

46   See *United States v Weizsaecker* (Ministries Case), XIV Trials of War Criminals 620–621, as quoted in Ramasastry (1998), at 417.

47   *United States v Weizsaecker* (Ministries Case), XIV Trials of War Criminals 621–622, as quoted in Ramasastry (1998), at 416.

2.2.2 *Criteria applied in tort cases under the US Alien Tort Claims Act (ATCA)*

Under the ATCA,[48] aliens can claim compensation for torts committed in violation of the law of nations or a treaty to which the US is a party. Since the landmark decision in *Filártiga*,[49] where a US court decided that the ATCA provided US courts with jurisdiction over all violations of universally accepted international human rights norms regardless of the nationality of the parties, the ATCA has been explored as a potential tool for holding multinational companies liable for human rights violations abroad.[50] In the context of ATCA litigation, the case closest to the situation of loans which are used in order to commit *ius cogens* violations is that of *Khulumani*.[51] In *Khulumani*, a lawsuit was brought against many different companies for their collaboration with South Africa's apartheid regime. The plaintiffs demanded compensation from multinational companies of different sectors, including various private banks. One of the arguments of the plaintiffs was that 'apartheid would not have occurred in the same way without the participation of the defendants.'[52] With regard to the responsibility of the banking sector for apartheid crimes, it was argued that the loans to South Africa's government were made:

> to finance expenditures, including military and security expenditures.[53] ... Moreover, any transfer of capital to South Africa had military implications: loans to the railways and harbours systems assisted in the mobilization of the armed forces; trade financing provided the computers and telecommunications equipment necessary to the efficient functioning of a modern army; financing for housing projects perpetuated the segregated housing of apartheid.[54]

The complaint also cites a statement of South Africa's former Prime Minister Jon Foster, according to whom 'each bank loan, each new investment is another brick in the wall of our continued existence'.[55] And the President of the South African Reserve Bank is quoted as having stated that: 'if the international association of bankers should effectively shut South Africa off from the international trade and payments system, that would be a far more powerful sanctions measure than the trade restrictions which foreign governments imposed.'[56]

The banks were not accused of having themselves committed apartheid related crimes, but instead of aiding and abetting the apartheid regime by supplying the government with the financial means that enabled it to commit specific offences,

---

48   28 USCA § 1350: The district courts shall have original jurisdiction of any civil action by an alien for a tort only, committed in violation of the law of nations or a treaty of the United States.

49   *Filártiga v Peña-Irala*, 630 F2d 876 (CANY 1980).

50   For an analysis see, for example, Joseph (2004); Van Schaack (2004).

51   *In re South African Apartheid Litigation*, 346 FSupp2d 538 (SDNY 2004).

52   Khulumani complaint and jury trial demand, www.cmht.com/casewatch/cases/apartheid-cmpl.pdf, at para. 268.

53   Ibid., at para. 407.

54   Ibid., at para. 422.

55   Ibid., at para. 391.

56   Ibid., at para. 424.

as well as providing the general financial basis that sustained the apartheid system. Translated into the language of *Furundzija*, the argument seems to be that without the bank loans, the apartheid regime would not have had the means to finance the expenditures that were used for the maintenance of the suppression of the black population; that the loans made a substantial contribution to the stability of the regime and the *ius cogens* violation to which its very existence amounted; and that the quotes of apartheid officials demonstrate that the international banks had been in a position to influence the commission of apartheid crimes by either withholding or providing financial support for the government.

Apartheid was condemned by the UN General Assembly as a crime against humanity;[57] any collaboration with the apartheid regime was proclaimed to be 'a hostile act against the oppressed people of South Africa and a contemptuous defiance of the United Nations and the international community';[58] the UN Security Council had issued an arms embargo against South Africa;[59] and the General Assembly had urged all states 'to induce transnational corporations, banks and financial institutions to withdraw effectively from South Africa.'[60] Thus, apartheid was regarded as deserving particular international condemnation, and there was ample evidence of the UN's position with regard to the apartheid regime and economic collaboration with it. In this particular context, it can therefore easily be established that the banks knew where their money went and what it was used for.

Nevertheless, in *Khulumani*, the US court rejected the tort claim, as the banks and other defendants had not been directly involved in the international law violations committed by the apartheid regime.[61] The court regarded the actions of the bank as not going beyond doing business with a state that was engaged in international law violations and relied on the holding in *Bigio* to argue that 'an indirect economic benefit from unlawful state action is not sufficient' for the purpose of establishing liability under the ATCA.[62] The court did not analyse the question of whether the defendants had aided and abetted the apartheid crimes, as it rejected the idea that aiding and abetting international law violations could give rise to liability under the ATCA.[63]

In *UNOCAL*,[64] on the other hand, it was accepted that aiding and abetting might trigger liability under the ATCA if there was 'knowing practical assistance

---

57 See International Convention on the Suppression and Punishment of the Crime of Apartheid.

58 General Assembly Resolution, Policies of Apartheid of the Government of South Africa: Economic Collaboration with South Africa, A/RES/31/6.H, 9 November 1976.

59 Security Council Resolution, The Question of South Africa, S/RES/418, 4 November 1977.

60 General Assembly Resolution, Policies of Apartheid of the Government of South Africa: Comprehensive and Mandatory Sanctions Against the Racist Regime of South Africa, and Imposition, Co-ordination and Strict Monitoring of Measures Against Racist South Africa A/RES/44/27 C & D, 22 November 1989.

61 *In re South African Apartheid Litigation*, 346 FSupp.2d 538 (SDNY 2004), at 549.

62 *Bigio v Coca-Cola Co.*, 239 F3d 440 (2d Cir 2000), at 449.

63 *In re South African Apartheid Litigation*, 346 FSupp2d 538 (SDNY 2004), at 549–551.

64 *Doe v UNOCAL*, 395 F.3d 932 (9th Cir 2002).

or encouragement which has a substantial effect on the perpetration of the crime',[65] which would be the case where a company hired Myanmar military to provide security for its pipeline construction and build infrastructure around it, knowing that the military would commit human rights violations in this context, including resorting to forced labour.[66] Thus, in *UNOCAL* the reprehensible conduct of the company went beyond making profitable deals with a regime that violated international law and rather consisted in actively cooperating with the military and encouraging it to commit *ius cogens* violations.[67] In *Talisman*, it was suggested that unlike the case of a banker who made 'loans that were used by an enterprise which exploited slave labour ... here plaintiffs allege that Talisman worked directly with the government in its policy of "ethnic cleansing" and provided material aid to its efforts. In such cases, liability may follow.'[68] Thus, again a direct co-operation with the regime concerning the commission of its violations of international law was required, and the mere granting of a loan was not regarded as sufficient to trigger liability under the ATCA. This was recently confirmed in the latest *Talisman*[69] decision, where the court granted the defendant's motion for summary judgement. The court argued that in order to demonstrate that the defendant aided and abetted an international law violation, it would need to be shown that to the defendant's knowledge, the principal violated international law; that 'the defendant's acts had a substantial effect upon the success of the criminal venture'[70] and that the defendant was aware of this. Most importantly for current purposes, the defendant needs to act with intent to assist the violation, 'that is [that] the defendant specifically directed his acts to assist in the specific violation.'[71] In particular, the court rejected the suggestion that the fact that Talisman paid royalties to the Sudanese government, knowing that it purchased weapons to target civilians and displace them, would be sufficient to establish liability for aiding and abetting the government's international law violations: 'The connection between the payment of royalties and the Government attacks on civilians is simply too indirect to permit the payment of royalties itself to serve as circumstantial evidence of an intent to assist in the Government's commission of war crimes and crimes against humanity.'[72] Thus, it seems as if to succeed, the plaintiffs would have needed to establish 'that when Talisman ... paid royalties, it "specifically directed"

---

65   Ibid., at 951.

66   Ibid., at 952.

67   For other cases of more direct involvement of the defendants in human rights violations see *Wiwa v Royal Dutch Petroleum Co.*, 2002 WL 319887 (SDNY 2002); and *Presbyterian Church of Sudan v Talisman Energy, Inc.*, 244 FSupp2d 289 (SDNY 2003).

68   *Presbyterian Church of Sudan v Talisman Energy, Inc.*, 244 FSupp2d 289 (SDNY 2003), at 322.

69   *Presbyterian Church of Sudan v Talisman Energy, Inc. and Republic of Sudan*, (2006) WL 2602145 (SDNY).

70   Ibid., at 26.

71   Ibid.

72   Ibid., at 33.

those payments to the Government's procurement of weaponry to target civilians and displace them.'[73]

It then seems obvious that the only link that in most cases can be established between loans and *ius cogens* violations, that is that banks made loans to regimes which violate *ius cogens* norms, would not be enough to generate tort liability of the banks under the ATCA for the violation of *ius cogens*, unless a more direct involvement of the bank with the regime and the acts that amount to a violation of *ius cogens* could be shown in individual cases.

2.2.3 Approach of the International Law Commission in the context of state responsibility

In the context of its work on providing Articles of State Responsibility,[74] the ILC in Article 16 addressed the question of aid and assistance in the commission of an internationally wrongful act. The article reads as follows:

> A State which aids or assists another State in the commission of an internationally wrongful act by the latter is internationally responsible for doing so if:
>
> a) That State does so with knowledge of the circumstances of the internationally wrongful act...

In its commentary to Article 16, the ILC explains that: 'The assisting State will only be responsible to the extent that its own conduct has caused or contributed to the internationally wrongful act.'[75] With regard to the requirement that responsibility for aid and assistance requires 'knowledge of the circumstances of the internationally wrongful act', the ILC comments that '[a] State providing material or financial assistance or aid to another State does not normally assume the risk that its assistance or aid may be used to carry out an internationally wrongful act,'[76] and unawareness of the intended use of the aid for wrongful purposes would preclude responsibility of the aiding state. Moreover, the aid must be given with a view and intent to facilitate the commission of the wrongful act, and it must have significantly contributed to it.[77] It seems that the criteria for state responsibility under international law are very similar to those developed by the US courts in the context of establishing tort liability under the ATCA.

2.2.4 Consequences for the validity of loans

It remains to be examined what the outcome of the analysis of the principles of criminal law, tort law and the law on the international responsibility of states means for the argument that debts could be odious and the underlying contracts void, if

---

73   Ibid.
74   See GA Res 56/83 (2001), Annex.
75   ILC Report A/56/10 (2001), at 155.
76   Ibid., at 156.
77   Ibid.

they assist a despotic regime in violating *ius cogens* provisions. Given the purpose behind criminal and tort liability and state responsibility, that is to establish and react to responsibility for unlawful and/or wrongful behaviour, the focus, both with regard to the responsibility of the principal and that of the accomplice, is not on the violation of the *ius cogens* norm itself. Instead, in order to justify criminal or tort liability and state responsibility, in addition to a violation of a *ius cogens* norm, the behaviour and state of mind both of the principal and of the accomplice are essential. The invalidity of a treaty or contract because of a violation of *ius cogens* has a different objective, as it intends to reverse existing *ius cogens* violations.[78] What is important is accordingly simply whether or not, from the perspective of the international community, a treaty violates such fundamental principles that it cannot be regarded as valid and enforceable. The parties' intentions or behaviour cannot usually influence the outcome of this assessment, as violations of *ius cogens* norms need to be terminated and, if possible, reversed, whether or not this violation was intended by the borrower and/or the creditor. This consideration is reflected in Article 53 of the Vienna Convention on the Law of Treaties according to which treaties that violate *ius cogens* are invalid without further requirements of intentionality, fault etc.

Another consequence of the different purposes of criminal and tort liability and state responsibility, on the one hand, and challenging the validity of a contract, on the other, is that in order to establish such liability, it is essential to determine the significance of the accomplice's contribution, as this will usually form the basis for delineating individual liability in each case. This individual element, however, cannot be important in the context of determining whether or not a contract is invalid, as what is relevant here is not the link between the individual and the violation, but rather that between the contract and the violation. Consequently, what counts is not whether and to what extent the individual, through his/her behaviour accompanied by the required state of mind, contributed to the violation, but instead whether the contract did. In the context of determining the validity of a loan agreement, the focus accordingly does not, as in cases in which criminal, tort or state responsibility needs to be established, lie on the act of assistance and the state of mind of the lender, but instead exclusively on whether or not the loan contributed to the *ius cogens* violation. To demonstrate that the loan contributed to the violation is essential, as there would be no reason to regard a loan as invalid because of a *ius cogens* violation committed by one of the parties, the borrowing state, unless this violation bears a relation to the contract.

As the *Khulumani* complaint graphically demonstrates, not only the link between the loan agreement and the *ius cogens* violation, but also the link between the use of the funds and the *ius cogens* violations might be indirect, at least in all cases in which the incoming money is not directly used for committing the violation, but instead serves the state budget as a whole. Of course, the more directly the loan is linked to the *ius cogens* violations committed by the borrowing regime, the easier it will be to establish that it contributed to them.[79] However, the argument presented

---

78   See Article 71 of the Vienna Convention on the Law of Treaties.
79   For a discussion see also McBeth (2005), at 24–25.

in Chapter Three in the context of the discussion of how to determine whether loans benefited the people of a country that is governed by an oppressive regime[80] equally applies here: a distinction according to which a loan is only regarded as significant for the *ius cogens* violation if the borrowed money is directly used for the prohibited purpose, but not where it is used for acceptable purposes as a consequence of which other resources are freed and can then be used to facilitate or commit the *ius cogens* violations, is not convincing. A loan can make a contribution to a *ius cogens* violation whether or not the money lent to the regime is directly used to finance this violation; whether it facilitates the violation by adding to the financial resources of the regime; or whether it makes it possible by having a stabilizing effect on the political position of the regime. It is, for example, possible that a loan that directly financed torture equipment or operations has a significant effect on the commission of torture, but the same might also be true, though this would be more difficult to establish, for a loan that enables a regime to remain in power and carry on with torture practices. Particularly in the latter type of cases, one could argue that individual loans will only very rarely have a discernible effect in that sense, and that the effect on the commission of *ius cogens* violations indirectly following from bank loans will more likely only become evident when looking at the totality of incoming funds. However, at least in the specific case of South African apartheid, Jon Foster's statement that 'each bank loan, each new investment is another brick in the wall of our continued existence'[81] points towards the significance of individual loans and provides *prima facie* evidence of their importance for the consolidation of the regime, and accordingly the facilitation of the *ius cogens* violations inherent in apartheid.

This would mean that in many cases banks could see loans declared to be odious simply on the basis that they were made to regimes that commit *ius cogens* violations, thus for doing business with such a regime, an outcome rejected by the Nuremberg Tribunal in the context of criminal liability,[82] and the US court in *Khulumani* in the context of tort liability. The *Khulumani* court pointed towards an important ideological debate that would be triggered by such a suggestion, which is that on what is the best attitude towards trade with and investment in countries with a dubious human rights record. The court explicitly rejected the idea that the fact of doing business with the apartheid regime constituted a violation of international law for the purposes of ATCA litigation, pointing out that such a finding would adversely affect:

> the policy of encouraging positive change in developing countries via economic investment. ... In a world where many countries fall considerably short of ideal economic, political and social conditions, this Court must be extremely cautious in permitting suits based upon a corporation's doing business in countries with less than stellar human rights

---

80   See Chapter Three, 3.2, supra.
81   Khulumani complaint and jury trial demand, www.cmht.com/casewatch/cases/apartheid-cmpl.pdf, at para 391.
82   *United States v Weizsaecker* (Ministries Case), XIV Trials of War Criminals 621–622, as quoted in Ramasastry (1998), at 416.

records, especially since the consequences of such an approach could have significant, if not disastrous, effects on international commerce.[83]

This suggests that the approach developed here will in all likelihood be unacceptable to all those who regard trade with regimes that commit *ius cogens* violations, including those that were as blatant and as widely and strongly condemned as those of the apartheid regime, as acceptable or even desirable. It would also probably be objected that such an approach might have a negative impact on developing countries and their access to the international financial market. However, it should not be forgotten that what is under discussion here is no more than the suggestion that contracts might be invalid and unenforceable if they make a contribution to *ius cogens* violations, that is acts that are regarded as so reprehensible by the whole international community that they cannot be tolerated. An application of the odious debts doctrine to cases in which principles that are commonly accepted to be part of *ius cogens* are violated by a state would not hinder trade or investment, but instead only make sure that trade and investment do not have the effect of enabling or facilitating such violations. However, one important problem that would need to be resolved is where to draw the line between loans that contribute to *ius cogens* violations, and those that alleviate their effect for the people of the relevant state.[84] If it were accepted that loans to regimes that commit *ius cogens* violations will in all likelihood at least indirectly facilitate these violations, a presumption could be applied in favour of the odiousness and consequent invalidity of such loans, unless it can exceptionally be shown that the loan did not even have such an indirect effect. This would require a determination of the regimes to which such a presumption could be applied, that is which regimes qualify as committing *ius cogens* violations. While this would include judgments on the policies of regimes, to invite the international community and potential lenders to beware of dealing with regimes that violate *ius cogens* is different from asking them to make a democracy assessment as sometimes suggested in the context of the traditional odious debts doctrine.[85] After all, despite all its uncertainties, the concept of *ius cogens* is recognized as part of international law, and it has at least a core content on which wide agreement exists, while it is not a requirement of international law that a regime be democratic.[86]

However, it is submitted that a seriousness threshold should be applied with regard to the *ius cogens* violations of the relvant regime. The ILC's Articles on State Responsibility distinguish between serious and other breaches of state obligations

---

83   *In re South African Apartheid Litigation*, 346 FSupp2d 538 (SDNY 2004), at 554. For comparable arguments see also Joseph (2004), at 52.

84   See the discussion by Talmon (2006) at 106 of the ICJ's advisory opinion in *Wall in the Occupied Palestinian Territory* (2004) ICJ 136, where he suggests that it is not at all clear what follows from the obligation not to assist Israel in maintaining the situation created by the creation of the wall, as it is, for example, open whether this would include financial assistance to alleviate the effects of the wall for the Palestinian people.

85   See Chapter Three, 3.2, supra.

86   See, for example, Ipsen (2004), at 428–430. See also *Military Activities in and against Nicaragua (Nicaragua v US)*, (1986) ICJ Rep 14, at 133. But see Cassese (2005), at 395; Franck (2000); Fox (2000), at 90.

arising under peremptory norms of international law (Articles 40 and 41) and attach particular consequences to the former. A serious breach is defined as one that 'involves a gross or systematic failure by the responsible State to fulfil the obligation' (Article 40(2)). A systematic violation is one that is 'carried out in an organized and deliberate way ... the "gross" refers to the intensity of the violation or its effects.'[87] Similar considerations should be applied in the context of loans.

As a tentative conclusion, it can then be said that while it faces many difficulties, ranging from the complexity of the legal argument to practicalities and the fact that its political implications make it very unlikely that such a concept will find widespread acceptance, it would nevertheless be possible to develop an odious debts doctrine based on violations of *ius cogens* norms with contours that are clear enough to make it workable. However, in addition to the many problems that needed to be overcome to reach this conclusion, many questions remain with regard to the further consequences of such a doctrine, as well as potential implementation mechanisms.

2.3 Implementing the ius cogens based approach

Given that an analogy with Article 53 of the Vienna Convention on the Law of Treaties was used in order to develop an alternative approach to odious debts that focuses on *ius cogens* violations, it seems consistent to look at Article 71(1) of the Convention when examining the consequences of the fact that a contract is odious and therefore void. Article 71(1) is mainly concerned with reversing the effects of a *ius cogens* violation. In the case of treaties in which future *ius cogens* violations are agreed, the consequence would presumably simply be that they are declared void and would therefore be unenforceable. Where a treaty was already executed and this violated *ius cogens* norms, the effects of these violations would have to be reversed. However, it is not so clear that Article 71(1) provides a useful framework for dealing with invalid loan contracts. If a loan contract substantially contributes to the violation of *ius cogens* by the borrowing state, the effects of *ius cogens* violations that were facilitated by that loan cannot be reversed by declaring the nullity of the contract after the loan was already paid out. This effect could only be achieved if the invalidity were to be invoked before the money was made available to the debtor.

However, the invalidity of such contracts would presumably have a significant deterrence effect, in that lenders are not likely to make loans that could contribute to a regime's *ius cogens* violation if such contracts were void and they would accordingly have to fear either losing their money, or being reduced to claims for restitution. This is in line with the frequently made suggestion that given the uncertainties surrounding some aspects of the concept of *ius cogens* in general, its main effect is to deter future *ius cogens* violations and to encourage compliance with *ius cogens* norms.[88] However, in the specific context of sovereign loans, this effect can only be achieved where creditors have a clear idea of the situations in which this consequence might arise, and which they therefore need to avoid. The doctrine

---

87   ILC Report A/56/10 (2001), at 285.
88   See, for example, *Prosecutor v Furundzija* (Case No: IT-95-17/1-T), paras 154–157; Cassese (2005), at 205; Rozakis (1976), at 19.

should therefore only be applied where either the loan itself exceptionally violates *ius cogens*, or where the creditors are aware, or should be aware, that the loans are made to a regime that is know for its violations of *ius cogens* norms.

One of the attractions of an odious debts doctrine that is based on *ius cogens* violations is that where a contract violates *ius cogens*, it is not only void, but it can moreover not be ratified.[89] Thus, not only the original loan transactions taken up by dictators who violate *ius cogens* norms would be invalid, but the restructuring and refinancing agreements referring to debt that falls into this category could not be regarded as valid ratifications of these loans. This would resolve one of the main problems of the traditional odious debts doctrine in the context of which it is much more difficult to develop an argument that the odiousness of a debt survives its restructurings or trading on secondary markets.[90] Furthermore, many argue that no limitation period applies to claims based on a violation of *ius cogens*,[91] which would be significant with regard to potential claims for restitution of payments made on such loans.

It is evident that such an approach would have very far-reaching practical implications. If there was no period of limitation, and odious debts could not be recognized, then all cases of debt restructuring and refinancing that took place over more than the past 25 years of debt crisis would need to be re-examined as to their potential invalidity. While this does not seem like a scenario that will make the recognition of the doctrine particularly attractive, it should not be forgotten that these consequences follow from a violation of principles that are recognized as peremptory in international law, and from which no derogation is allowed. It might be objected that the invalidity of the original loan contracts as well as of all subsequent debt restructurings would unfairly harm individual bondholders who in good faith obtained bonds without having had anything to do with the original odious loan transactions. However, it is submitted that where the original loan violated *ius cogens* principles, to allow the recognition of such loans in the interests of the bondholders would undermine the concept of odious debts based on *ius cogens* violations, as the consequences of the odiousness could then be avoided by restructuring the original debt. This does not mean that good faith bondholders will end up with nothing, as the fact that the debt is odious does not itself resolve the question of how the transaction is to be reversed and to what extent they might have claims for compensation against the financial institutions from which they obtained the bonds,[92] or claims for restitution.

---

89   Brownlie (2003), at 490.

90   See Chapter Three, 4, supra.

91   Kadelbach (1992), at 65; Fischer-Lescano (2003), at 235; Talmon (2006), at 107. See also *Prosecutor v Furundzija* (Case No: IT-95-17/1-T) for the specific case of torture. But see Sinclair (1984), at 224, who argues that there is no clear legal principle to this effect.

92   See also "Galli, Hugo y Otro c/ PEN – s/ Amparo Ley 25.561", 6 April 2005, per Justices Zaffaroni and Lorenzetti, at para. 16. For successful claims in a different context, against banks that sold Argentinian bonds to inexperienced investors, such as pensioners, without sufficiently explaining the inherent risks of such a transaction, see,

According to the Vienna Convention on the Law of Treaties, the invalidity of a treaty is not the automatic consequence of a *ius cogens* violation, but it must rather be invoked by the party that wants to see the treaty terminated on those grounds. Where the other party disagrees, international tribunals need to be involved in order to settle the dispute. This mechanism is only available to the states that are parties to the Convention,[93] and it is limited to the situation to which the Convention applies, that is treaties between states, so that it does not help in the context of a *ius cogens* violation encouraged by a contract concluded between a state and a private party. Thus, in order to make this doctrine workable at the international level, some mechanism similar to those suggested in the context of the traditional odious debts doctrine,[94] with all the problems that entails, would be necessary. However, the tribunal that would be needed in order to decide these claims would at least have the framework of *ius cogens* to resort to, instead of having to make decisions on issues such as whether or not a debt was beneficial to the people of the debtor state.

Alternatively, given the status of the rules and principles of public international law in the domestic law of some jurisdictions, it could be argued that the national courts of some countries have the power to take the issue of *ius cogens* violations into consideration when examining the validity of a claim for debt repayment according to its domestic law. In Germany, for example, Article 25 of the German Constitution states that: 'The general rules of public international law form part of the federal law. They take precedence over the laws and directly create rights and duties for the inhabitants of the Federal territory.' The general rules of public international law to which Article 25 of the German Constitution refers include, but go beyond, norms of *ius cogens* status.[95] Individuals as well as foreign states who are parties to judicial proceedings in Germany can demand that courts take these principles into account when making their decisions, and courts moreover have to consider them *ex officio*.[96] Where a court decision violates such principles, this decision can be challenged by the means of a constitutional complaint.[97] Accordingly, if an odious debts argument were based on a *ius cogens* violation, and proceedings for debt repayment were to be brought in Germany, German courts would have to take account of the *ius cogens* violation when determining the validity of the loan agreement.[98] This gains particular

---

for example, OLG Bamberg, decisions of 2 June and 17 July 2006 (Az. 5 U 246/05); for Italy see, for example, *Clarín*, 20 March 2005.

93   Warbrick (2003), at 205; Ruffert (2006), at 301. See also *Case Concerning Armed Activities on the Territory of the Congo (Democratic Republic of Congo v Rwanda) (Provisional Measures)*, Order of 10 July, (2002) ILM 41, at paras 74–75.

94   See Chapter Three, 5, *supra*.

95   See Geiger (2002), at 162 with further references; von Münch and Kunig-Rojahn (2001), at para. 6 to Article 25.

96   BVerfGE 46, 342 (1977), at 363.

97   See, for example, BVerfGE 23, 288 (1968), at 300; Geiger (2002), at 169; von Münch and Kunig-Rojahn (2001), at para. 24 to Article 25.

98   In Germany, NGOs raised a comparable point in an *amicus* brief to the Federal Constitutional Court. Bondholders had brought proceedings for debt repayment against Argentina, after the country defaulted on its debt. Argentina did not question the validity of the loans, but invoked inability to pay based on economic necessity, and the court

importance when bearing in mind the reluctance of debtor states to repudiate debts as odious. Claims for debt repayment against debtor states who are in default, which will usually take place in the courts of creditor states, would then provide a good opportunity to raise and apply the doctrine. However, this might trigger the same objections that are raised against the American ATCA litigation, that is that to allow the national courts of a country to assume the role of a universal watchdog for worldwide human rights or *ius cogens* violations faces legitimacy problems and gives rise to the worry that national courts of a country might use international human rights language to pursue the interests of their own country and impose their own interpretation of international human rights standards upon other countries.[99]

To summarize, an approach to the odious debts doctrine that applies to loans which involved a violation of *ius cogens* has many advantages over the odious debts doctrine as traditionally understood. In particular, it is able to resolve some of the problems that make the latter unworkable and undesirable: no international tribunal the legitimacy and impartiality of which would be highly contentious would necessarily need to be created to decide the issue, as they could also be decided by national courts when hearing claims for debt repayment; if international tribunals were to be instated in order to decide the issue, they could base their decisions on the concept of *ius cogens*; the odiousness of loans does not depend on an international evaluation of whether or not specific loans were beneficial to the people of a country that was ruled by an oppressive regime; and most importantly, the invalidity of the original loan transactions would extend to all subsequent restructurings of that debt. It is submitted that to focus on *ius cogens* violations moreover implies how to decide the question of whether the doctrine of odious debts should be limited to the case of state succession, or extend to that of regime change. If what makes a debt odious in a given case is the violation of international law thereby committed, then there is no reason to distinguish between cases of state succession and cases of regime change. Indeed, it should not even matter whether there was any change at all, either in the form of state or of regime change, as the debt would even be odious if the regime that contracted the loan to finance its *ius cogens* violations remained in power. This could, of course, lead to the undesirable consequence that when borrowing money for international law violations, states would know that they will not have to repay such loans, which might encourage such borrowing. However, if these principles were to become recognized and enforced, lending practices would in all likelihood change quickly.[100]

---

referred the question of whether economic necessity was a principle of international law to the Federal Constitutional Court. The *amicus* brief argued that the issue of necessity was not relevant, as the court should have declared the loan contracts void because they violate ss. 134 and 138 of the Civil Code (according to s134, a contract that violates a legal prohibition is void, and s138 attaches the same consequence to a contract that violates good morals). The Federal Constitutional Court decision is still pending.

99   See Flauss (2006), at 387–389 with further references.

100 But see Norwegian Ministry of Foreign Affairs (2004), which argues at 20 that 'both debtor and creditor must clearly be responsible for ensuring that loans are financially justifiable.'

3 Odiousness of debts because of violations of international law principles that are not part of *ius cogens*

Another issue that should be addressed in the context of a discussion of an odious debts doctrine with an international law focus is whether it is justified to limit such a doctrine to cases of *ius cogens* violations. A consequence of this limited approach is to accept that only principles that are recognized as part of *ius cogens* would trump *pacta sunt servanda*, and the underlying message is clearly that where the principle of *pacta sunt servanda* stands in conflict with international law principles that have not reached the standard of *ius cogens*, the sanctity of the contract will automatically prevail. This implies that there is not even a need for balancing the conflicting interests in such cases, so that it seems as if *pacta sunt servanda* stands below *ius cogens*, but above all other principles of international law. Given, for example, that important principles such as that of the right to development are not universally regarded as forming part of *ius cogens*, under this approach the sanctity of a loan agreement prevails even if it violates the right to development or other international law principles of fundamental importance to the people of debtor states.

This, however, is in line with the approach taken by the Vienna Convention on the law of Treaties which only allows for the invalidity of a treaty in cases of *ius cogens* violations, but not where it is incompatible with other international law principles. Furthermore, the doctrine of odious debts aims to provide no more than a tool which helps exceptionally to invalidate contracts where an intolerable violation of international law occurred. This is not to say that loan contracts would automatically be valid if they 'only' violate principles of international law that are not part of *ius cogens*, but instead merely that this would then not be a case of invalidity under the odious debts doctrine. However, these contracts could nevertheless be invalid for other reasons.[101]

Of course, it might be possible to develop an odious debts doctrine based, for example, on violations of the right to development, and to restrict it to creating 'the obligation of all states to international solidarity and social justice [which] is violated if states require or grant public credits or secure private credits with public guarantees for investments that are demonstrably unproductive and inimical to development.'[102] However, given the controversy surrounding the recognition of the right to development as a right[103] instead of a mere programmatic statement,[104] and the uncertainty of the content of such a right and the corresponding obligations on states, if one were to include such a contentious issue into the doctrine of odious

---

101 For example because of their unconstitutionality under domestic constitutional law, or their invalidity under contract law.

102 Frankenberg and Knieper (1984), at 433. For an expansion of the odious debts doctrine to include the right to development as outlined in Article 55 of the UN Charter, though in the context of investment rather than debt agreements, see Wabnitz (1986), at 662.

103 For an overview see, for example, Ipsen (2004), at 440–443; see also Harris (2004), at 770–771.

104 Leyendecker (1988), at 195.

debts, this would risk making an already difficult concept completely unworkable.[105] Similarly, the doctrine should not be broadened so as to include all principles of international law and to invite a balancing in each case of conflict, as problems not that dissimilar to those identified in the context of the ideological debate on how to define beneficial purposes of debts[106] would then presumably arise. The same applies to the recent suggestion to give shape to an odious debts doctrine by delineating 'case groups', that is by adopting an approach similar to that found in national systems in the context of determining under what circumstances contracts are void because they violate good morals.[107] Here, if the focus goes beyond *ius cogens*, for example by including the provisions of human rights treaties, it will be difficult to reach any agreement on what 'good morals' might be at the international level, or on how to determine the factors that render a debt odious.[108]

4 Application of the doctrine of odious debts to the case of Argentina

The example of Argentina will now be used to examine how the odious debts doctrine might work in specific cases. In Argentina, it is frequently argued that the country's foreign debt is in large parts odious and does for that reason not have to be repaid. To give some recent examples of how the doctrine was used in Argentina, in 2004, and again in March 2006, bills rejecting Argentina's foreign debt were introduced in Congress. The 2004 Bill was entirely based on the odiousness of the debt, and Article 1 (out of two) of the Bill stated that: 'The whole foreign debt contracted by the military dictatorship shall be declared odious.' The reason given for this was that the possibility that citizens could exercise control over the acts of government was dramatically reduced, if not abolished, under the military regime. Article 1 of the Bill introduced in March 2006 is formulated in slightly more general terms, stating that: 'The foreign public debt contracted by the military dictatorship shall be declared to be absolutely void.' The explanatory notes to the Bill then *inter alia* refer to the doctrine of odious debts to justify the declaration of the nullity of the sovereign debt.

The discussion in Argentina frequently links reference to the odious debts doctrine in its traditional form with other international law arguments. However, in order to use Argentina as an example at which to test the potentiality and limits of the two forms of the odious debts doctrine, they will be applied separately.

---

105 This is not to say that development focused challenges to certain loans should be dismissed, but simply that this should take place as a separate debate.

106 Chapter Three, 3.2, supra.

107 See Christoph Paulus (2005a), at 95–102.

108 For a suggestion of such an approach, based loosely on Article 3.10 of the UNIDROIT Principles of International Commercial Contracts, www.unidroit.org/english/principles/ contracts/principles2004/blackletter2004.pdf, see Christoph Paulus, (2005a).

4.1 Odiousness under the traditional odious debts doctrine

When applying the traditional odious debts doctrine to Argentina's debt that was taken up by the military regime, it could be argued, first of all, that the people did not consent to the taking up of the debt. The loan agreements were concluded in a situation in which Congress was dissolved and all decisions, including those regarding the taking up of sovereign debt, were taken entirely by a regime that had seized power without being democratically elected and that did not leave any room for democratic participation.[109] It is sometimes suggested that there was widespread popular agreement with the military coup in 1976, given the desire to see an end of the disastrous political situation of the country under the government of Isabel Perón prior to the military coup.[110] However, even if this were true, it would not alter the fact that there was no possibility for the people to express opposition, let alone participate in the decision-making processes, and that the regime governed the country, and carried out its economic policies of which the indebting of the country was an important part, after having brutally repressed large parts of the political parties, the unions, and in fact any opposition to its policies that would otherwise have made the carrying out of these policies difficult, if not impossible.[111] It thus seems plausible that the Argentinian people did not consent to the military government in general, or the loan transactions, in particular.

Unless one accepts the view that to grant loans to military dictatorships can never be beneficial, a thorough investigation of the individual loan transactions would be necessary in order to determine their unbeneficial nature, facing the problem that no clear criteria exist according to which such an assessment could be carried out. However, according to a World Bank report, large parts of the debt taken up by Argentina between 1975 and 1983 was contracted to finance capital flight and to pay for arms and non-declared imports.[112] An agreement could probably be reached that at least the capital flight, and probably also the arms purchases and undeclared imports, did not benefit the interests of the country. It is very likely that the creditors were aware of the fact that the debt was taken up by a military regime that governed the country without the consent of the people, and in many cases they will also have been aware of the fact that the loans were not used for the benefit of the Argentinian people.

If the doctrine of odious debt in its traditional form were recognized by international law; included cases of regime change; and agreement could be reached, and proof provided, for the allegation that the debt was unbeneficial to the Argentinian people, large parts of Argentina's debt that was taken up by the military regime would qualify as odious.[113] However, as argued above, even if all these *ifs* could be overcome satisfactorily, the real problems have only just started. The decisive problems would then be the lack of a procedure through which the

---

109 See Chapter Two, 1, supra.
110 See, for example, Dreyfus, (2006).
111 See, for example, Feinmann (2006), at 84.
112 World Bank, Economic Memorandum on Argentina, 22 June 1984, at 17–19.
113 See also Plan Fénix (2004).

doctrine could be enforced, and the question of the extent to which the doctrine can be applied to Argentina's restructured debt, as the country no longer repays the debt in its original odious form, but rather the debt that was restructured by a variety of democratic regimes.

4.2 Odiousness because of a violation of ius cogens

If, on the other hand, the *ius cogens* centred variant of the odious debts doctrine were to be applied to the case of Argentina's debt, the analysis would have to focus on the question of whether the debt was taken up in order to violate imperative norms of international law, or whether the loans at least contributed to the commission of such violations.[114] The loans contracted by the Argentinian military regime were largely made to pay for the financial policies of the military regime, capital flight, and arms purchases.[115] It is submitted that if at all, it will only be possible to establish a direct link between loans and *ius cogens* violations with regard to the loans made for arms purchases, but such a finding would depend on the purposes for which arms were bought, and on how they were used. More promising for a repudiation of parts of Argentina's debt based on *ius cogens* violations might be the more far-reaching argument that the loans were made to a regime that violated *ius cogens* norms, and that they indirectly contributed to these violations. As a first step, it would then need to be examined to what extent the Argentinian military regime did, in fact, commit *ius cogens* violations. While there might be other potential violations of *ius cogens* norms committed by the military dictatorship, the most obvious relevant activities of the regime would be those related to torture and forced disappearances, whose commission by the Argentinian military dictatorship is well documented.[116]

There is widespread agreement that the prohibition of torture forms part of *ius cogens*,[117] but to determine the exact point in time at which the prohibition of torture became recognized as part of *ius cogens* is difficult. In the context of an analogy with Article 53 of the Vienna Convention on the Law of Treaties, this is, however, significant, as contracts are only void if they violated *ius cogens* at the time when they were concluded. Thus, it would need to be established that during the government of the latest Argentinian military regime, that is between 1976 and 1983, the prohibition of torture was already regarded as a peremptory norm of international law. The difficulty in establishing at what time the prohibition on torture was recognized as part of *ius cogens* is to some extent reflected in the House of Lords decision in *Pinochet*.[118] Lord Goff's speech, for example, seems to indicate that he did not think

---

114   This was taken for granted by Fischer-Lescano (2003), at 235.

115   World Bank, Economic Memorandum on Argentina, 22 June 1984, at 17–19.

116   See, for example, CONADEP, *Nunca Más* (1984).

117   See, for example, Brownlie (2003), at 489; *Prosecutor v Furundzija* (Case No: IT-95-17/1-T), at paras 155–157. See also the US decisions on the issue in the context of litigation under the ATCA, for example *Siderman de Blake v Republic of Argentina*, 965 F2d 699 (9th Cir 1992), at 714. And for the position of the IACHR see, for example, *Michael Domínguez v US*, Case 12.285, Report No.62/02, at para. 49.

118   *Regina v Bow Street Metropolitan Stipendiary Magistrate And Others, Ex Parte Pinochet Ugarte* (No. 3) [2000] 1 AC 147.

that the prohibition of torture outside of armed conflict reached *ius cogens* status before 'well after 1989'.[119] Lord Hope and Lord Hutton were of the opinion that the prohibition of torture had acquired *ius cogens* status by 29 September 1988.[120] As this was not relevant for the decision they had to reach, they left open at what exact point before that date they thought the *ius cogens* nature of this concept materialized. Lord Millett suggested that this had already been the case in 1973,[121] and based this, *inter alia*, on the view that the UN Convention against Torture and other Cruel, Inhuman and Degrading Treatment or Punishment 1984 did not outlaw torture and the other practices the Convention refers to, but instead aimed at strengthening their prohibition which predated the Convention.[122] In *Siderman*, in the context of a claim under the ATCA, a US court found that the torture committed by the Argentinian military regime constituted a violation of *ius cogens*.[123] Although the court did not specifically address the issue of when the prohibition of torture turned into a norm of *ius cogens*, the statement seems to imply that the court assumed that the *ius cogens* character of the prohibition was already recognized at the time when the torture was committed. This brief overview demonstrates that it might be controversial whether or not the prohibition of torture was part of *ius cogens* at the time when the relevant loan agreements were contracted between the Argentinian military regime and the country's creditors.

Another potential *ius cogens* violation committed by the Argentinian military regime could be that of crimes against humanity in the form of forced disappearances of persons, which would again raise the question of whether and at what time this was recognized as a norm of *ius cogens*. As early as 1978, both the UN General Assembly,[124] and the Inter-American Commission on Human Rights (IACHR),[125] expressed their concern about the policies of forced disappearances with all the human rights implications they entailed. In its country report on Argentina in 1980, the IACHR emphasized in the introduction that: 'The Commission believes that the problem of the disappeared is one of the most serious human rights problems that Argentina faces.'[126] Both the Inter-American Court of Human Rights (I/A Court H.R.), and the IACHR have repeatedly stressed that forced disappearances and the various criminal offences inherent therein, are condemned by norms of *ius cogens* status,[127] but did not indicate since when they regarded this to be the case. In Argentina, the

119 Ibid., at 211. See also De Wet (2004), at 118.
120 Ibid., at 247 and 260–262, respectively.
121 Ibid., at 276.
122 Ibid., see also Lord Hutton, at 260–261. Both relied on Burgers and Danelius (1988), at 1, when making this point.
123 *Siderman de Blake v Republic of Argentina*, 965 F2d 699 (Cal. 1992), at 717.
124 GA Res.33/173 of 20 December 1978.
125 Annual Report 1978, Part II.
126 OEA/Ser.L/V/II.49, Doc. 19 corr.1.
127 See, for example, *Michael Domínguez v US*, Case 12.285, Report No.62/02, IACHR, at para. 49; *Barrios Altos Case (Chumbipuma et al. v Peru)*, 14 March 2001, I/A Court HR, at para. 41; *Case of the Serrano Cruz Sisters v El Salvador*, 23 November 2004, I/A Court HR, at para. 105. See also *Wiwa v Royal Dutch Petroleum Co.*, 2002 WL 319887 (SDNY 2002), at 9; and Grammer (2005).

issue has recently received a lot of attention in the course of criminal trials against individuals for their involvement in forced disappearances and the various criminal offences inherent therein. Both in *Clavel*[128] and in *Simón*,[129] the Argentinian Supreme Court specifically addressed the issue of *ius cogens*. In *Simón*, Justice Boggiano argued in this respect that forced disappearances fall under the definition of crimes against humanity; that they violate *ius cogens*;[130] and that 'the norms of *ius cogens* that penalize crimes against humanity have been in force from time immemorial.'[131] Justice Maqueda equally suggested that crimes against humanity in the form of forced disappearances were already prohibited during the latest military dictatorship by norms of *ius cogens* character.[132] Whether this is a universally accepted view remains to be tested.

If the prohibition of torture, that of forced disappearances, or both, were found to have already been recognized as *ius cogens* norms in the period of 1976–1983, loans made to the Argentinian military regime could be invalid to the extent to which they contributed to the regime's *ius cogens* violations. This would require an evaluation of what role the loans played in the *ius cogens* violations committed by the regime, for example in the form of providing it with the means to finance the repression that resulted in torture and forced disappearances, or in the general form of strengthening its position and keeping it in power. As the Odious Debts Bill 2004 emphasizes, the consequence that Argentina's debt is odious derives from 'the special link between crimes against humanity and the process of indebtedness'. In this context, research into the link between the *ius cogens* violations of the Argentinian regime and its economic policies, including the excessive taking up of loans, would be necessary in order to establish such a link. Where no direct link between loan and *ius cogens* violations can be established, a presumption of odiousness could nevertheless apply which could be rebutted if it can be shown that the loans did not at least indirectly contribute to the *ius cogens* violations.

If parts of Argentina's debt were to be regarded as odious on this basis, to restore the situation that would have existed without the violation of *ius cogens* norms would be rather complex, given the amount of debt restructurings; the variety of bondholders; and the chain of creditors who over the years had some involvement in the process,[133] but this is no reason to uphold the *status quo* that developed in violation of imperative norms of international law. More importantly still, Argentina would not be free to assume these debts, given the inadmissibility to recognize acts that violate *ius cogens*.

---

128 "Arancibia Clavel, Enrique Lautaro s/homicidio calificado y asociación ilícita y otros –causa No.259", Argentinian Supreme Court (24 August 2004).
129 "Simón, Julio Héctor y otros s/ privación ilegítima de la libertad, etc. –causa No. 17.768", Argentinian Supreme Court (14 June 2005).
130 Ibid., at paras 38 and 40. See also Justice Maqueda, at para. 49.
131 Ibid., at para. 43.
132 Ibid., at para. 89.
133 See also Fischer-Lescano (2003), at 238.

5 Conclusion

In this chapter, an attempt was made to give the odious debts doctrine a new focus by moving away from the traditional emphasis on notions of consent of and benefit to the people, to those of violations of imperative norms of international law. This change of perspective has various consequences. A doctrine based on *ius cogens* violations provides clearer criteria than the traditional doctrine of odious debts, and it overcomes one of the fundamental weaknesses of the doctrine in its traditional form in that it would extend to restructured debt. On the other hand, given the narrow scope of *ius cogens* in current international law, the potential applicability of the doctrine would be very limited. Indeed, some of the cases that would probably have fallen under the traditional odious debts doctrine, such as the use of borrowed money for the personal enrichment of dictators, would not necessarily be covered by the *ius cogens* based doctrine.[134]

The analysis of the debt taken up by the Argentinian military regime showed some of the problems that arise when applying the doctrine to past contracts because of the difficulties in establishing at what point in time a norm was accepted as part of *ius cogens*. More complicated still would be to unravel all transactions that were made over many years with regard to an originally odious loan transaction. Taking further into account the complexity of the legal arguments on which this doctrine is based, and the fact that it is admittedly unlikely that it would be applied to, or in fact invoked in the context of debt that was incurred in the past and forms the basis of the debt problem of the developing countries, one could be inclined to reach the conclusion that this doctrine is not worth developing any further, as other legal mechanisms would still have to be found in order to address the problem of the debt of developing countries more broadly.

However, while the main potential of such a doctrine would clearly be its prospective application, if it were to be recognized, one of the purposes behind the original odious debts doctrine, that is to change lending practices, could be achieved. While the underlying assumption that the mere fact of doing business with a regime that violates *ius cogens* norms could lead to the invalidity of a loan transaction will in all likelihood mean that the doctrine will not be greeted with enthusiasm by large parts of the international community, it is exactly this focus that makes it attractive, as the doctrine challenges the assumption that it is only a moral, but not a legal obligation not to contribute to such violations.[135] Furthermore, to the extent that the content of *ius cogens* might gradually expand, such a doctrine might see its scope of application increase.

Nevertheless, leaving aside the political and ideological contentiousness of the ideas developed in this chapter, it needs to be borne in mind that an odious debts doctrine based on *ius cogens* violations leaves open many questions that would have to be addressed before it could have a chance of becoming operable. However, in the absence of consensus regarding the question of how *ius cogens* might be

---

134 See also Christoph Paulus (2005b), at 59.
135 But see *United States v Weizsaecker* (Ministries Case), XIV Trials of War Criminals 621–622, as quoted in Ramasastry (1998), at 416.

extended to legal issues beyond those that are governed by the Vienna Convention on the law of Treaties, it is legitimate that '[a]nswers are mostly given in a piecemeal approach'.[136]

---

136   Tomuschat (2006), at 426.

Chapter Five

(Un)Constitutionality of Debts Taken Up by Unconstitutional Regimes

1 Introduction

Given the very limited possibilities to challenge the validity of the foreign debt of developing countries that was taken up by dictatorial regimes and passed onto their democratic successors under international law, it is important to examine to what extent the domestic law of the debtor countries can fill the gap and provide legal mechanisms according to which the binding nature of this debt can be questioned. This chapter will concentrate on constitutional issues. Using Argentina as an example, it will analyse the validity of Argentina's public foreign debt according to Argentinian constitutional law.

In Argentina, many legal objections against debt repayment are based on constitutional arguments, and one of the points frequently insisted on in this context[1] is that of the unconstitutionality of the foreign debt on the ground that it was not incurred or recognized by the constitutionally competent state organ, which would be the legislative (Article 75(4) and (7) of the Argentinian Constitution). The analysis accordingly has to start with an examination of whether the debt contracted by the military regime was incurred by the constitutionally competent organ. However, even though it will be argued in the course of this chapter that this was not, in fact, the case, the discussion cannot stop there. Rather, given that since the return to democracy at the end of 1983, the various democratic governments that ruled Argentina all consistently repaid, refinanced, rescheduled and restructured the debt inherited by the military regime, it needs to be examined to what extent the operations performed by constitutionally legitimate governments might have healed the original invalidity.

In order to address the constitutional issues of whether the debt was contracted by the competent organ and for constitutional purposes,[2] it needs to be determined when the debt was contracted, for what amount, for which purposes, by whom, and by the means of which acts. None of these facts are easy to establish. First of all, at least the debt taken up by the latest military regime between 1976 and 1983 was largely not even properly documented. Secondly, the sovereign debt was taken up in such a variety of ways, and restructured so many times by different legal instruments over the past decades, that to analyse the constitutionality of each of the loan transactions

---

1   See, most recently, the Bill presented to the Argentinian Congress by some NGOs on 24 March 2006, which suggests to declare the nullity of the public foreign debt.

2   The latter question being the subject of Chapter Six.

would by far exceed the possibilities of this book. The constitutional analysis will accordingly limit itself to an examination of some of the loan transactions that seem important for an assessment of the constitutional issues around Argentina's sovereign debt.

Given that in the context of its sovereign debt, Argentina to a large extent accepted foreign jurisdiction and waived sovereign immunity, it could at first sight be thought that an analysis of Argentinian domestic law in this area is a moot point, as the validity of the debt arrangements will in many cases be determined according to foreign law. However, even if the relationship between Argentina and its creditors is largely governed by foreign law, it does not follow that national law is therefore unimportant for the assessment of the validity of the loan contracts. First of all, even to the extent that the loan contracts are governed by foreign law, the issue of authority, that is whether or not the state was validly represented when the contract was concluded, will usually be governed by the national law of the debtor state.[3] Furthermore, the validity of waiving sovereign immunity and of agreeing that the loan contracts are governed by foreign law is in itself controversial in Argentina,[4] so that it might be possible to convince Argentinian courts to hear cases challenging debt repayment, and to apply Argentinian law in order to decide whether or not the loan contracts are valid. More generally, an evaluation of the validity of the existing sovereign debt according to Argentinian law can assist in identifying core issues around the taking up of sovereign debt, such as which organs are and should be allowed to contract debt; for what purposes; and where the limits should be set, which is important with a look towards future debt contracting.

A legal analysis of these issues faces the difficulty that not much case law examining the constitutionality of Argentina's debt exists. Furthermore, there is only a relatively scarce academic legal discussion of the constitutionality of Argentina's sovereign debt, which is particularly surprising when bearing in mind the fundamental importance of the issue for the country. As might be expected, given the highly political nature of the topic, among those who do provide such an analysis, many different views on how to apply the Constitution in the context of sovereign debt are put forward, and there does not seem to exist much agreement on the underlying legal and constitutional principles.

2 The debt taken up by the military regime

To examine the exact legal basis of the different loan transactions that took place under the military dictatorship and to assess their constitutionality would be a very complicated task. This is partly because of the sheer number of different loan

---

3   See, for example, Delaume (1967), at 130; Stone (2006), at 299–300. This also seems
     to have been assumed by the English Court of Appeal in *Marubeni v Mongolian
     Government* [2005] EWCA Civ 395, [2005] 1 WLR 2497, at 2508–2509 per Carnwath
     LJ with regard to the issue of authority of state representatives.

4   See Conesa (2004), at 1002. In favour of the validity of such clauses see, for example,
     Goldschmidt (1982), at 847; for an overview of the different positions in Argentina see
     Oschmann (1993), at 268–271.

transactions that were entered into under that regime, and partly because the Central Bank of Argentina, the main institution involved in all matters surrounding foreign debt, did not keep a record of the transactions related to the country's foreign debt during that period.[5] However, in the context of examining the constitutionality of the debt taken up by the military government, it might suffice to establish, as a general matter, that under that regime, Argentina's foreign debt was not contracted through parliamentary legislation. Indeed, the first acts of the military regime that took power on 24 March 1976 were to enact the 'Statute for the Process of National Reorganization', to dissolve Congress,[6] and to remove the Supreme Court Justices from their office, entrusting the President with the new appointments to that court.[7] Thus, the constitutionally prescribed system of separation and distribution of powers was replaced by a system that conferred almost unlimited powers onto the executive. In the context of the taking up of sovereign debt this is of the utmost importance, as the Constitution provides in Article 75(4) that Congress is the organ that is competent to contract loans. During the military regime, the involvement of Congress in all matters concerning the taking up of foreign debt as required by Article 75(4) of the Constitution was not complied with, and the debt was instead contracted by the means of executive regulations and decisions of Central Bank executives.[8]

This raises, as a first issue, the question of the constitutional validity of acts of *de facto* regimes that do not respect formal constitutional requirements, or that change them. Not very surprisingly, during the *de facto* period, the Supreme Court in its new composition recognized the *de facto* regime and accepted the necessity to disregard to some extent the constitutional principle of separation of powers and to entrust the President with additional powers.[9] Thus, during the military dictatorship, the highest judicial forum sanctioned, at least in some instances, the exercise of power by a military regime even though it violated the Constitution that was in force when it took power.

Whether or not governmental acts of a military regime have any legal validity beyond the actual term of office of the *de facto* regime is not so clear. In the course of Argentina's history of military coups that resulted in *de facto* regimes, a whole *de facto* doctrine dealing with this issue developed.[10] What is important for current purposes is to establish how, according to this doctrine, it can be determined whether an act carried out, or regulations or statutes[11] enacted by the military regime are valid

---

5   See statement of expert witnesses Valle and Trocca in "Olmos, Alejandro S/denuncia", causa N°14.467, 13 July 2000, Juzg. Nac. Crim. y Corr. Fed., n. 2., www.cadtm.org/ IMG/rtf/sentencia_olmos.rtf; see also Naylor (1994), at 144–148.

6   Zarini (1999), at 901.

7   Ibid., at 897.

8   See García Lema (2004), at 959.

9   "Ercoli, María Cristina s/Recurso de Hábeas Corpus", 16 November 1976, Fallos 296:372; "Lokman, Jaime s/habeas corpus en su favor" 10 November 1977, Fallos 299:142.

10   For an overview and discussion see, for example, Bidart Campos (1992), at 505–539; for an interesting jurisprudential approach see Nino (1983).

11   The *de facto* executive called some of the legal instruments it issued statutes, even though they came about without any involvement of Congress.

and can create rights and correlative binding obligations beyond the *de facto* period. While *de facto* regimes can take acts and issue laws that are necessary in order to fulfil their governmental tasks, the validity of these acts is not absolute. Once a *de facto* regime has come to an end, measures taken in violation of constitutional principles need to be confirmed by a subsequent democratic government in order to be regarded as constitutional and thus valid.[12] In the words of the Supreme Court, 'the validity of provisions and acts emanating from the *de facto* executive power depends on the explicit or implicit recognition by the constitutionally elected government that succeeds it.'[13]

2.1 De facto *doctrine and acquired rights*

While, in principle, the legal status of the loan transactions undertaken by the military regime in disregard of constitutional requirements might therefore depend on whether or not the relevant acts and legal instruments were later legitimized by the democratic successor government, it is controversial whether the power of the democratic successor government to reject laws and acts of a *de facto* regime goes as far as taking away rights that third parties, in this instance the country's creditors, acquired on their basis. No case law exists that discusses the point of acquired rights in the context of sovereign debt. However, some Supreme Court decisions deal with the issue of acquired rights in other contexts, mainly that of academic appointments. The issue that occupied the Supreme Court in various cases was whether the democratic government could, by repealing the *de facto* law on the basis of which individuals had been appointed to permanent academic posts, invalidate these appointments and extend the applicability of the newly introduced procedure for access to academic posts to them and the posts they held. Thus, the question was whether the appointment made by a *de facto* executive based on *de facto* legislation created a right that could not be taken away by the new democratic government.

The Supreme Court adopted two contradictory approaches in this regard. In *Herraiz*,[14] the most recent decision on this point, the majority of the Argentinian Supreme Court held that to the extent that acquired rights might thereby be affected, statutes enacted by democratic governments that repeal *de facto* legislation cannot have a retroactive effect, 'as these rights are, by their nature, inalterable and cannot be abolished by a subsequent law without harming the property right recognized in Article 17 of the Constitution.[15] In this respect, it is not possible to make a distinction

---

12　　Bidart Campos (1992), at 510–512, 519 and 522.

13　　"Dufourq, Felix E.", 27 March 1984, Fallos 306:174, at para. 2; see also "Provincia de Formosa c. Estado nacional", LL-1991-B-506, at 512; "Aramayo, Domingo R.", 14 February 1984, Fallos 306:72, at para. 3.

14　　"Herraiz, Héctor Eduardo c/ Universidad de Buenos Aires s/ nulidad de resolución", 27 December 1996, Fallos 319:3378.

15　　Article 17: Property may not be violated, and no inhabitant of the Nation can be deprived of it except by virtue of a sentence based on law. Expropriation for reasons of public interest must be authorized by law and previously compensated ...

between *de facto* and *de iure* laws,'[16] because the provisions dictated by *de facto* governments have full validity until they are repealed. Disregarding previous Supreme Court decisions where the exact same issue had been decided differently,[17] it was alleged that these principles represented case law that had been consistent over 37 years.[18] In one of the decisions quoted to demonstrate that point,[19] the Court had, for example, held that:

> the acts of *de facto* governments are valid or 'can be legitimized' by their 'real effectiveness', which means that they have imperative force and govern as long as they are not lawfully repealed or revoked; and while they are in force, they generate subjective property rights ... 'Every other solution would lead to uncertainty and confusion' (Fallos: 169:309, at 318), that is, to a crisis of legal certainty, which is one of the worst threats that can hang over an organized society.[20]

Thus, the argument seems to be that even though the democratic government can repeal *de facto* laws, so that their validity is subject to the democratic government's attitude towards them, as long as they are not revoked, they have exactly the same status and effect as other laws, and can therefore create constitutionally protected subjective rights which cannot even be disregarded in order to achieve a return to 'institutional normality'.[21] This means that the principle of legal certainty on which the individual can rely is regarded as more important than all other considerations, including the fact that the very same principle of legal certainty is adversely affected by the disruption of the constitutional order through a *de facto* regime and the existence of rights and obligations that were created in disregard of constitutional principles.

---

16   "Herraiz, Héctor Eduardo c/ Universidad de Buenos Aires s/ nulidad de resolución", 27 December 1996, Fallos 319:3378, at para. 7.

17   "Budano, Raúl Alberto c/Fac. Arquitectura s/amparo", 9 June 1987; Fallos 310:1045; "Gamberale de Mansur, María Eugenia c/Universidad Nacional de Rosario s/nulidad de resolución", 6 April 1989, Fallos 312:435.

18   "Herraiz, Héctor Eduardo c/ Universidad de Buenos Aires s/ nulidad de resolución", 27 December 1996, Fallos 319:3378, at para. 8. However, as Petracchi points out in his dissent in "Hector José Carlos Gaggiamo v Provincia de Santa Fe", 19 November 1991, Fallos 314:1477, at para. 3, the significance of the fact that this was the Supreme Court's approach during a long period is questionable because many of these precedents were decided by Supreme Court Justices who had been appointed by *de facto* regimes.

19   "Console de Ulla, Ángela Marta v Universidad de Buenos Aires /Carrera de psicología", 18 December 1990, Fallos 313:1483.

20   Ibid., at para. 5. See also "Godoy, Oscar Eduardo v Universidad Nacional de La Plata s/ nulidad de acto administrativo /ordinario", 27 December 1990, Fallos 313:1621, at para. 4; and "Hector José Carlos Gaggiamo v Provincia de Santa Fe", 19 November 1991, Fallos 314:1477.

21   "Console de Ulla, Ángela Marta v Universidad de Buenos Aires /Carrera de psicología", 18 December 1990, Fallos 313:1483, at para. 5. This also seems to be the opinion of Bidart Campos (1985), who argued that rights that were acquired on the basis of *de facto* laws cannot be revoked by Congress, but can be reviewed by the courts in case they are affected by unconstitutionality, at 341. See also Comadira (2003), at 113, note 363.

It is submitted that it is not convincing that although laws might be revoked by the democratic government because they were not enacted by the constitutionally required procedure, rights acquired on their basis receive full constitutional protection, just as if they had been acquired under a law that was enacted by the constitutionally competent organ.[22] Instead, as the Supreme Court explained in *Budano*,[23] while in normal times, the inviolability of acquired rights is of fundamental importance in order to give adequate protection to individual rights, and to guarantee legal certainty, different considerations apply in the case of a disruption of the constitutional order by a *de facto* regime. This is because if rights thus acquired could not be revoked by the democratic regime, the latter could not redress the distortions of the Constitution that occurred under the military dictatorship. Therefore, just like the laws on which they are based, acquired rights cannot be absolute, but are instead subject to the democratic government's powers to restrict their exercise in defence of other rights granted by the Constitution and to uphold 'the supremacy of the full validity of the Constitution itself in relation to its hemiplegic and distorted application during the military regime.' Furthermore:

> not to award the constitutional government the legal power to annul the validity of acts of the *de facto* regime that continue to have an effect would imply ... to limit harmfully its possibilities to achieve the consolidation of the democratic system and, moreover, it would mean to attach to the acts of the *de facto* power all effects that can only be reasonably attributed ... to legitimate acts of *de iure* powers. ... The illegitimate act – and no one can doubt that this is what acts dictated by a *de facto* legislator are – ... cannot, nor should it, impose its validity beyond the time and manner which the restored constitutional government free from outside interference permits. ... [The constitutional government] finds itself influenced, on the one hand, by the obligation to uphold legal certainty, and on the other, by the imperative need to restore the institutions that were infringed ... and to provide the consolidation of the republican principles.[24]

Thus, rights acquired on the basis of *de facto* laws are 'precarious rights',[25] in that, unlike rights obtained under a constitutionally legitimate regime, they can be reviewed and curtailed by Congress, at least where their non-reviewability would mean that the consequences of *de facto* acts continue to have an effect in the newly restored democracy. As Fayt convincingly explained in his dissenting opinion in *Gaggiamo*, if *de facto* laws were to create absolute subjective rights, 'the powers that were set up in conformity with the imperatives of the National Constitution would be turned into servants of those who unlawfully held these positions, and their mandates would be prolonged indefinitely and intangibly.'[26] If the attempt to re-establish the rule of law were conditioned that way, it would turn into an illusionary act.

---

22   See also Ekmekdjian (1995), at 402–404.
23   "Budano, Raúl Alberto c/Fac. Arquitectura s/amparo", 9 June 1987; Fallos 310:1045.
24   "Gamberale de Mansur, María Eugenia c/Universidad Nacional de Rosario s/nulidad de resolución", 6 April 1989, Fallos 312:435.
25   Ibid. See also Ekmekdjian (1995), at 403.
26   "Hector José Carlos Gaggiamo v Provincia de Santa Fe", 19 November 1991, Fallos 314:1477, at para. 7.

When applying these principles to loan agreements entered into by the military regime, one might be tempted to argue that there are substantial differences between the cases of academic posts and loan transactions. The employment contract of an academic creates an ongoing relationship, in that the academic is obliged to fulfil their work obligations at a continuous basis, and the state is under the equally continuous obligation to pay the monthly salary. It follows that the appointment to a permanent academic post based on a *de facto* law clearly continues to have legal effects in democratic times in that, unless these appointments can be cancelled, the new government would have to accept this ongoing relationship, assume the obligations thereby created, and, more importantly, would be stuck with the appointments made by the *de facto* regime. This would perpetuate a situation created by the *de facto* regime and restrict the democratic government's freedom to make academic appointments according to its own criteria.

The loan agreements entered into by the *de facto* government, on the other hand, are legal transactions under which one of the parties, the creditor, was under the one-off obligation to provide a loan, which it will have performed while the military regime was still in power, whereas the Argentinian state had to perform its own obligations at a later point in time, namely when the debt matured. Given that the creditors already fulfilled their part of the deal, it needs to be asked whether it is appropriate to apply the principles developed in the academic appointment cases to loan transactions. In the former case, the decision of the democratic government not to recognize the *de facto* laws on which they were based presumably only had an effect for the future, but did not in any way affect the relationship between the state and the academic with regard to the performances already fulfilled on both sides. Thus, what the democratic government is taking away is the expectation that the position created by the *de facto* regime will continue to be protected under future democratic governments, but it does not retrospectively revoke the rights of the academic to counter-performance for their work during the military government itself. In the loan cases, on the other hand, if the democratic government could unilaterally repudiate the contractual relationships with the creditors, the democratic state would be freed of its obligation to repay the loans and to pay the interests agreed, and the creditor who already performed their obligations, would accordingly lose the right to counter-performance.

It is submitted that the considerations on which the decisions in *Budano* and *Gamberale* were based, should nevertheless be applied in this context. This is because the underlying assumption, that is that rights acquired under a military regime are not absolute, but instead subject to review by the democratic government given that they lack full constitutional legitimacy, can be generalized. Indeed, outside of the specific context of academic appointments, it has been argued more generally that:

> provisions dictated by a *de facto* regime do not benefit from the presumption that their content is just, which applies to norms that emanate from democratic procedures that operate within the margin of certain basic rights ... Given the precariousness of the

validity of norms of an autocratic origin, they do not generate acquired rights before their legitimacy was corroborated by the competent constitutional organs.[27]

It is submitted that particularly in the context of sovereign debt, this provides a sensible solution. While the creditors have the expectation that the state will honour its 'obligations', it needs to be borne in mind that they were aware that they were dealing with a *de facto* regime that lacked constitutional legitimacy. The people of the country, on the other hand, who would be obliged to honour these contracts if they were to be regarded as valid, were not represented in these transactions in the way prescribed by the democratic Constitution. If the rights the creditors acquired in their dealings with the *de facto* regime were absolute and therefore binding on the democratic government, this would mean that the rights of the creditors would automatically outweigh all considerations that a government would normally, by the terms of its Constitution, be expected to take into account when contracting debt, namely the interests of the country and its citizens as defined by the Constitution. Given that the creditors' rights came about without a democratic government having made such an assessment, the democratic government must have the chance to redress this situation by reviewing it. Indeed, as Corti observed:

> Its beneficiaries usually employ, with apparent invocation of the Constitution – which was previously deprived of its national, democratic and progressive characteristics – the principle of acquired rights in order to save their privileges, circumstances and "rights" (deliberately in inverted commas) supposedly obtained under the protection of legislation that is manifestly irregular, both because of its formally unrepresentative origin, and because of its content, which more often than not, stands in conflict with the economic and social interests of the community.[28] ... Indeed, a democratically organized national community can hardly see itself forced to accept the validity or inalterability of the so-called *de facto* laws or alleged acquired rights based on them, to the extent that one or the other affect essential questions of sovereignty, significant collective goods, or fundamental human rights.[29]

These considerations are important in the context of the sovereign debt contracted by the military regime. If the contracts had to be accepted as valid and as conferring absolute rights on the creditors, the newly democratic state would have been obliged to fulfil its part of the agreement. It is then obvious that these contracts have continuing effects for the Argentinian state after the return to democracy, and it is submitted very substantial ones, given that the economic, political and social fate of Argentina is very closely linked to the debt problem inherited by the military regime.

It then remains to be decided according to which criteria Congress can review and decide to discard acquired rights. As the rights acquired under *de facto* regimes do not receive full constitutional protection, the applicable standard cannot be the strict

---

27   Nino (1983), at 945–946.
28   Aristides Corti (1984), at 971.
29   Ibid., at 973. This, he suggests, is in line with the principles reflected in the Civil Code, where acquired rights are protected, but those which emanate from illegitimate acts have an inherent initial weakness (Article 2664).

standard according to which acquired rights can usually only very exceptionally be restricted.[30] On the other hand, the principle of legal certainty which concerned the Supreme Court so much in *Herraiz, Godoy* and *Console de Ulla*, does have a role to play in this context, but not because legal certainty is a value in itself, but instead because:

> There are, nevertheless, certain aspects of those considerations that refer to social peace and to certainty that remain applicable to *de facto* provisions even after the democratic form of government was restored ... A multitude of private, public and international relationships, the general and indiscriminate disregard of which is not convenient, are intertwined with these provisions. The validity of these provisions creates expectations in people, and these expectations give rise to individual plans and situations that are not easily reversed without producing a situation of uncertainty.[31]

It can accordingly be argued that even though these expectations do not create rights, they indicate the existence of interests that cannot simply be ignored. While

> it is true that he who developed expectations based on a title conveyed by someone who did not have the legitimacy to do so, did this at his own risk, there is no reason to cause him harm by frustrating these expectations where they are not incompatible with the rights of others.[32]

Thus, the expectations created by *de facto* laws 'should be respected if they are not in conflict with genuine rights of others or with significant interests of society.'[33] What would then be needed in order to justify a democratic government's decision to repeal the *de facto* laws and acts on the basis of which Argentina's creditors claim repayment of the loans they made, including interest, is a balancing of the interests involved on both sides. As part of this assessment, it needs to be borne in mind that even if the democratic government can decide not to recognize these transactions as valid, this does not mean that the creditors automatically lose all their rights and with them the money they already made available to the state. All it means is that the agreement reached between the *de facto* regime and the creditors will then not be transformed into a binding contract between the Argentinian state and the creditors, so that the creditors cannot have any rights against the state, including the right to debt repayment, based on those void transactions. As in all cases in which a performance was made in the absence of a valid legal relationship, the question of restitution would then be dealt with by the principles of unjust enrichment.[34]

Consequently, what Congress could have done after the return to democracy was to debate whether the various loan contracts that had ongoing effects were compatible with the interests of the Argentinian society. This issue is separate from the question of whether the loan transactions made by the military government might

---

30   See Article 18 of the National Administrative Procedure Act. See also Comadira (2003), at 55–81.
31   Nino (1983), at 942.
32   Ibid., at 942.
33   Ibid., at 945–946.
34   For a discussion see Chapter Seven, 1.4, infra.

be void because they violated other constitutional or legal principles, for example because they were tainted with fraud.[35] Even if these obligations were not affected by any other legal or constitutional defects, Congress could thus have decided not to recognize them, for example based on the assessment that the extreme debt burden inherited by the military government severely limited its political freedom and put the country into a relationship of dependence on agreements with foreign creditors and IFIs, thereby restricting the country's sovereignty. The consequence that the relationship of the Argentinian state and its creditors would then have been governed by the principles of unjust enrichment instead of by the loan agreements would have been beneficial for Argentina, as the main reason that made the debt unsustainable were the contractually agreed floating interest rates that increased dramatically at the beginning of the 1980s.[36]

If the doctrine of acquired rights then does not stand in the way of Congress' freedom to reject or recognize the acts and laws of a *de facto* regime in the context of Argentina's sovereign debt, it now needs to be examined whether Congress did, in fact, recognize this debt as valid.

2.2 Recognition of the debt by the democratic successor government

The sovereign debt taken up by the military regime was never explicitly recognized by the Argentinian Congress. That the debt was implicitly recognized is sometimes questioned on the grounds that the incoming democratic government explicitly rejected the relevant factual, administrative and legislative acts of the military regime. In support of this view, Act 23.062,[37] which was enacted in 1984, is mentioned as a law by which Congress rejected all administrative acts and provisions of the *de facto* regimes, including those referring to Argentina's sovereign debt.[38] However, the text of the statute, its context and its application by the courts[39] suggest that the statute does not have such a general scope of application, but instead only applies to acts and norms which had the purpose 'to judge, or impose sanctions upon, the members of the constitutional powers' (Article 1), and to other cases of political persecution during the *de facto* period.[40] Thus, the Act does not seem to address the issue of the sovereign debt contracted by the military regime.

Another statute that could be relevant in connection with the country's sovereign debt is Act 23.854 by which Congress rejected the investment accounts referring to the period of the military regime, that is 1976 to 1983. In this context, it needs to be explained that according to the Argentinian Constitution, Congress has the power to approve the budget and at the end of each financial year, to approve or

---

35 A conclusion that is often drawn from the findings of Justice Ballesteros in "Olmos, Alejandro S/denuncia", causa N°14.467, 13 July 2000, Juzg. Nac. Crim. y Corr. Fed., n. 2., JA 2001-I-514.

36 See Chapter Two, 1, supra; also Buckley (1999), at 22.

37 Boletín Oficial 19/07/84.

38 See, for example, Olmos (2004), at 58–59.

39 See, for example, "Brieba, Rodolfo J.", Supreme Court, 20 December 1984, Fallos 306:1844.

40 See, for example, Bianchi (1984); Bidart Campos (1992), at 513–514.

reject the investment accounts (Article 75(8)).[41] This way, Congress can exercise both prospective and retrospective control over the way in which the executive uses the budget. In *Brunicardi*,[42] the Attorney General suggested that the rejection of the investment accounts in Act 23.854 invalidated the regulations and statutes by the means of which the military regime had introduced the bonds that were at issue in that case (Regulation 1334/82 and Act 22.749). However, the Supreme Court was of the opinion that the rejection of the investment accounts did not, in itself, affect the validity of any legal acts or relationships that date back to the military regime.[43]

While it is then questionable that the acts of the military regime with respect to the sovereign debt were explicitly rejected by Congress, it remains to be examined whether there was at least an implicit recognition of these acts, as required by the *de facto* doctrine in order for the relevant acts to be valid. It might be possible to regard the servicing of the debt by the Alfonsín government, or the restructuring of the debt, for example through the issuing of new bonds, as a recognition of the validity of the underlying obligation. With regard to the latter, the Supreme Court's decision in *Brunicardi* has some significance. In that case, a bondholder challenged the constitutionality of Regulation 772/86 and of ministerial resolutions and communications of the Central Bank based on that regulation. The bonds he was holding had been issued under the military regime through Regulation 1334/82, which was one of the legal instruments by the means of which the state assumed the debt of private Argentinian companies, and at the same time modified the conditions of the original loan. In 1986, the terms of the bonds were again altered, this time by the democratic government through Regulation 772/86. According to the Court, 'the modification by the federal executive through Regulation 772 of 23 May 1986 of the terms of the obligations assumed towards the foreign creditors in 1982 ... had the effect of an implicit ratification as it involved a recognition of the validity of those obligations.'[44]

Given that Regulation 772/86 had been issued by the executive, it seems to follow that the Supreme Court was of the opinion that the executive branch of the democratic government can validly ratify the debts taken up by the *de facto* regime. This was justified with reference to the fact that Congress gave this ratification its blessing by approving the relevant budget acts.[45] The approach of the Supreme Court in *Brunicardi* therefore seems to be based on the assumption that the executive, with marginal congressional involvement, can validly ratify acts of *de facto* regimes in

---

41 For an explanation of the political significance of this power and some of the legal issues arising in this context see, for example, Padilla (1985); and Roberto Thompson (1985).

42 "Brunicardi, Adriano Caredio c/ Estado Nacional (BCRA) s/ cobro S.C. B.592.XXIV.", 24 February 1997, Fallos 319:2886.

43 However, many interpret the rejection of these investment accounts to mean that Congress thereby refused to recognize the sovereign debt. The Odious Debts Bill 2004, for example, refers in its explanatory notes to Act 23.854 as evidence that the debt was not recognized by Congress upon return to democracy.

44 "Brunicardi, Adriano Caredio c/ Estado Nacional (BCRA) s/ cobro S.C. B.592.XXIV", 24 February 1997, Fallos 319:2886, at para. 9.

45 Ibid.

areas in which, as will be seen in a moment, Congress has the exclusive constitutional competence.

However, it is submitted that a more profound analysis of these two issues – the constitutionality of a delegation of powers onto the executive, and the exact scope of congressional involvement that is required by the Constitution in this matter, is necessary. This is because even if one could regard the payment of the debt and/or its restructuring, as a factual recognition of the acts of the military regime from which this debt originated, a recognition by a democratic government that has the function of healing the prior unconstitutionality of an act by a *de facto* regime can only have this effect if it is itself in accordance with constitutional requirements. Otherwise, the democratic government could, by the means of an implicit recognition of the acts of a *de facto* regime, award them constitutional legitimacy without taking into account the limits the Constitution imposes on its own acts. Even if one were to argue that a tacit recognition of the laws and acts of *de facto* regimes by Congress in the sense that these laws are valid until they are repealed or amended is sufficient,[46] it is submitted that Congress' passivity in the relevant area can only have such a validating effect if the Constitution does not specifically require an active step in the matter, as might be the case in the context of Congress' role to settle the payment of the country's public debt.

Thus, while the payment of the debt and its restructuring clearly indicate a factual recognition of the underlying obligations, it nevertheless needs to be analysed whether this results in the legal validity of these obligations. Before coming back to this issue, it will first be examined which role the Constitution assigned to Congress in this context.

3 Constitutional competence with regard to sovereign debt

The Argentinian Constitution regulates the distribution of powers between the different state organs. With regard to Argentina's sovereign debt, the issue of constitutional competence comes up in two different contexts. First of all, the question arises which constitutional organ is competent to contract foreign debt. Secondly, it needs to be examined which organ has the competence to renegotiate, restructure and generally regulate the payment of the existing debt. Article 75 establishes in which areas Congress has the exclusive competence.[47] Article 75 contains two different sections dealing with questions of public debt. First of all, in s 4, Article 75 empowers Congress to borrow money on the credit of the Nation, thus clarifying that it is the legislative, not the executive, that has the power to indebt the country by taking out loans. S. 7 of Article 75 empowers Congress to settle the payment of the

---

46   See dissent in "Soria, Silverio Florencio v Dirección Nacional de Vialidad", 2 April 1985, Fallos 309:338, per Fayt and Belluscio, at para. 5. For an interesting comment on the dissenting opinion in *Soria*, and the validity of *de facto* laws more generally, see Negretto (1991).

47   In Argentina, Congress is synonymous with the legislative and consists of two Houses, Senate and the Chamber of Deputies.

domestic and foreign debt of the Nation. Thus, only Congress can validly indebt the country, and only Congress has the power to settle the payment of such debt.

3.1 What does it mean to settle the payment of the debt?[48]

In this context, it needs to be determined what involvement of Congress the Constitution requires in the context of the country's sovereign debt. While it is more or less clear what is meant by contracting debt, there is a lot of controversy with regard to what is meant by 'settling' the payment of the debt. As this raises complex issues, Article 75(7) will first be analysed in general before coming back to the role of this provision in the specific context of recognizing the debt of the military regime.

In order to understand the meaning of the powers conferred upon Congress in the context of sovereign debt, it might be instructive to have a quick look at the relevant constitutional history. Both of the relevant sections of Article 75 were already included in the Constitution of 1853, which, with amendments, is still in force today. As a constitutionalist explained in 1897, the two different sections of what was then Article 67 of the Constitution[49] express two ideas: that Congress was awarded the competence to recognize the pre-existing debts of Buenos Aires and the various provinces, and that the competence with regard to all future debts was vested in Congress.[50] The historical purpose behind Congress' competence to settle the debt was described as follows:

> In those times of struggles, the internal debt and the external debt seemed to be so obscure, so abstruse that it was not possible to know its exact amount and importance. It seemed necessary to consolidate the obligations of the State, and in order to make a meticulous examination of the value of the loans, especially given that the power to take up loans had been conferred upon Congress, and the consolidation in some ways forms part of these tasks, it was prudent to determine that it would be the prerogative of Congress to settle the payment of the debts contracted within and outside of the Nation.[51]

This seems to confirm the view that settling the payment of the debt involves its examination and the determination of its amount, in order to provide Congress with the knowledge that is an essential prerequisite of developing policies both with regard to the payment of such debt, and with regard to deciding how much new debt the country can reasonably afford. The historical context furthermore suggests that the power to settle the payment of the debt was given to Congress in order to ensure that in the case of debt that was incurred, prior to the coming into force of the Constitution, by an organ other than Congress, Congress would retrospectively be involved in settling the payment of such debt. Indeed, with regard to pre-constitutional debt, the importance of Congress' involvement in the issue of public debt can be explained

---

48   The following part draws, to some extent, on Michalowski (2006), 309–316.
49   Article 67(3) and (6), respectively. These are the relevant articles in the context of assessing the constitutionality of any debt that was taken up before the changes introduced by the constitutional reform of 1994 came into force.
50   González (1959), at 437.
51   Montes de Oca (1927), at 230.

by the consideration that the people can only be expected to pay debt taken up in the name of the country if Congress, as the representative of the people, at least retrospectively accepts it as binding.[52] With regard to the controversial question of what is meant by 'settling' the payment of the debt, the history of the provision thus indicates that what is required is a recognition of the pre-existing debt by Congress after an examination of its origins and amount. This interpretation finds support in the fact that in the 19th Century, Congress passed various statutes recognizing pre-constitutional debts.[53]

It remains to be discussed what, if anything, can be inferred from the history of the provision for its significance and interpretation in present times. First of all, given that s. 7 survived the constitutional reform of 1994, even though it is not very likely that there are any more payments of public debts in need of settlement that refer to the pre-constitutional period,[54] it seems as if the provision cannot be regarded as exclusively applicable to the pre-constitutional debt and therefore redundant in present times.[55] Instead, the general consideration on which the provision was historically based, that is that debts that were contracted outside of the constitutionally foreseen procedure need to be assessed by Congress before they can be regarded as binding the country, points towards the applicability of Article 75(7) to the situation that a public debt was not incurred by Congress, but instead by a *de facto* regime that governed the country and indebted it without constitutional authority. If Article 75(7) then requires a congressional recognition of this debt,[56] it follows that Congress would have had the task to settle the payment of the debt taken up by the military dictatorship, including an analysis of its origins and a determination of its scope.

In present times, an argument for a more far-reaching role of Article 75(7) beyond such exceptional situations could be made. Given Argentina's reality, that is that because of the extremely high external indebtedness, the country is not in a position to satisfy all of the claims of its creditors whenever payment of interests or principal becomes due, it could be argued that Congress can only meaningfully carry out its tasks with regard to the country's sovereign debt if, when making decisions on the payment of the debt, a careful analysis takes place of how to prioritize the different obligations of the state. Not only does this require decisions on how to rank the obligations towards the different creditors, but also on how to balance the claims of the creditors against the state's obligations to protect the rights and interests of its people.

However, many dispute that Article 75(7) of the Argentinian Constitution has this content and requires an involvement of Congress in the settling of the payment of the debt that goes beyond providing the budget with which the debt can be repaid. They suggest instead that Congress can validly settle the payment of the public debt by approving the budget acts which annually determine the budget of the Argentinian

---

52   Lozada (2002), at 249–252; Sola (2005), at 32.
53   González (1959), at 437.
54   Mastrorilli (1984), at 833; Lozada (2002), at 251.
55   García Lema (2004), at 957. But see Dalla Via (2004), at 311.
56   Juliá (2002), at 165; Lozada (2002), at 252; Mastrorilli (1984), at 833.

State, and which routinely include a provision assigning a certain amount of money to the payment of the country's foreign debt.[57] Alternatively, the payment of the debt can be settled by approving measures according to which the original debt is restructured.[58] The main reasons behind this interpretation of Article 75(7) are that it reflects constitutional practice and provides the most practicable solution. With regard to the former point, it is true that for decades the Argentinian constitutional practice with regard to the payment of the sovereign debt has been that the executive sets the underlying policies and carries out the necessary negotiations with the country's creditors, and that Congress approves the budget act which provides the resources for the debt repayment thus negotiated. However, the consistency of a practice does not make it constitutional.

It seems as if the main problem with a more profound involvement of Congress in this matter is seen in the fact that in the light of the impossibility to repay all of the country's sovereign debt when it becomes due, debt servicing usually involves renegotiations and restructuring. As a consequence, the word 'settle' is in this context interpreted as requiring an interaction between Congress and the creditors,[59] a task which, given its complexity, it is alleged a collegiate organ such as Congress cannot fulfil.[60] The suggestion is instead that Congress should and does fulfil its task of settling the payment of the debt by approving that which the executive negotiates, just as in the context of international treaties, which are negotiated by the executive but then need to be ratified by Congress. In this respect, it was suggested that Article 99(11), which gives the President the competence to conclude and sign 'treaties, concordats and other agreements[61] required for the maintenance of good relations with international organizations and foreign powers', extends to the negotiation of the foreign debt,[62] an interpretation of the Constitution which was said to be supported by Article 27 of the Vienna Convention on the Law of Treaties,[63] according to which a state cannot invoke the provisions of its own laws as a justification for its failure to perform a treaty. Thus, according to this interpretation, in the context of sovereign debt, the Constitution provides for the following division of powers: the executive negotiates the debt, and the legislative approves the budget.[64] In approving the budget act, Congress incidentally approves the settling of the debt that was carried out by the executive in negotiation with the country's creditors through the provision of resources for the debt repayment thus negotiated, and/or through the recourse to new loans as part of the budget.[65] Thus, many seem to think that in order to fulfil the task

---

57   García Lema (2004), at 961. With regard to the comparable situation of contracting debt pursuant to Article 75(4), see Villegas, Bruno and Piaggio (2004), at 1025; Quiroga Lavié (2000), at 387.

58   García Lema (2004), at 961.

59   See also Bidart Campos (2001), at 1280.

60   See also Dalla Via (2004), at 312–313; Gelli (2005), at 28; and Gelli (2003), at 551; Vanossi (1985).

61   The original text says 'negociaciones'.

62   Gelli (2005), at 28; Ekmekdjian (1993), at 462; Vanossi (1985).

63   Dalla Via (2004), at 312.

64   Ibid., at 313.

65   Ekmekdjian (1993), at 462.

of settling the debt, Congress does not even need to authorize the debt negotiations carried out by the executive in advance, beyond setting aside the funds for debt repayment in the respective budget acts, nor set the framework within which these negotiations should take place.[66]

The view that Congress settles the payment of the debt by annually approving the budget act seems to find some support in the Supreme Court's decision in *Brunicardi*.[67] There, the Court argued that the parliamentary debate of the budget made it possible to know Congress' opinion with regard to the servicing of the country's debt. It therefore did not trouble the Court that the actual alterations to the bonds issued by the military regime were made in the form of executive regulations and not parliamentary statutes. From the fact that Congress did not adopt the suggestion of a minority in Parliament which wanted to include into the text of the budget acts explicit references to a direct involvement of Congress in the context of settling the public debt, the Court concluded that Congress accepted the practice whereby the executive exercised all faculties concerning the foreign debt and Congress' involvement was reduced to the annual debate of the budget dedicated to the payment of the foreign debt.[68] This approach seems to have been confirmed by the Supreme Court in the recent decision of *Galli*,[69] where the Court implies, without providing an analysis for this position, that Congress simultaneously exercises its powers to settle the debt and to approve the budget when ratifying executive regulations in the area of public debt in the annual budget acts.

However, that Congress accepts a practice does not automatically make it constitutional,[70] so that it is nevertheless necessary to analyse whether the arguments that to 'settle' the payment of the debt means no more than to approve the budget prepared by the executive are constitutionally sound and convincing. One argument on the basis of which this view was rejected is that Article 75 of the Constitution makes a clear distinction between Congress' power to approve the budget, a power conferred by s. 8 of Article 75, and the power to settle the payment of the public debt pursuant to s. 7 of Article 75. S. 7 of Article 75 would be superfluous if it could be exercised simply by approving the budget, that is by the very same act with which Congress fulfils its task of fixing the budget under Article 75(8). Instead, settling the payment of the debt needs to be something qualitatively different from the mere

---

66   Vanossi (1985). Some go as far as saying that the only moment in which Congress can possibly exercise its task of approving the negotiation of the country's debt is in the context of approving the budget, so that Article 75(7) does not have any independent content that goes beyond the task of approving the budget according to Article 75(8) and is accordingly redundant; see Dalla Via (2004), at 311.

67   "Brunicardi, Adriano Caredio c/ Estado Nacional (BCRA) s/ cobro SC B592.XXIV", 24 February 1997, Fallos 319:2886.

68   Ibid., at para. 10.

69   "Galli, Hugo y Otro c/ PEN – s/ Amparo Ley 25.561", 6 April 2005, at para. 17 per Justices Maqueda and Highton de Nolasco; and at para. 8 per Justices Zaffaroni and Lorenzetti.

70   See, for example, the holding in "Verrocchi, Ezio Daniel c/ Poder Ejecutivo Nacional – Administración Nacional de Aduanas s/ acción de amparo", 19 August 1999, Fallos 322:1726, at paras 8–10.

approval of a budgetary item. Neither can Congress' involvement in the contracting or settling of the public debt be reduced to approving the relevant international treaty in which the terms of the debt were agreed between the Argentinian Government and the creditor, as here again, two distinct constitutional faculties of Congress would otherwise merge into one.[71] It could then be concluded that the practice according to which it is the executive that contracts the foreign debt and regulates the terms and conditions of its payment, whereas Congress does no more than approve the relevant treaties and allocate the funds necessary for these purposes within the budget, is a mutation of the Constitution.[72]

Another argument might be added. As pointed out above, those who want to reduce Congress' involvement to the approval of the budget act regard the 'settling' of the payment of the debt by Congress as impossible, because settling the payment requires a negotiation, a task that is naturally in the hands of the executive.[73] However, the analysis of the historic origins of the provision suggested that settling was understood as examining the debt and determining its scope, which involved the auditing of debts that were not taken up by Congress. In the context of the debt inherited by the military regime, to settle the payment of the debt would then not mean to negotiate with the creditors, but rather, prior to the negotiation stage, to audit the debt, something Congress can do perfectly well. In addition to guaranteeing a democratic auditing of a debt that was not taken up by a democratically legitimized body, this is the only possibility to enable Congress to make sure that such debts are only repaid if the underlying transactions were in accordance with constitutional principles.[74]

Even Vanossi, one of the first constitutionalists[75] to advance the theory that Congress' involvement in settling the payment of the debt should be reduced to the approval of the budget act, suggested that:

---

71   Bidart Campos (1992), at 126; see also Mastrorilli (1984), at 833; and Bazán Lazcano (1986), at 970–971.

72   Bidart Campos (1992), at 127. The approach suggested in *Brunicardi* and by some constitutionalists also leaves open questions of delegation of power, as it could only be constitutional if, in addition to reducing the meaning of settling the payment of the debt to the approval of the budget, it would not violate the system of distribution of powers envisaged by the Constitution, an issue to be discussed at 3.2, infra.

73   Dalla Via (2004), at 312–313; Gelli (2005), at 28; and Gelli (2003), at 551; Vanossi (1985).

74   Vanossi (1985) argues that while it might be possible to interpret Article 75(7) so as to give Congress the power to regulate the payment of the sovereign debt, this would go against constitutional practice and could therefore only apply to future circumstances, but not affect and invalidate executive acts in this matter prior to the passing of a law that reflects this change of approach. This is an amazing interpretation, as it suggests that constitutional practice stands above the Constitution itself; see also Bazán Lazcano (1986), at 976.

75   Interestingly, his legal analysis was not published in a legal journal, but in a daily newspaper, a fact which demonstrates the general importance of the issue for the public.

But always and in all cases it is Congress that brings together the means by which to make the relevant payments. This means to say or to recognize that Congress could in extreme cases refuse such payments if the debt had not been [validly] contracted or if there had been a fraud.[76]

However, it is submitted that if Congress' involvement is reduced to the approval of the budget act, then it is next to impossible for Congress to determine that the budget that is set aside for the payment of the debt, or part of it, is used for the fulfilment of obligations that are based on fraudulent transactions. Instead, it seems that suggesting that Congress has the power to reject the payment of debts in case of irregularities to some extent requires that Congress first examines the legitimacy of the debt before such an assessment can be made, thereby giving support to the view that to settle the debt means more than to make available the budget for its payment. On the other hand, to explain the contemporaneous significance of Article 75(7) by the fact that to settle the debt means no more than to renegotiate and restructure it, would imply that Congress might approve the budget for repaying a debt that was never scrutinized as to its constitutionality, a fact which at least in the context of the debt taken up by the military dictatorship, which has its questionability written all over it,[77] cannot be satisfactory.

The difference between settling the payment of the debt as suggested here, and the mere approval of budgetary positions is that the latter only refers to setting aside a certain amount of money for a specific purpose, but does not include, as should the former, a thorough and detailed analysis of the origins of such loans, their destination, conditions and any other point that is important in order to perform the task of effectively auditing the foreign debt that was contracted by an organ other than Congress, and to determine future policies in this regard.[78] To settle the payment of the debt would then refer to all decisions about transactions in this context, including cuts, guarantees, securities, refinancing of the debt, the period of payment, and interest rates.[79] Given that Article 75(7) of the Constitution is aimed at involving Congress retroactively in scrutinizing those foreign debts that were not contracted by Congress itself in order to decide whether it is justified that the country assume the payment of such debt, Congress cannot fulfil this task by approving something as part of the budget the exact circumstances of which it ignores and never debated.[80]

Indeed, looking, for example, at the provisions of one of the budget Acts particularly mentioned in *Brunicardi* as sufficient for Congress to fulfil its tasks under Article 75(7), they state no more than that the executive is authorized to contract loans up to the amount mentioned in the Act; that to that effect it can emit titles of debt in the form and for the amounts it deems appropriate; and that it can restructure and modify the amounts necessary for the amortization of debts within

---

76   Vanossi (1985).
77   See, for example, the findings in "Olmos, Alejandro S/denuncia", causa N°14.467, 13 July 2000, Juzg. Nac. Crim. y Corr. Fed., n. 2., JA 2001-I-514.
78   Juliá (2002), at 166; see also Lozada (2002), at 260–261; Bazán Lazcano (1986), at 971.
79   Mastrorilli (1984), at 832; see also Juliá (2002), at 165.
80   Lozada (2002), at 261–262.

certain specified financial limits.[81] However, the Budget Act does not contain any detail beyond these very general authorizations in respect of particular debts.

With regard to Congress' tasks of settling the payment of debts that were not contracted by military regimes, it was already suggested above that in a situation in which the debt burden is such that a repayment of all debts when they become due is impossible, to settle the payment of the debt requires decisions that go beyond simply approving budgetary items. In particular, it needs to be decided in this context how to prioritize the various obligations, that is the obligations towards the different creditors, but also whether and to what extent precedence should be given to the obligations towards the country's foreign creditors over those towards the people in times of very serious social problems and high poverty rates.

A settling of the payment of the debt in the sense suggested here has never taken place. In 1984, the Alfonsín Government convened an Investigative Committee of Senate whose task was to investigate the economic illegalities and irregularities that occurred between 1976 and 1983. This could have been a first step towards enabling Congress to perform its task of settling the payment of the country's foreign debt based on the findings of this Committee. However, the Committee's mandate was terminated in 1985 before it could fulfil its mission,[82] and Alfonsín, in fact, suggested that it had only in a very small number of cases been possible to prove the illegitimacy of the debt, so that a distinction between legitimate and illegitimate loans proved to be unfeasible.[83] When Justice Ballestero decided in 2000 to send his findings in *Olmos*, including all expert witnesses' reports, to Congress to make available to both Houses of Parliament the outcome of the most thorough investigation into the development of the country's foreign debt under the last military regime that has been undertaken so far,[84] a parliamentary debate of the issue did not take place. From all this follows that the payment of the debt taken up by the military regime was never settled by Congress in the constitutionally required way. Given the practice of reducing the involvement of Congress to the enactment of the budget acts, it is submitted that the same is true with regard to most of the subsequent acts of debt renegotiation, restructuring, repayment and even contracting.

To summarize the analysis so far, many constitutionalists as well as the Supreme Court are of the opinion that in order to fulfil its tasks of contracting and settling the country's sovereign debt, the Constitution requires from Congress no more than to approve the relevant provisions of the annual budget acts. Others argue, it was submitted more convincingly, that at least in the context of debt that was not contracted by Congress, so that Congress was not involved in an assessment of its constitutionality when the obligation was entered into, such debt needs to be audited by Congress. In addition, in a situation in which it is impossible to service all of the debt when it matures, to settle the payment of the country's debt requires more profound decisions than those to provide the sums to repay the debts when they

---

81 See, for example, Articles 10, 13 and 15 of the Annual Budget Act 1987 (Act 23.526).
82 Juliá (2002), at 174–180.
83 In *¿Por qué doctor Alfonsín?* at 169–171, as quoted in Galasso (2003), at 270.
84 "Olmos, Alejandro S/denuncia", causa N°14.467, 13 July 2000, Juzg. Nac. Crim. y Corr. Fed., n. 2., JA 2001-I-514.

become due. In particular a policy assessment of how the interests of the various creditors and those of the country and its people can best be maximized is necessary, something that is currently carried out by the executive, not by Congress.

3.2 Delegation of powers

While the questions of what it means validly to settle the country's debt, and to what extent powers with regard to public debt can be delegated overlap to some extent, they also raise separate issues. Even if to settle the payment of the debt is understood in the sense suggested here and not in the way in which the predominant opinion in Argentina defines it, it could still be argued that Congress might validly delegate some of its powers in this context onto other constitutional organs. On the other hand, even if settling the debt involved no more than to approve the annual budget, it needs to be decided whether current practice respects the system of distribution of powers as laid down in the Constitution, that is whether Congress can validly delegate such far-reaching powers as those of regulating all the details with regard to these debts, onto the executive.[85]

3.2.1 General principles of delegation of powers

Before analysing the specific situation of sovereign debt, the Argentinian system of distribution and delegation of powers first needs to be outlined in general. As was already explained, the Argentinian Constitution regulates the distribution of different powers to different organs. Article 75 lists the areas in which Congress has the exclusive competence, whereas Article 99 deals with the powers of the President.

Prior to the constitutional reform of 1994, the Argentinian Constitution did not contain any provisions specifically allowing for a delegation of powers. However, the President did (and still does) have certain powers to enact regulations. First of all, they can make autonomous regulations in areas of their exclusive competence. The President also has the power to issue regulations in emergency situations. As Article 99(3) states in its present form:

> The Executive shall in no event issue provisions of a legislative nature, in which case they shall be absolutely and irreparably null and void.

> Only when due to exceptional circumstances the ordinary procedures foreseen by this Constitution for the enactment of laws are impossible to be followed, and when the provisions do not refer to criminal issues, taxation, electoral matters, or the system of the political parties, he may issue regulations on grounds of necessity and urgency, which shall be decided by a general agreement of ministers who shall countersign them together with the Chief of the Ministerial Cabinet.[86]

---

85   As suggested by the Supreme Court in "Brunicardi, Adriano Caredio c/ Estado Nacional (BCRA) s/ cobro SC B592 XXIV", 24 February 1997, Fallos 319:2886, at para. 4.

86   With regard to the procedure to follow in such situations, Article 99(3) goes on to state that: 'Within the term of ten days, the Chief of the Ministerial Cabinet shall personally submit the decision to the consideration of the Joint Standing Committee of Congress,

Furthermore, according to Article 99(2), the President can issue regulations that are 'necessary for the enforcement of the laws of the nation', but without altering the content of the underlying legal provisions. The Supreme Court interpreted this provision so as to permit that the legislative delegate regulatory powers onto the executive. In the leading case of *Delfino A.M. y Cía*,[87] the Supreme Court stated that: 'There is a fundamental distinction between the delegation of powers to make statutes, and that which confers a certain authority on the executive or an administrative body to enable it to regulate the necessary details for their execution. The former cannot be done, the latter is allowed.'[88] Thus, according to case law, it is unconstitutional that Congress authorizes another organ to perform the functions the Constitution has vested in Congress.[89] What is, on the other hand, constitutional is that Congress exercises its constitutional powers in an area of its competence, but does so in a form that leaves room for the executive to become active in the same area, within the framework set by Congress.[90] Many constitutionalists agreed that this case law was, in fact, based on an unconstitutional interpretation of the powers contained in Article 99(2), given that what the Court sanctioned in various decisions were in reality not provisions of a merely regulatory/procedural nature, but instead regulations that governed substantive matters, thereby going beyond that which is necessary for the execution of the underlying parliamentary statute.[91]

In 1994, a new provision, Article 76, was introduced which now expressly deals with the delegation of powers from Congress to the executive and states as follows:

> (1) The legislative powers shall not be delegated to the executive save for specified matters of administration and public emergency, with a specified term for their exercise and within the framework of the delegation set by Congress.

Article 76 needs to be seen in conjunction with Article 100(12) which vests in the Chief of the Ministerial Cabinet the power 'to countersign regulations enacted on the basis of powers delegated by Congress, which shall be under the control of the Joint Standing Committee.' In this context, it needs to be stated that this Joint Standing Committee has only been created in July 2006, that is 12 years after the constitutional reform.[92] Before, these regulations were controlled by a Joint Committee which

---

which shall be composed according to the proportion of the political representation of the parties in each House. Within the term of ten days, this committee shall submit its report to the plenary meeting of each House for its specific consideration and it shall be immediately discussed by both Houses. A special law enacted with the absolute majority of all the members of each House shall regulate the procedure and scope of Congress' participation.' This special law required by Article 99(3) was only enacted in July 2006 (Act 26.122), that is 12 years after the constitutional reform which introduced Article 99(3) in its current form. During this period, many issues of utmost importance for the country were dealt with by regulations of necessity and urgency.

87   "Delfino A.M. y Cía", 20 June 1927, Fallos 148:430.
88   Ibid., at 435.
89   Bidart Campos (1992), at 28.
90   Ibid., at 31.
91   See, for example, Quiroga Lavié (2000), at 234–235.
92   See Act 26.122.

was not established in the form prescribed in the Constitution.[93] What consequences this has for the validity of the regulations issued according to Article 76 is not at all clear. It has been suggested that if the control required by Article 100(12) is not exercised, the regulations are unconstitutional and void.[94] However, since the constitutional reform in 1994, many matters have been regulated by emergency regulations according to Article 76 and Article 99(3), and the courts never questioned their validity on the basis that the constitutionally prescribed control had not been exercised. This seems to show how little impact the procedural provisions of the Constitution have in practice.

The content and significance of the new Article 76 are controversial. Indeed, the opinions of constitutionalists as to whether the provision restricts or confirms the former practice and Supreme Court case law, vary.[95] The most important issues when trying to determine to what extent delegations can be valid in the context of Argentina's sovereign debt is to define which matters fall under the terms 'specified matters of administration and public emergency', and what the requirements for a valid framework of delegation are. Both of the exceptions from the general prohibition on delegating legislative powers onto the executive, that of 'specified matters of administration' because of its vagueness, and that of 'public emergency' because of the political instability Argentina suffered in the course of its constitutional history, could potentially be interpreted very widely. However, given that Article 76 starts off with a prohibition on the delegation of legislative powers, it seems as if the exceptions need to be interpreted narrowly.[96] Otherwise, the exception would turn into the rule, and the general prohibition to delegate legislative powers would be undermined.[97] With regard to 'specified matters of administration', it has been suggested that the

---

93   Badeni (2001), at 923.
94   Colautti (1996), at 861; see also Comadira (2003), at 245. The Supreme Court's argument that the passivity of the legislator to create the framework required by the Constitution for the exercise of the emergency powers by the executive under Art.99(3) could not prevent the executive from exercising them, as otherwise the legislature could, by mere omission, take away powers the constitution vested in the executive (see "Rodríguez, Jorge, Jefe de Gabinete de Ministros de la Nación s/ plantea cuestión de competencia", 17 December 1997, at para. 13; but see "Verrocchi, Ezio Daniel c/ Poder Ejecutivo Nacional – Administración Nacional de Aduanas s/ acción de amparo", 19 August 1999, Fallos 322:1726, at para. 14, per Justice Petracchi, concurring), cannot work in the context of Article 76. Here, the emergency powers are delegated onto the executive by Congress, and in that case there is no reason to allow Congress to do so without creating the constitutionally required controls.
95   For the different views see, for example, Quiroga Lavié (2000), at 533–536; Ekmekdjian (1997), at 710; Palazzo (1999), at 1271; Gelli (1999), at 1282. For a detailed discussion see also Bianchi (1996), at 764–773. The Supreme Court held in this respect that the reform intended to restrict the practice that existed before the constitutional reform, see "Verrocchi, Ezio Daniel c/ Poder Ejecutivo Nacional – Administración Nacional de Aduanas s/ acción de amparo", 19 August 1999, Fallos 322:1726, at para. 8.
96   "M. Langenauer e Hijos S.A. y A.G. c. Estado nacional" CNFed. Contencioso administrativo, sala IV, 18 November 1999, LL 2000-D, 576, at 579.
97   Ekmekdjian (1997), at 713–714; Comadira (2003), at 264.

use of the word 'specified' prohibits generic or ambiguous delegations.[98] In respect of emergency regulations, the interplay of Article 99(3) which gives the President the power to enact them, and Article 76 which allows Congress to delegate such powers onto the executive, has been interpreted in a way that the powers under Article 99(3) only come into play when the emergency is such that it prevents Congress from enacting an empowering statute. Moreover, the delegation of emergency powers overrides and excludes the President's powers under Article 99(3).[99]

Agreement seems to exist with regard to some of the basic requirements an empowering provision needs to meet in order to be constitutional. The legislative must determine clearly the contours of the policy which the executive needs to implement when making the regulation.[100] Where possible, the empowering statute should state the objective of the legislation, the basic principles that need to be applied, and the margin within which the executive can take regulative decisions.[101] This means that the legislative cannot give the executive a 'blank cheque' with regard to the regulations that can be issued based on the delegation, but that instead the executive can only validly 'complete' a norm already 'planned' by the legislature.[102]

After having thus outlined the general principles of delegation of powers in Argentinian constitutional law, it remains to be examined how this applies to the specific situation of sovereign debt. As already stated, in many, if not most, cases, both the taking up of new debt and the restructuring of existing debt took place through executive regulations which were usually confirmed by Congress, through the approval of the annual budget acts and investment accounts; or in some cases by the means of specific statutes. However, it is submitted that whatever the practice, if the executive becomes active in the area of sovereign debt, this would only be constitutional if it was either based on a valid delegation of powers according to Article 76, or based on the President's own powers under Article 99(2) and (3). Here, it needs to be remembered that Congress cannot validly delegate to the executive its powers to settle the country's foreign debt as such. What Congress could, on the other hand, in principle do is delegate the competence to negotiate the terms of repaying, refinancing or renegotiating the old debt, as these seem to be administrative tasks that normally belong to the executive's responsibilities, as long as Congress sets the policy framework within which these activities are to take place,[103] something which logically has to precede any activity of the executive in this area.[104] Some examples will now be analysed to see how matters of delegation of powers were dealt with in the context of Argentina's sovereign debt.

---

98   Gelli (1999), at 1283; for an interesting analysis of how to determine 'matters of administration' see Comadira (2003), at 265–267.
99   "Provincia de San Luis c Estado Nacional", *La Ley*, 2003-B, 537, at paras 26–30; Bianchi (1996), at 771; Sabsay (2004), at 625–627.
100 "Domínguez, Luis v SAICF Kaiser Aluminio", 9 June 1971, Fallos: 280:25, at para. 5; see also Colautti (1996), at 858; Badeni (2001), at 924.
101 Quiroga Lavié (2000), at 540.
102 Sabsay and Onaindia (2004), at 246.
103 See also Badeni (2001), at 924; Ekmekdjian (1994), at 462.
104 See also Giuliani Fonrouge (2004), at 981–983.

3.2.2 Restructuring of bonds under Alfonsín

During the Alfonsín government, several operations concerning the country's sovereign debt took place. In 1985, for example, an important part of the debt was consolidated through Guaranteed Refinancing Agreements, and in 1987 another important debt refinancing was carried out.[105] One of the operations undertaken under Alfonsín was that of the restructuring of the bonds with which the military regime had assumed the foreign debt of private debtors. While it is arguably not the most important instance of debt restructuring that took place under Alfonsín, it will nevertheless be used as an example because it is the only case which triggered a Supreme Court decision.

In *Brunicardi*, a case already mentioned several times, the Supreme Court had to assess the constitutionality of Regulation 772/86 which altered the terms of bonds that had originally been created by the military regime when assuming the foreign debt of private Argentinian companies. The Supreme Court stated that the fact that the democratic government modified the terms of the bonds issued by the military regime in 1982 must be regarded as an implicit ratification and recognition of the validity of the original obligations that were thereby altered.[106] The Court did not have a problem with the fact that the restructuring took place by the means of executive regulations, instead of by statute. In this respect, the Court opined that Congress had accepted the practice whereby the executive exercised all faculties concerning the foreign debt and Congress' involvement was reduced to the annual debate of the budget dedicated to the payment of the foreign debt.[107] As there was no valid empowering statute that might have served as the basis of Regulation 772/86, the Supreme Court argued that Act 24.156, which was enacted by the Menem government in October 1992, even though not applicable as an empowering statute for regulations issued in 1986, nevertheless demonstrated the continuing will of the government (that is presumably the Menem government, not that of Alfonsín who was in power when the relevant regulations were issued) to accept the practice under consideration.[108] From all this followed that Regulation 772/86 and the administrative acts based on it, were constitutional.[109]

The Attorney-General had reached a similar conclusion, though based on slightly different considerations. He suggested first of all that an empowering statute was not necessary for Regulation 772/86, as 'the executive, over and above those powers that Congress can delegate onto it in the matter under litigation, has sufficient powers to administrate according to its vision of reality.' When the executive can demonstrate that the payment of the debt was impossible and that it was therefore necessary in the

---

105 For more detail see Silva (h.) (1992), at 838; see also Giuliani Fonrouge (2004), at 968 and 1007–1008.

106 "Brunicardi, Adriano Caredio c/ Estado Nacional (BCRA) s/ cobro SC B592 XXIV", 24 February 1997, Fallos 319:2886, at para. 9.

107 Ibid., at para. 10. See also Rodríguez Galán and Girardi Gutiérrez (1997), at 1279.

108 Ibid., at para. 14. See also Rodríguez Galán and Girardi Gutiérrez (1997), at 1275–1276.

109 Ibid., at para. 15.

public interest to take restructuring measures, he argued, 'it is not valid to prevent the executive from reacting in the general interest according to its own assessment of this prevailing reality.'[110] He went on to say that even if his view of the powers of the executive were not accepted, the lack of any legislative intervention prior to the enactment of Regulation 772/86 did not make it unconstitutional, as the approval of the investment accounts for 1986 and the approval of the subsequent budget acts that set aside funds for the payment of the rescheduled debts turned this into an academic question.

Both the Court's and the Attorney-General's opinions give rise for concern. The Court suggests that the discrepancy that exists between the distribution of powers as provided for in the Constitution and the actual practice adopted with regard to all acts concerning the country's foreign debt is not problematic because the practice received Congress' approval. This is surprising, given that within a system of a written constitution that expressly allocates different tasks to different constitutional organs, the question of whether or not constitutional requirements have been complied with cannot depend on the attitude of the different organs, but instead depends on whether or not the constitution regards such practices as acceptable. Thus, Congress and the executive cannot, even by mutual agreement, circumvent the constitutionally determined distribution of powers, and powers that the Constitution assigned to Congress cannot be vested in the executive, unless the Constitution itself allows for such a delegation of powers.[111]

It is accordingly not sufficient to state that a practice is constitutional because Congress accepts it as such, but it needs to be assessed instead whether or not the practice according to which Congress' involvement is reduced to approving the Budget Act constitutes a delegation of power that is in compliance with the Constitution. This would require that the relevant budget acts provide a delegation of powers onto the executive that complies with the requirements set out above, that is outlines the general framework and policy decisions based on which the executive can then make further and more detailed regulations. However, the budget acts usually contain no more than a general authorization to use certain specified funds for the purpose of debt repayment or restructuring as the executive sees fit, without going into any more detail. If this is the only involvement Congress has in the matter, such a broad delegation of powers does not seem to be sufficiently specific to justify the conclusion that Congress thereby sets the framework within which the executive can become active and negotiate and restructure the country's debt, including by the means of legislative regulations. In the light of the impossibility to service all the debt when and as it becomes due, it is submitted that for a delegation to be valid, it needs to contain some indication as to how to prioritize among the many debt

---

110   Ibid., at 8.

111   This follows, for example, from "Verrocchi, Ezio Daniel c/ Poder Ejecutivo Nacional – Administración Nacional de Aduanas s/ acción de amparo", 19 August 1999, Fallos 322:1726, at paras 8–10. For a US Supreme Court decision stating that Congress cannot validly confer a power onto the President outside of what the Constitution regards as valid, before first changing the Constitution, see *Clinton v City of New York*, 524 US 417 (1998), at 449 per Justice Stevens, and at 451–452 per Justice Kennedy, concurring.

repayment obligations and according to which criteria, as it can otherwise hardly be said that it is Congress that makes the underlying legislative decisions.

Coming back to *Brunicardi*, even more problematic is the view expressed by both the Court and the Attorney-General that the subsequent approval of investment accounts, future budget acts or a future statute can somehow retrospectively validate a regulation that was not based on a valid empowering statute at the time of its enactment. This flies in the face of the principle of distribution of powers as provided for in the Constitution. Neither does this practice comply with the principles which were developed by case law and are now codified in Article 76 of the Constitution, as it accepts a delegation of powers only where it is based on an empowering statute that sets out the legislative policy, which logically requires that the empowering statute predates the exercise of the powers it authorizes.[112] The only exception would be emergency regulations issued under the powers in Article 99(3), but this did not apply to the circumstances of *Brunicardi*.

The Attorney-General did not rely on any constitutional provision to support his opinion that the executive can issue regulations in the area of bond restructurings based on 'powers to administrate according to its vision of reality' or on the necessity to regulate the matter 'in the general interest according to its own assessment of this prevailing reality.' It seems that the only possibility would be to base this view on Article 99(1) which states that the President is the supreme head of the country and in charge of its general administration. However, as the power in the area of contracting and settling the payment of sovereign debt is expressly vested in Congress, it is submitted that the executive cannot have genuine powers to regulate this area unless validly authorized by Congress to do so.

Another piece of legislation which is often mentioned as legitimizing a delegation of powers onto the executive in matters of sovereign debt and to which the Supreme Court referred in *Brunicardi*[113] is the Ministries Act, promulgated as a *de facto* law, but then amended by regulations first under Alfonsín (Regulation 132/83), and then under Menem (438/92). It confers powers onto the Secretary of the Economy 'to authorize operations of internal and external credit of the public sector'(s. 20(13)). If the statute were to be interpreted as conferring such wide ranging powers onto the Secretary of the Economy as those to issue new bonds and to determine their terms and conditions, this would mean that instead of executing parliamentary policies, the executive determines these policies, thereby assuming powers that are vested in Congress. This would go beyond the powers envisaged by Article 76 and Supreme Court case law preceding this provision. Moreover, it is not obvious that a provision that regulates the competencies of the Secretary of the Economy has the effect of delegating legislative powers from the legislative onto the executive. Instead, it seems more convincing to understand the relevant provisions of this statute as

---

112 See, for example, "Franco, Rubén Oscar y otros v Estado Nacional /Mrio. de Defensa s/personal militar y civil de las FF.AA. y de seguridad", 19 August 1999, Fallos 322:1868, at para. 14; "M. Langenauer e Hijos S.A. y A.G. c. Estado nacional" CNFed. Contencioso administrativo, sala IV, 18 November 1999, LL 2000-D, 576, at 579.

113 Although with a view to the original regulations issued by the military regime, not with regard to those issued by the Alfonsín government to restructure said bonds.

effecting the distribution of competencies within the executive[114] and as providing an authorization to negotiate the sovereign debt and enter into agreements, always within the framework set by, and subject to the approval of, the legislative.[115]

While without undertaking a detailed examination of all the operations concerning the restructuring of sovereign debts under the Alfonsín government, it cannot be decided whether or not this conclusion applies to all of them, it is submitted that the preceding analysis shows that at least with regard to the bonds at issue in the case of *Brunicardi*, there are substantial doubts that they were restructured in compliance with the constitutional principles of delegation of powers. In this particular context, the fact that the Court accepted the constitutionality of the operations without requiring any policy decisions of Congress that go beyond approving the relevant budget and investment accounts is all the more significant when bearing in mind that what was under examination was the private debt that the Argentinian state assumed under the military regime, and with regard to which many irregularities were highlighted, for example in the decision in *Olmos*.[116] The Court thus seems to have taken the view that debt repayment and restructuring are mainly questions of how much money is available for and was dedicated to debt servicing, and went out of its way to uphold the regulation as constitutional, even though the principles of delegation of power needed to be significantly stretched in order to back such a conclusion. The case in *Brunicardi* was brought by a bondholder who sought a declaration that the original bonds issued by the military regime were valid, while the restructured bonds were not. This would have given the Court the opportunity to pronounce itself first of all with regard to the validity of the original bonds by examining both their procedural and substantive constitutionality, and then to analyse the constitutionality of the bonds issued by the Alfonsín government based on the outcome of that analysis. Unfortunately, this opportunity to perform a profound legal analysis of issues surrounding the debt taken up by the military regime was lost, and it was instead taken for granted that this debt had created a binding obligation.[117]

3.2.3 Debt restructuring under Menem – the Brady bonds

The most important debt restructuring that took place during the Menem government was the Brady Plan[118] which restructured 23,000 million dollars of debt stock, and

---

114   Mastrorilli (1994), at 833–834; see also Bazán Lazcano (1996), at 972.
115   García Lema (2004), at 960.
116   "Olmos, Alejandro S/denuncia", causa N°14.467, 13 July 2000, Juzg. Nac. Crim. y Corr. Fed., n. 2., JA 2001-I-514.
117   Another important feature of the decision in *Brunicardi* which is not relevant to the issues under discussion here is that the Court held that the particular bonds at issue had not been issued *iure gestionis*, but instead by an exercise of sovereign powers, as the state thereby assumed the debt of private Argentinian companies. Because of this, the Court concluded that the state could unilaterally change the terms and conditions of the bonds in cases of a financial emergency, see "Brunicardi, Adriano Caredio c/ Estado Nacional (BCRA) s/ cobro SC B592 XXIV", 24 February 1997, Fallos 319:2886, at paras 16–19.
118   For a detailed description of the Brady Plan see Silva (h.) (1992).

8,600 million dollars of interest.[119] This operation, which was of huge importance for the country, was mainly carried out by the means of executive regulations. First, Regulation 2321 of December 1992 authorized the Secretary of the Economy, Domingo Cavallo, to sign in representation of the Argentinian state all contracts and instruments necessary for the restructuring of the debt in accordance with the Brady Plan. Through Regulation 407, Menem approved in 1993 all contracts and legal instruments that Cavallo had signed in this context. The regulation explains that the approved operations were necessary in order to fulfil the country's legal obligations, and that they would achieve a reduction of both the debt stock and future interests. With regard to the legal bases of these operations, it was stated that:

> In accordance with the competencies conferred by Article 86(1) of the Constitution; Article 48 of Act 16.432, incorporated into Act 11.672, the Permanently Complementing the Budget Act, and modified by Article 7 of Act 20.548; Articles 10 and 17 of Act 24.061; Articles 11 and 24 of Act 24.191; and Article 65 of Act 24.156, the executive is authorized to make the present regulation.

This very impressive looking list of empowering provisions needs some further scrutiny. Article 86(1) of the Constitution (now Article 99(1)), stated that the President is the supreme head of the country and in charge of its general administration. It was already argued above that from this it cannot follow that the President has the power to enact regulations in areas in which Congress has the exclusive constitutional competence.[120] Acts 24.061 and 24.191 are the Budget Acts of 1992 and 1993, respectively, and the relevant articles contain no more than general authorizations with regard to the sovereign debt, but without any specific instructions concerning the Brady Plan or the restructuring operations thereby planned. Article 7 of Act 20.548 that modified the Act Permanently Complementing the Budget, provides the executive with a general authorization, in stating that:

> Whenever it may be convenient to facilitate the mobilization of capital in the internal or external market for the purpose of establishing or expanding public utilities or activities which directly or indirectly are related to utilities of such nature, by means of legally authorized works or developments, or making investments which are fundamental for the economic development of the country, declared to be in the national interest by law or by the executive power, the latter is authorized to contract loans with economic financial international agencies of which the Republic of Argentina is a member, or with agencies or entities of other governments, provided they conform to usual terms and conditions and to provisions of the respective basic agreements and regulations pertaining to loans.[121]

---

119 See also Chapter Two, 3, supra.
120 See also "M. Langenauer e Hijos S.A. y A.G. c. Estado nacional", CNFed. Ctenciosoadministrativo, sala IV, 18/11/1999, LL 2000-D, 576, at 579; "Rodelia SA.A. c. Inspección General de Justicia", 22 September 1999, LL 2000-A 141, at 143.
121 As translated in Mairal (1987), at 150. The provision further empowers the executive to secure obligations assumed by public or private enterprises with a guarantee of the Nation.

It is submitted that this incredibly broad enabling provision does not adequately outline the policies which the executive has to follow when taking up loans, particularly bearing in mind that the executive itself is empowered to determine that the loan it intends to contract is in the national interest. However, instead of being struck down as unconstitutional, the application of this provision has been extended beyond the words of the statute itself, in that the term 'government' was interpreted as being synonymous with 'country'. As a consequence, the provision was said not to be restricted to debt with IFIs and foreign governments, but it was rather also applied to loans with foreign private banks.[122]

Act 24.156 (Financial Administration and the Control Systems of the National Public Sector Act), which was enacted in the context of the restructuring of Argentina's public debt under the Menem Government, and was regarded by the Supreme Court in *Brunicardi*,[123] and later in *Galli*[124] as a valid empowering statute, authorizes the executive in its Article 65 to 'carry out operations of public credit in order to restructure the public debt by the means of consolidating, converting or renegotiating it, to the extent that this involves an improvement of the original amount, maturity and/or interest rates.' While the executive cannot make any operations with regard to the public debt unless they have been contemplated and specified in the relevant budget act (s. 60 of Act 24.156), operations with IFIs are expressly excluded from this requirement. Article 56 of the Act defines public credit as

> the faculty of the state to take up debt with the aim of obtaining the financial means to carry out productive investments; to address issues of evident national necessity; to restructure its organisation or to refinance its liabilities, including interests. It is prohibited to carry out operations of public credit to finance operative costs.

While Article 56 has been praised[125] because it implements the limits on operations of public credit set by Article 4 of the Constitution,[126] it is submitted that that is not entirely accurate. This is because Article 56 includes the restructuring and refinancing of debt, which is not envisaged by Article 4.[127] Article 65 of Act 24.156 sets at least some framework for the activities of the executive in the area of public debt, as it requires that all operations in this context need to involve some improvement of the original conditions, and further makes the validity of these operations dependent upon their inclusion in the relevant budget act. It could therefore be thought that this delegation complies with Article 76 of the Constitution. However, it is submitted that Article 65, even when seen together with the provisions of the budget acts, is nevertheless too general to serve as a valid basis for a delegation of powers. The provision does not give any indication as to what is regarded as an improvement of

---

122 Mairal (1987), at 151.
123 "Brunicardi, Adriano Caredio c/ Estado Nacional (BCRA) s/ cobro SC B592 XXIV", 24 February 1997, Fallos 319:2886, at para. 14.
124 "Galli, Hugo y otro c/ PEN – s/Amparo Ley 25.561", 6 April 2005, at para. 8 per Justices Zaffaroni and Lorenzetti.
125 García Lema (2004), at 962.
126 For a detailed discussion of Article 4 see Chapter Six, 1, infra.
127 See the discussion ibid.

the terms of the debt. As it refers to an improvement of 'the original amount, due dates and/or interest rates', this gives the executive a very wide discretion with regard to the policies to adopt, as it could decide to focus on the improvement of one of the three elements to the detriment of the others. This is then not a delegation that sets a clear policy framework. Furthermore, that the very same provision can authorize the executive to perform debt restructurings under such different circumstances as the Brady Plan, the *megacanje* under De la Rúa in 2001, and the debt restructurings carried out by the Kirchner government in 2005, demonstrates that it is a blanket provision rather than an empowering statute that adequately outlines the specific policies to be performed in the respective situations, a deficit which the respective budget acts with their lack of policy specifications cannot cure. Indeed, under Article 65, Congress' role is largely reduced to rubberstamping whatever the results of the executive's negotiations might be by making available the necessary funds in the budget act. With regard to the debt with IFIs, the empowering statute does not even require that.[128]

Leaving aside the doubts about the constitutionality of Article 65 as an enabling statute, in order to comply with that provision, the operations carried out under the Brady Plan would need to have improved Argentina's debt. It was already stated that as a consequence of the Brady Plan, Argentina's creditors changed from a number of easily identifiable international banks to a multitude of anonymous bondholders,[129] and that in actual fact, between 1992 and 1993, the debt increased by 6.8 per cent due to the costs of the Brady Plan.[130] Whether or not there was really an improvement as required by Article 65 would then depend on how improvement is interpreted in this context. It could be argued that all of the various Brady bonds brought an improvement on at least one of the elements listed in Article 65, so that they would be covered by Article 65. This, however, only supports the view expressed above that an overall assessment in each case of debt restructuring is needed in order to evaluate the effects of the operation as a whole on the country's debt situation, something that it is submitted needs to be performed by Congress prior to authorizing the executive to act upon this assessment. Thus, a more specific enabling provision should be required for each case of debt restructuring in order to provide a sufficiently concrete framework for the executive.

3.2.4 Mega swap under De la Rúa/Cavallo in 2001

Another important example of a debt restructuring operation is the so-called *megacanje* (mega swap) initiated again by Domingo Cavallo, this time as De la Rúa's Secretary of the Economy. In Regulation 648 of 2001, the operation was

---

128   It is then impossible to understand the opinion that this provides a constitutional delegation of powers, but see García Lema (2004), at 962.
129   Galasso (2003), at 295; Kulfas and Schorr (2003), at 21. In 1989, the creditors of Argentina's foreign debt were international banks (61.1 per cent), IFIs (around 20 per cent), and only about 10 per cent of the debt was owed to individual bondholders, see Galasso (2003), at 293.
130   Kulfas and Schorr (2003), at 23.

justified on the grounds that the maturing of large amounts of the sovereign debt over the following four years would cause significant financial needs, and that the swap aimed to resolve this problem by postponing the maturity of the debt. The legal basis of this operation, in this case involving a sub-delegation of the respective powers onto the Secretary of the Economy, was seen in Article 65 of Act 24.156, and in the fact that 'the presentation of new instruments in exchange of titles of public debt existing in the market in order to cancel them is a common operation in the financial markets.' In addition, the executive relied on the general authorization in the Budget Act 2001; Article 16 of Act 11.672, and on its own powers under Article 99(1) and (10) (Article 99(10) empowers the President to oversee 'the performance of the duties of the Chief of the Ministerial Cabinet as regards the collection of the revenues of the Nation, and their investment according to the law or budget of national expenditures').

Here, again, an important debt restructuring operation was carried out by the executive, with minimal congressional involvement. With regard to the enabling provisions mentioned, in addition to what was already stated before and equally applies here, Article 16 of Act 11.672 empowers the executive to take up loans with IFIs for certain purposes specified in that provision and is therefore of limited relevance in the context of the *megacanje*. That the executive can have the power to perform operations that fall, according to the Constitution, under the exclusive competence of Congress, based on the fact that the relevant act is 'a common operation in the financial markets' is not exactly convincing. Nor does the fact that something is a common operation in the financial markets say anything about the question of which constitutional organ has the competence to regulate it.

As the *megacanje* postponed the maturity of the debt, but increased its stock considerably,[131] the IMF's chief economist's assessment at the time was that while the mega-swap would save the country 12,000 million dollars of debt repayment between 2001 and 2005, this came at the cost of additional debts of 66,000 million dollars as of 2006.[132] Thus, again the question of how to interpret Article 65 of Act 24.156 needs to be asked, and, more importantly, in whose responsibility this evaluation should lie, as it would once more be possible to justify a formal compliance with the Act on the grounds that the operation involved an improvement with regard to the maturity of the debt, though at the cost of increasing the overall debt stock. The validity of the *megacanje* has been questioned in judicial proceedings, although in the context of criminal proceedings for fraud and the diversion of public funds initiated against then President De la Rúa, then Secretary of the Economy Domingo Cavallo, and David Mulford, an American banker who was heavily involved in the planning and carrying out of the operation. With regard to the issue of whether the *megacanje* had been based on irregular procedures, the General Auditors of the Nation, a body created by Article 85 of the Constitution and having the task of controlling the public sector, provided three different reports. Concerning compliance with Article 65 of Act 24.156, some of the auditors suggested that it was not sufficient that one of the

---

131 Ibid., at 46–47; Galasso (2003), at 344; IMF's Independent Evaluation Office's Report (2004), at 90.
132 Mussa (2002), at 65–66.

three factors, that is amount, maturity and interests of the debt, would be improved by the operation concerned, as in addition the situation would have to be looked at in its entirety to decide whether or not the operation brought an improvement as required under Article 65.[133] While two of the Auditors General were of the opinion that the operation had taken place 'outside of the normative framework of our legal system and was harmful to the financial interests of the Argentinian state,'[134] the others did not take a stance on this issue, and the experts appointed by the defence, unsurprisingly, came to a different conclusion. They argued that even though the debt stock had increased by 55,000 million dollars, the *megacanje* had a positive effect in that it helped to avoid a greater evil, namely the default. Leaving aside that the *megacanje* only postponed the default by a few months, it is submitted that this argument demonstrates in absolute clarity the problems with a delegation in the form of Article 65, as an assessment of what constitutes an improvement and what are the greater evils is a complex decision that should be made by Congress itself. The judge, however, adopted a literal interpretation of Article 65 and came to the conclusion that the executive had been empowered to improve one of the conditions mentioned in Article 65, which it had done, so that the *megacanje* did not fall outside of the empowering statute.[135] However, given that the Constitution entrusts this assessment in Congress, the constitutionality of the delegations based on which the *megacanje* was carried out, and of the *megacanje* itself, is very questionable.

3.2.5 Debt management under Kirchner

Moving on to the government of President Kirchner, which started in 2003, it first needs to be remembered that when Kirchner came into power, the Public Emergency and Reform of the Monetary System Act (Act 25.561) which was enacted in January 2002 as a reaction to the acute economic and financial crisis was still in force. This Act, which declared the public emergency in social, economic, administrative, financial and monetary matters, delegated powers onto the executive to make emergency regulations until December 2003, *inter alia* in order to 'create the conditions for economic growth that is sustainable and compatible with a restructuring of the public debt' (Article 1(3)). While it can hardly be doubted that an emergency situation existed in January 2002, these powers have since been prolonged on an annual basis,

---

133   See the opinion of Auditors General Fernández and Arias, and the opinion of Auditor General Palacios, in "Cavallo, Domingo Felipe y otros s/defraudación contra la administración pública" (2003), but see the opinion of Auditors General Fadel, Folica and Fragoso, ibid., who do not express themselves as to whether a global approach needs to be taken when evaluating if there was, in fact, an improvement with regard to the debt according to Article 65.

134   See the opinion of Auditors General Fernández and Arias, ibid.

135   Ibid. Based on new expert evidence, he since changed his mind and came to the conclusion that the *megacanje* was, in fact, detrimental to the interests of the country and he decided that the criminal proceedings should continue, as the prosecution has made a *prima facie* case against the accused. See "Cavallo Domingo Felipe y otros s/ abuso de autoridad y violación a los deberes de funcionario público", 28 September 2006.

despite a significant improvement of the economic situation over the last few years, and a stabilization of the political situation. Indeed, the Kirchner Government itself, when justifying its policy to repay the debt with the IMF, stated in December 2005 that 'a situation of fiscal solvency can be noticed which allows to secure the economic strength in the light of possible unfavourable external scenarios.'[136] Nevertheless, the emergency powers delegated onto the executive in order to resolve the crisis were consistently prolonged, most recently by Article 1 of Act 26.077 of January 2006 until 31 December 2006.

Under Kirchner, two main important operations in the context of sovereign debt have so far taken place: a considerable debt restructuring operation in 2005, and the payment of all debts with the IMF on 3 January 2006.

(a) Debt restructuring

The debt restructuring needs to be seen in the context of Argentina's default on all foreign debt other than with IFIs as of December 2001. As already explained in Chapter Two,[137] after long and painful negotiations, Argentina submitted an offer to its creditors to restructure the debt that was in default, applying a large cut on the principal of the debt, which was eventually accepted by 76 per cent of the country's creditors. These operations were mainly performed by the means of executive regulations and resolutions. Many of the details of the operations were contained in Regulation 1735/04, where the following bases for the regulation were mentioned: Regulation 256/02 which was issued based on Act 25.561, and conferred upon the Secretary of the Economy the power to undertake the steps and negotiations necessary in order to restructure the sovereign debt; Article 65 of Act 24.156; the Budget Acts of 2002, 2003 and 2004 which authorized the executive via the Secretary of the Economy to restructure the sovereign debt there mentioned, and imposed upon the executive the obligation to inform Congress at a quarterly basis of the progress of the negotiations and agreements; Article 99(1) and (2) of the Constitution; and Article 16 of Act 11.672. In the context of the operation, a statute, Act 26.017, was enacted to regulate some details, such as a prohibition directed towards the executive to reopen the swap and take up negotiations with hold-out creditors once the date at which the bondholders could accept the swap had passed.[138]

The main reasons given for the restructuring of the debt in default were that it was necessary in order to consolidate the financial situation of the Argentinian state, and to normalize the relations with the country's creditors. By drastically reducing the number of bonds; of currencies in which they were issued; and of jurisdictions that were applicable to them, the negative impact on fiscal, financial and economic

---

136   Regulation 1601/05.
137   Chapter Two, 5 and 6, supra.
138   Sola (2005) suggests at 35 that this prohibition to negotiate is unconstitutional in that it violates Article 75(7). This is because according to him, to settle the payment of the debt means to try and find solutions to the debt problem when faced with a situation of a hypothetical default. The Act, he argues, does the opposite in that it stands in the way of solving the problem of non-payment.

matters of the state would be diminished. As in the past, the new instruments of public debt include foreign jurisdiction clauses and a waiver of sovereign immunity. The Secretary of the Economy was authorized to approve and sign all acts that were necessary to implement the operation, and his Ministry empowered to assume the expenses arising. With regard to the validity of the delegations, not much needs to be added to the analyses provided in the context of the previous debt restructurings. However, to use the emergency powers conferred by Act 25.561 in a situation in which the existence of an emergency can be seriously questioned, puts the validity of this delegation in serious doubt. Furthermore, the delegations contained in the Act itself, as well as in Regulation 256/02, raise constitutional concerns, given their extreme generality and breadth.[139]

(b) Payment of the debt with the IMF

As was explained in Chapter Two, Argentina had a longstanding relationship with the IMF, which was rather jovial throughout the Menem period, as Menem was regarded as the star pupil of the IMF,[140] but turned more conflictive since De la Rúa took over in 1999 when the country found itself in a desolate financial situation which then continuously worsened. The IMF at first, though according to its own accounts reluctantly, supported the economic policy of the De la Rúa government and reached several credit agreements with Argentina. However, in December 2001, when it became obvious that the collapse of both the government and the convertibility regime was imminent, the IMF changed its policy and declined all further loans. The period of the Duhalde government (January 2002 to May 2003) was characterized by drawn out and complicated negotiations with the IMF to reach a Stand-By Agreement. The difficulties continued under the Kirchner government, when the IMF made all agreements subject to conditions such as that the charges of the privatized public services, for example gas, electricity etc., should be increased,[141] and the debt in default renegotiated. After the debt restructuring in 2005, this was changed to a demand that an offer needed to be made to the hold-out creditors.[142] When the negotiations turned more and more difficult, the Kirchner government decided to pay the debts with the IMF when they matured, instead of negotiating any refinancing agreements. In December 2005, President Kirchner took the surprising step of announcing the repayment of all of the outstanding debt with the IMF, even that which was not then due, in one payment with Central Bank reserves, and this was carried out in January 2006.

---

139 Hernández (2004) suggests at 351 and 380–383 that the delegation conferred upon the executive by the means of Act 25.561 is far too broad to be compatible with Article 76.

140 IMF's Independent Evaluation Office's Report (2004), at 12.

141 For example when insisting on legislation authorizing an increase of the charges for their services, see Amadeo (2003), at 151. See also, for example, *Clarín*, 2 December 2005.

142 See, for example, *Clarín*, 27 November 2005.

To this effect, Regulations 1599/05 and 1601/05 were issued on 15 December 2005. Regulation 1601/05 stated that the costs of the existing financial agreements with the international organisms exceeded the returns achieved on the reserves; that the policy of reducing the foreign debt adopted by the Government allowed to obtain more flexibility in designing and executing economic policies, and that it was therefore necessary and appropriate to use Central Bank reserves to pay the debt with the IMF. According to the Government, it was authorized to adopt this policy and to empower the Secretary of the Economy to take the necessary measures to carry it out, by Article 99(1) of the Constitution, and Article 6 of Act 23.928.

The reference to Article 99(1), empowering the President with the general administration of the country, shows that this payment was regarded as a general matter of administration, and not as a settling of the payment of the debt which would require the involvement of Congress. Given the important effects of this measure for the country, this view must be questioned. With regard to litigation against the country in foreign courts and arbitral tribunals such as ICSID, for example, Argentina's defence of economic necessity might be seriously undermined by this payment, and the preferential treatment of the debt of the IMF raises particular issues where this extends to debt that had not matured. Furthermore, whether to repay a debt before it is due can be justified in the context of the country's precarious social situation,[143] is another issue that would have deserved a debate in Congress. More importantly still, it needs to be taken into account that in repaying the debt to the IMF in full, the government accepted its obligation towards the IMF in its totality,[144] even though there are many indications for the IMF's responsibility or at least co-responsibility for the country's economic crisis. It could, for example, be questioned whether the loans made to the De la Rúa government in full awareness of the fact that they would finance capital flight and indebt the country even more,[145] are loans that need to be repaid in full. By making the payment, the government, prior to any analysis of the underlying issues performed by Congress, lost the opportunity to raise these issues.[146]

Coming back to the question of whether the payment to the IMF complied with constitutional requirements, Article 6 of Act 23.928 to which the executive referred is not an enabling provision, but instead a provision, newly amended by Regulation 1599/05, which provides that the federal reserves that are freely available can be used for repaying obligations with IFIs, as long as the monetary effect of such a measure would be neutral. This means that Regulation 1599/05 changed various provisions of a statute, Act 23.928 regulating the Central Bank reserves, and thereby introduced a fundamental change in fiscal policy, in order to provide the legal framework

---

143 See Chapter Six, 2, infra.

144 For a study of the IMF's responsibility with regard to Argentina's economic crisis see Cafiero (2005).

145 See in this respect, Chapter Two, 4. A co-responsibility of the IMF can, for example, be inferred from the findings of the IMF's Independent Evaluation Office's Report (2004), at 53–54; see also Bluestein (2005), at 203.

146 But see Bohoslavsky (2006a), who argues that the President paid under protest which leaves open the possibility to claim compensation from the IMF for the damage its loans and conditionalities inflicted on the country.

without which this 'measure of general administration', as the payment to the IMF was characterized, could not have taken place. The government argued that given the commercial and current account surplus on the balance of payments, and the country's fiscal solvency, it was justified to use parts of the reserves in order to fulfil obligations with IFIs. It was then stated that because this was a case of exceptional circumstances which made it impossible to comply with the constitutional procedure for the enactment of statutes, the matter needed to be regulated as a matter of urgency and emergency, based on the President's competence for such measures under Article 99(3). Thus, the executive changed a statute by an emergency regulation through which it empowered itself to carry out what it regarded as a matter of general administration. A few days later, this regulation was ratified by Congress,[147] as required by Article 99(3).

It is impossible to see the urgency and emergency of the measure, given that the debt that was paid had in large parts neither matured when the regulations were issued, nor when the actual payment was made. Why, given that Congress was in session and there was no need to act swiftly,[148] this was a case of exceptional circumstances which made it impossible to comply with the constitutional procedure for the enactment of statutes is anybody's guess. It is submitted that it cannot be sufficient to make a general allegation of exceptional circumstances, without specifying exactly what they are and why they require executive emergency measures, in order for a regulation based on Article 99(3) to be constitutional. However, even more disturbing is the fact that Congress ratified this regulation, given its unconstitutional nature. This demonstrates several points. In Argentina, the abuse of the executive's emergency powers under Article 99(3) is so normal that it is almost regarded as a normal way of governing.[149] Furthermore, the constitutional system of separation of powers which is based on the idea of delimiting the power of the various organs by introducing control mechanisms that act as checks and balances,[150] can only work if Congress, even when the President has a comfortable majority in both Houses, takes its tasks seriously, instead of docilely ratifying whichever governmental policy is put before it, whether or not it is constitutional.

---

147   Act 26.076.

148   These are the only reasons for which the executive can make use of its emergency powers under Article 99(3), see "Verrocchi, Ezio Daniel c/ Poder Ejecutivo Nacional – Administración Nacional de Aduanas s/ acción de amparo", 19 August 1999, Fallos 322:1726, at para. 9.

149   One of the main arguments of the government in the recent parliamentary debates on the legislation concerning the regulations of urgency and emergency (Act 26.122), and the super-powers vested in the Chief of the Cabinet of Ministers (Act 26.124), the constitutionality of which was questioned by the opposition, was not that these statutes are, in fact, constitutional, but that they do no more than give a statutory basis to what has been the consistent practice over many years. See, for example, *Página* 12, 9 July 2006, at 7; *Clarín*, 6 and 12 July.

150   "Verrocchi, Ezio Daniel c/ Poder Ejecutivo Nacional – Administración Nacional de Aduanas s/ acción de amparo", 19 August 1999, Fallos 322:1726, at paras 7–8.

3.2.6 Concluding remarks

It has been demonstrated that the common practice adopted in Argentina in the context of debt negotiations is not in line with the principles of the Constitution concerning the delegation of powers, because the enabling statutes, at least in the cases examined above, are far too general to comply with the requirements of Article 76.[151] In this respect, it can be seen that Argentinian constitutional reality in the context of sovereign debt does not have much to do with the text of the Constitution itself, or with general constitutional doctrine in this area.[152] Congress' involvement is regarded as a mere formality, and even as a formality it is reduced to a level that lies below the threshold of what is required by the Constitution. To insist on compliance with procedural constitutional requirements in this context might seem like meaningless constitutional formalism. However, as the example of Argentina shows, the sovereign debt is one of the main problems of the country, and the way in which the debt problem is handled is essential for most other political decisions, and for the social situation of the country and its citizens. It is submitted that given their far-reaching effects for the future of the country, it is therefore significant that decisions such as major debt restructurings are taken by the democratically legitimized organ, Congress, after a thorough debate of the different options and their respective advantages and disadvantages, and based on the values contained in the Constitution.[153] It is particularly important that these policy decisions reflect a balancing of the various constitutionally protected interests that are at stake, which in a democratically organized state is more likely to happen if the decision is taken by Congress, where a multitude of societal groups and interests are represented. In line with the constitutional requirements of a valid empowering statute, this can be achieved if Congress, prior to any executive activities with regard to the foreign debt, sets the policy framework within which such activities are to take place, and then decides whether or not to approve the outcome of these negotiations either through a specific statute, or in the context of approving or disapproving the relevant budget.[154] Thus, it is submitted that Congress must be involved not just in setting aside the money needed for fulfilling obligations entered into by the executive, but must rather provide, through empowering provisions, a clear framework for the negotiating position of the Argentinian State.[155] If the empowering statute does not contain such clear guidelines, the delegation itself, and also executive regulations that are based on it, would be unconstitutional.

The current practice does not reflect these constitutional principles, as there is a significant qualitative difference between Congress debating and designing

---

151 But see Palazzo (1999), at 1271, who argues that Article 76 does not seem to prohibit the existing constitutional practice with regard to delegations of rather general powers in the context of settling the payment of the sovereign debt.

152 For a critical discussion of similar trends in the US see Morrison and Hudec (1993), at 102–110.

153 See also Horacio Corti (2002), at 44.

154 Mastrorilli (1984), at 835–836; see also García Lema (2004), at 960.

155 Mastrorilli (1984), ibid.

the policies with regard to the country's sovereign debt, on the one hand, and the executive merely informing Congress of the outcome of debt negotiations, agreements, payments and restructurings, and inviting Congress to approve the budget act that contains the financial details of these policies, on the other. If Congress plays along and delegates ever broader powers onto the executive[156] and accepts whatever decisions the executive regards as necessary in the context of renegotiating and restructuring the country's foreign debt, this means that the executive can, and regularly does, take decisions of fundamental importance for the country without a prior debate and without wide societal and parliamentary participation,[157] and that these decisions are taken in violation of the constitutionally prescribed principles of distribution of powers.[158]

Another observation needs to be added. It seems as if almost from the beginning of the return to democracy, the issue of debt repayment was not one of sovereign decision-making by the Argentinian legislative in fulfilment of its constitutional mandate, but instead turned into a power game between the government of the country, on the one hand, and its creditors; the G7 governments as protectors of creditor interests; and IFIs, on the other. In addition to raising sovereignty issues, this fact had an important effect on domestic constitutional practice. What could, for example, be observed in the most recent Argentinian debt saga is that based on its role as the prime negotiator with international organizations such as the IMF, the government put more and more pressure on Congress to delegate extensive powers onto the executive and to reduce its own role to rubberstamping legislation proposed by the executive. On 14 February 2003, for example, the newspaper *Clarín* reported that Lavagna, the then Secretary of State for the Economy, urged Parliament with regard to the enactment of a bill on tax reforms, that 'if we change as much as one comma of what has been agreed with the IMF, the whole agreement falls through.' At the same time, government put a lot of pressure onto the judiciary not to question its emergency policies and not to put the negotiations and potential agreements with the IMF at risk. Indeed, the government went as far as accusing the Supreme Court judges of delaying any possible agreement with the IMF, as:

> those who observe the situation from the outside and need to provide the necessary funds will abstain from making available funds to a country whose judges do not seem to understand that to resolve partially the problem of this or that deposit holder means to delay indefinitely the overall solution and to jeopardize even more a system in crisis.[159]

Thus, the necessity to reach agreements with the IMF in the context of debt renegotiations was used as a justification to turn the executive into the main actor that determines all policies, and to discipline and control the other branches of government.

---

156 For the most recent delegation of super-powers onto the executive, see Act 26.124, which was promulgated on 7 August 2006 and vests the Chief of the Cabinet of Ministers with powers to change the allocation of parts of the budget without referring the matter to Congress.
157 See also the discussion of these policies by Natanson (2006).
158 In this sense, see also Nino (2005), at 224.
159 *Clarín*, 31 October 2002. In a similar vein, see, for example, Rivera (2002), at 1135.

However, it is submitted that it does not say anywhere in the Constitution that negotiations and agreements with IFIs and other creditors stand above constitutional principles, so that these arguments could only have legal validity if the procedures thereby suggested were in compliance with the Constitution, and it was demonstrated that this is not, in fact, the case. Particularly in a situation of emergency, it is essential that the decisions taken with regard to foreign creditors, which at the same time necessarily affect the possibilities of protecting the rights of the country's citizens and therefore the interests of the nation as a whole, are taken in strict compliance with constitutional principles and due regard for constitutionally protected rights.[160] Exactly because of the attempts of IFIs and other creditors to interfere with the country's policies, it is important that the distribution of powers within the country is not undermined and that constitutional principles are upheld.[161]

4 Summary and conclusion

As the preceding analysis showed, several doubts exist in respect of the constitutionality of Argentina's foreign debt. The debt taken up by the military regime was not contracted by the constitutionally competent organ, Congress, and thus came about in disregard of constitutional principles, so that its validity would depend on whether or not it was later recognized by the democratic government. If the fact that the debt was originally not contracted by the constitutionally competent organ had been the only constitutional flaw affecting the debt taken up by the military regime, Congress would have been free to reject or recognize it, depending on its own assessment of which of the two options better served the interests of the country. This is because the whole point of the *de facto* doctrine is that Congress can decide whether or not to recognize as valid acts taken by *de facto* governments which, according to the Constitution, would have required the involvement of Congress. The doctrine of acquired rights would not have stood in the way of the freedom to reject the recognition of the debt, given that the loan agreements between the military regime and Argentina's creditors did not create rights for the latter that have the same status as rights that were granted by a constitutionally legitimized government. Instead, the original transactions generated no more than 'precarious rights' which can be revoked by the democratic government if they are in conflict with other constitutionally protected rights or interests. However, Congress never rejected the debt, but instead consistently authorized the repayment, renegotiation and restructuring of the debt that dated back to the military regime. It is thus difficult not to come to the conclusion that, at least factually, Congress recognized this debt as valid and binding.

Whether or not this recognition was constitutional is a different issue. With regard to the payment of the debt of the military regime by the subsequent democratic governments, Article 75(7) of the Constitution comes in which requires that Congress settle the payment of the country's public debt. It has been submitted that what this

---

160   For a discussion of the role of the judiciary in this context see Michalowski (2004).
161   See also Carty (1986), at 419.

means in the context of recognizing the debt taken up by a *de facto* regime is that Congress audit this debt as to its amount, the regularity of the circumstances under which it came about, and any other aspects that are important for the decision of whether or not such a debt should be assumed, or rejected, by the re-established democratic state. This, however, never took place, so that the debt was never recognized by Congress in compliance with constitutional requirements.

In respect of whether the repayment and restructurings of this debt by the democratic successor governments could be regarded as a constitutionally valid recognition of this debt, it was argued that Congress could, in principle, validly delegate the competence to negotiate the terms of repaying, refinancing or renegotiating the old debt, as long as Congress itself sets the policy framework within which these activities are to take place.[162] However, at least with regard to the debt restructurings analysed above, it was demonstrated that they were based on empowering statutes that were too broad to form the basis of a valid delegation of powers. Thus, they are themselves unconstitutional and can accordingly not constitute a valid recognition of the debt taken up by the military regime. Another consideration needs to be added. In the light of the view that to settle the debt requires, at least with regard to the debt that was taken up by the military regime, an analysis of the validity of this debt, it is doubtful that any delegation of powers in the context of negotiations, refinancing, restructurings etc. of this debt can be constitutionally valid before Congress has exercised its task of settling the debt. This is because before Congress has audited and accepted as binding a debt that was incurred in an unconstitutional fashion, this debt has not been legitimized. To delegate powers with regard to the payment of this debt would then mean that Congress gives the executive the power to dedicate the Nation's money to the fulfilment of an obligation the Nation has not as yet assumed in the constitutionally prescribed way. This can hardly be regarded as a legitimate and constitutionally valid expense,[163] particularly bearing in mind the many irregularities that took place in the context of the loan transactions of the military regime as evidenced in the decision of *Olmos*.[164] Thus, it is submitted that according to the preceding analysis, all acts of the Argentinian State with regard to repayment, refinancing and restructuring of the debt of the military regime are unconstitutional. Before an auditing of the debt by Congress has taken place, they amount to no more than a factual recognition of the debt that does not comply with constitutional requirements.

Given that in Argentina the acts of all organs of the state are subject to constitutional review by the courts,[165] the courts have the role and the power to control the compatibility of all decisions of the executive and the legislative with constitutional principles. This means that if proceedings for unconstitutionality were initiated, the courts could, and should, declare all acts aimed at debt repayment or renegotiation before the debt has been settled by Congress to be unconstitutional.

---

162   See also Badeni (2001), at 924.
163   See also Lozada (2002), at 256–257.
164   "Olmos, Alejandro S/denuncia", causa N°14.467, 13 July 2000, Juzg. Nac. Crim. y Corr. Fed., n. 2., JA 2001-I-514.
165   Zarina (1999), at 87–93.

While it is originally Congress' task to settle the payment of the debt, if Congress does not perform its task, and proceeds in a manner that is not in accordance with constitutional principles, it is the role of the courts to exercise judicial control over the acts or omissions of Congress. This includes that the current practice of assigning funds to debt repayment in the annual budget acts[166] could be struck down as unconstitutional by the courts. The same applies to enabling provisions which delegate powers onto the executive in the context of sovereign debt that go beyond what is regarded as acceptable by Article 76, particularly where the delegation is so broad that it in fact delegates onto the executive not only the power to carry out and regulate the details of policies adopted by Congress in the context of sovereign debt, but instead authorizes the executive to determine these policies itself. Unfortunately, the courts did not reach a decision on these issues in any of the judicial proceedings that were initiated over the years to prevent the various governments from performing acts aimed at paying, renegotiating or restructuring the country's foreign debt, or contracting new debt for this purpose, until Congress establishes the real amount of the debt and settles its payment with regard to the findings in *Olmos*.[167]

---

166   For a general discussion of the reviewability of the Budget Acts see Horacio Corti (2002), at 58 and 80.

167   For an extract of one of the petitions made to the courts to this effect see www. lanuevahuella.con.ar/temasnacionales/Acerbi_10.htm.

Chapter Six

Substantive Constitutional Limits with Regard to Sovereign Debt

We have seen that in Argentina, the constitution sets a formal and procedural framework with regard to the taking up of sovereign debt, regulating such issues as which organ is competent to contract sovereign debt and whether this needs to be done in a certain form in order to be constitutional. Some constitutions, including that of Argentina, in addition determine the purposes for which debt can only validly be contracted, and set limits as to the amount of debt that can be taken up. Constitutional and international human rights obligations, in particular obligations to protect economic, social and cultural rights, might also limit the freedom to contract or repay debt.

1 Purposes for which debt can be contracted

In Argentina, the Constitution does not include any provisions restricting the amount of debt that can be taken up. However, it contains an article that specifically deals with the purposes for which debts can be contracted. Article 4 of the Constitution, states that:

> The Federal Government provides for the expenditures of the Nation with the funds of the National Treasury ... of whatever loans and credit transactions Congress may order in case of national emergencies or for enterprises of national interest.

Thus, not only does the Argentinian Constitution regulate which organ has the competence to take up foreign debt (Article 75(4)), but it moreover defines the purposes for which this can be done. Congress is accordingly not free to take up debt for whichever reasons it sees fit, but can only do so within the limits of, and for the purposes laid out in Article 4.[1] The common justifications given for limiting the contracting of loans to these two situations is that in emergency situations which cannot be overcome with ordinary resources, considerations of solidarity justify that future generations can exceptionally be burdened with the repayment of such loans. With regard to the second purpose sanctioned by Article 4, where borrowed money is invested in projects which are intended to bring in future funds, it is not perceived

---

1   Sabsay and Onaindia (2004), at 32.

as problematic to burden future generations with repaying these loans, as the debt is then repaid by those generations that benefit from the projects.[2]

In 1897, Article 4 seems to have been regarded as an important and sensible provision. At least this is the impression one gets when looking at González's warning that:

> The abuse of the power to take up money on the credit of the state is one of the most serious that governments can commit, because it not only destroys the productive force of the people and the internal welfare, but can also put the reputation and honour of the Republic before other Nations at risk.[3]

Almost one hundred years later, in 1993, Ekmekdjian analysed the usual practice displayed by Argentinian governments as follows:

> In present times, the massive and indiscriminate use of public loans ... has distorted the clear constitutional precepts ... [L]oans are automatically renewed and ... used ... to settle the expenditures of ordinary administration, even without the prior authorization which Congress needs to give. ... It is normal that state dependencies 'pay' their debt ... with titles of public debt, transforming an administrative into a financial debt, which is an open and clear violation of the analysed constitutional precepts, unless it can be demonstrated that the supply of office utilities qualifies as 'enterprise of national interest.'[4]

And in 2003, Gelli stated that while in 1853, to contract public debt was intended to be an extraordinary measure, it since turned into an ordinary means to finance public expenditures.[5] It is surprising that even though there seems to be a clear understanding that the current practice violates the Constitution, constitutional law scholars who mention the unconstitutionality of current and past borrowing polices in the light of Article 4 do so only in passing, and without analysing the potential consequences of this for the legal status of such debts. Thus, it seems as if the same Article that was given such an important role over one hundred years ago, now, precisely in times of a debt crisis it was aimed to avoid, seems to have faded into insignificance.

In order to assess whether a provision such as Article 4 of the Argentinian Constitution is ignored or regarded as obsolete mainly because it has been disregarded so consistently; because it is no longer in touch with regular practice; or because it does not provide the adequate means to regulate the debt problem, it might be interesting to look at another country, Germany, which has a different, but nevertheless in some respects comparable provision in its Constitution. Article 115 of the German Constitution states that:

> (1) The borrowing of funds and the assumption of pledges, guarantees or other commitments, as a result of which expenditure may be incurred in future fiscal years, shall require federal legislative authorization indicating, or permitting computation of, the

---

2   Ekmekdjian (1993), at 294; González (1959), at 438; Villegas, Bruno and Piaggio (2004), at 1025; Dalla Vía (2004), at 303.
3   González (1959), at 439.
4   Ekmekdjian (1993), at 294; see also Dalla Vía (2001/2002), at 548–549.
5   Gelli (2003), at 40.

maximum amount involved. Revenue obtained by borrowing shall not exceed the total expenditures for investments provided for in the budget; exceptions shall be permissible only to avert a disturbance of the overall economic equilibrium. Details shall be regulated by federal legislation.

As is the case with Article 4 of the Argentinian Constitution, we are here faced with a constitutional provision which confers the competence of taking up debt on the federal legislative, and which at the same time sets some substantive limits to restrict this power. In the German constitutional discussion, one of the reasons given for the constitutional requirement of legislative approval of the debt is that of transparency,[6] another the fact that parliamentary involvement is regarded as the best guarantee for a debate of the underlying policies.[7] The latter argument seems to stand in stark contrast to the approach adopted in Argentina in the context of Article 75(7) of the Argentinian Constitution, as obviously in Germany it is felt that legislative involvement in debt related policies is essential, whereas in Argentina it is regarded by many as impossible.[8] However, this difference loses some of its significance when considering that in Germany, Article 115 is usually only applied to new credits, but not to cases where new debt is contracted in order to pay existing debt.[9]

As to the content of the provision, unlike Article 4 of the Argentinian Constitution, Article 115 of the German Constitution accepts that the taking up of loans is a normal way of funding state activities, but sets a limit in that the credits taken up in each financial year may not surmount the funds dedicated to investments in the budget act of that very same year. As long as the new debts are below the budget set for investments, the legislative has a large discretion to take up debt. However, if the debt exceeds the investment budget, the contracting of debt, as well as the budget act itself, is only constitutional if, exceptionally, the taking up of the debts is necessary to avert disturbances of the financial equilibrium.[10] The importance of the provision accordingly lies in the fact that it sets a presumption of unconstitutionality which the legislative needs to rebut, and it can only do so in the very limited circumstances in which the taking up of debt above the investment budget can exceptionally be justified with reference to the economic equilibrium of the country.[11] At least in theory, 'Article 115 binds the credit contract, to be entered into by the executive, to the budgetary planning reserved to the legislature, thus preserving the legislative function as the planning, future-oriented authority.'[12]

It is interesting to note that in Germany, the constitutionality debate surrounding sovereign debt is frequently linked to a discussion of concepts of democracy, as it is argued that governments need to show some reluctance and self-restraint in taking up debt, because they thereby create obligations which bind future governments and

---

6   BVerfGE 79, 311, 343 (1989); Paul Kirchhof (1986), at 346.
7   Bonner Kommentar-Hoefling/Rixen (2003), at para. 110 to Article 115; Paul Kirchhof (1986), at 358.
8   See Chapter Five, 3.1, supra.
9   Ferdinand Kirchhof (2002), at 1575.
10   Birk (1984), at 748.
11   Ibid., at 749.
12   Paul Kirchhof (1986), at 349.

inevitably limit their discretion.[13] However, this is controversial, as others object that the constitutional principle of democracy cannot impose a prohibition on the current government to bind future governments, as the fulfilment of its constitutional tasks often requires that a government take decisions that have consequences beyond its term of office.[14] However, it seems nevertheless uncontroversial that the main purpose behind the substantive limits set in Article 115 is to prevent the creation of an excessive debt burden for future generations.[15] Here, Article 115 needs to be seen in conjunction with Article 109(2) of the German Constitution which states that 'The Federation and the Länder shall have due regard in their budget management to the requirements of overall economic equilibrium.'[16] Article 109(2) is interpreted so as to impose a prohibition on over-indebting the country[17] and is thought to be violated if the debt reaches such an amount that it practically paralyses all economic and financial state activities and excludes any governmental room for manoeuvre in this respect.[18] The question remains whether constitutional provisions can achieve this goal, particularly in the context of financial crises.

In 1989, the German Federal Constitutional Court had to deal with some of the constitutional issues surrounding the above-discussed provisions of the German Constitution in norm control proceedings (proceedings in which the constitutionality of legislation is questioned), initiated by the opposition in the German Parliament against the Federal Budget Act 1981. When defining the situations in which loans can be constitutional even if they exceed the investment budget, the Court highlighted that it is not sufficient that it can be shown that such loans have become necessary because of a disturbance of the overall economic equilibrium. Instead, the legislative has the additional burden of demonstrating that the equilibrium is seriously disturbed and that the taking up of these loans is intended to restore the equilibrium as well as a suitable means to achieve this purpose.[19] Thus, the legislative needs to be able to provide a convincing explanation of how the taking up of loans will restore the economic equilibrium.[20]

Another interesting feature is the decision of the Constitutional Court of Berlin, again taken in the context of norm control proceedings initiated by the opposition, this time against the Berlin Budget Act 2002/2003. After a lengthy discussion the Court declared the Act to be unconstitutional and void, mainly based on the argument that the legislative had not sufficiently justified the suitability of taking up debts

---

13   See for example Birk (1984), at 749 with further references.

14   BVerfGE 79, 311, 339–340 and 345 (1989); Heun (1985), at 25–26; Höfling (1998), at 95–96.

15   VerfGH Berlin DVBl 2004, 308, 309; Heun (1985), at 15 with reference to the predominant opinion among German constitutionalists.

16   In Argentina, the task of assessing the impact of an external debt operation on the balance of payments lies with the Central Bank which needs to submit a report to this effect according to Article 60 of Act 24.156.

17   Birk (1984), at 748.

18   Janson (1983), at 143; Wendt and Elicker (2001), at 500–501.

19   BVerfGE 79, 311, 339–340 (1989); VerfGH Berlin DVBl 2004, 308; but see Janssen (1989), at 618.

20   Arndt (1990), at 346; Rossi (2005), at 270.

beyond the investment budget to overcome the extreme economic emergency the Land found itself in. However, the Court decided to declare the Act void only from the moment of issuing its decision, which means that during the remainder of the budget year no decisions could be based on that law, but instead had to be taken by the means of emergency powers. With regard to decisions already taken on the basis of the Act, the Court felt that in the interest of legal certainty and predictability they should stand, and therefore did not let the unconstitutionality of the Act stand in the way of its applicability in the past.[21] Given that emergency powers are much more limited than ordinary budgetary powers, to declare the Budget Act null and void and thereby to reduce the political leeway of the legislative might be a potential means to enforce compliance with constitutional precepts.[22]

It is submitted that a well-thought through constitutional provision which sets limits to the debt a country can take up, imposes a requirement of justification onto the legislative and makes debt decisions to some extent subject to judicial control, is, in principle, desirable in order to limit the debt a country can take up.[23] However, it cannot be ignored that even in Germany, compliance with this provision creates serious problems in the current financial and economic crisis of the country.[24] It might then be argued that constitutional limits to sovereign debt can only have a very limited effect. Moreover, Argentina's and Germany's situations in the context of sovereign debt are hardly comparable. However, it is submitted that particularly in a country such as Argentina that faces a serious debt crisis and as a consequence of this finds its sovereignty in economic, financial and political matters significantly reduced, constitutional provisions limiting the government's leeway to indebt the country, at least if taken seriously and, if need be, enforced by the courts, might not only help to avoid future debt crises, but furthermore assist in setting limits with regard to the demands foreign creditors can reasonably make, thereby reducing outside pressure if it can be shown that the demands cannot lawfully be fulfilled.

However, in this context, it would be of the utmost importance that the contracting of new debt in order to service old debt is not excluded from the relevant provisions. This issue has not received a lot of attention in Argentina, but has been debated within the framework of the German Constitution, and the predominant opinion in Germany seems to be that while loans contracted for the purposes of refinancing existing loans are regarded as 'borrowing' in the meaning of Article 115, so that a legislative authorization for their contracting is required, the limitation of Article 115(1)(2) only applies to new credits, but not to debt refinancing.[25] Refinancing credits largely seem to be regarded as financially neutral, as they neither bring in fresh money, nor affect the amount of public debt, and instead merely prolong the

---

21 VerfGH Berlin DVBl 2004, 308, 317. For a general discussion of why it might be the better approach to declare the unconstitutionality of budget acts as of the date of the court decision and not retrospectively, see Maunz (2005), para. 36 to Article 93.

22 Rossi (2005), at 272.

23 See also Richard (2005), who argues at 21 that external debt should only be taken up for productive purposes; Villegas (2002), at 142.

24 See the debate surrounding the constitutionality of the 2006 budget of the Merkel government, for example *Süddeutsche Zeitung*, 29 March 2006.

25 For an overview of the discussion see Lappin (1994), at 139–141.

maturity of existing debt.[26] However, it is submitted that to prolong the maturity of existing loans does have an effect on the amount of public debt, as the debt is then not cancelled as planned and the repayment obligations are projected further into the future, which might potentially limit the financial leeway of future governments.[27] This could also have an impact on obligations regarding the payment of interest. It is then submitted that the purpose behind Article 115, that is to limit the indebtedness of the state,[28] can better be obtained if debt refinancing is equally included in the balance between debts and investment expenses.[29]

This consideration can equally be applied to the issue of how Article 4 of the Argentinian Constitution should be interpreted.[30] If the Constitution, for the reasons mentioned above, limits the contracting of public debt to specific purposes, to exclude debt refinancing that involves new loans and therefore creates a higher debt burden, at least with regard to interest payment, without bringing new money into the country, is difficult to justify. What is more important in the Argentinian context is whether these constitutional limitations should be extended to debt restructurings, which, as was seen, almost always bring partial present relief at the cost of high interest payment in the future and/or acceptance of the debt stock way beyond its market value. It is difficult to conceptualize the applicability of Article 4 to debt restructurings, as long as they do not require the taking up of new debt in the form of refinancing loans in order to carry out the operation, although in the course of the legal challenge of Cavallo's *megacanje* of 2001, it was argued that by resulting in an overall increase of the debt stock, the restructuring operation amounted to the taking up of new debt, an argument rejected by the court.[31]

In *Brunicardi*, the Supreme Court mentioned Article 4, and suggested that Regulation 1334/82 dealt with loans in the meaning of that article.[32] Regulation 1334/82 was the legal instrument by the means of which the military government had assumed the private foreign debt of Argentinian companies as public debt by unilaterally issuing government bonds which changed the maturity of the original debt. It is difficult to learn much from the Courts cryptic words with regard to the scope of application of Article 4. All the Court suggested was that the loan in question was a loan 'which is included in the generic concept of funds of the National Treasury, namely "loans and credit transactions Congress may order in case of national emergencies or for enterprises of national interest (Article 4)."' While this shows that the Supreme Court thought that Article 4 was applicable, which is a sign that it did not regard the provision as obsolete, it is difficult to square this with the

---

26   Höfling (1998), at 173.
27   Lappin (1994), at 178.
28   BVerfGE 79, 311, 379 (1989); Lappin (1994), at 142–143.
29   Ferdinand Kirchhof (2002), at 1575.
30   According to García Lema (2004), Article 4 of the Argentinian Constitution does not
      distinguish between new loans and those that are taken up in order to refinance existing
      debt and is applicable to both situations, at 956.
31   "Cavallo, Domingo Felipe y otros s/defraudación contra la administración pública"
      (2003).
32   "Brunicardi, Adriano Caredio c/ Estado Nacional (BCRA) s/ cobro SC B592 XXIV", 24
      February 1997, Fallos 319:2886, at para. 6.

outcome in *Brunicardi*. The Court regarded the debt that was assumed by Regulation 1334/82 as binding, and not as unconstitutional, even though there was no indication that this debt was taken up for one of the purposes mentioned in Article 4.

Coming back to the analysis of the constitutionality of the debt taken up by the military regime, it was seen in Chapter Two that according to a World Bank estimate, 44 per cent of the debt taken up by Argentina between 1975 and 1983 was contracted to finance capital flight; 33 per cent to pay interest to foreign banks, and 23 per cent to pay for arms and non-declared imports.[33] In the light of the preceding analysis of Article 4, it seems difficult to argue that any of this debt was then contracted for the purposes mentioned in that provision. Thus, if Article 4 were applied instead of ignored, it would follow that this debt was not contracted for constitutionally acceptable purposes.

2 Economic and social rights considerations

Economic and social rights considerations might also have a role to play in the context of the constitutionality of debt policies, both with regard to the use of borrowed money, and more generally with regard to borrowing and repayment policies. According to the Argentinian Constitution, all acts, legislative or executive, that violate constitutional rights and principles, including social and other human rights, are unconstitutional. Argentina not only ratified the relevant international treaties that require the protection of economic, social and cultural rights, but moreover gives some of these treaties, including the International Covenant on Economic, Social and Cultural Rights (ISCESR), the International Covenant on Civil and Political Rights (ICCPR), the Universal Declaration of Human Rights (UDHR), and the Convention on the Rights of the Child (CRC), constitutional status (Article 75(22) of the Argentinian Constitution). This means that all state acts must not only be compatible with the human rights guarantees included in the Argentinian Constitution itself, but also with the provisions of those international treaties to which the Constitution granted constitutional status. Thus, a state act or omission that violates any of the obligations imposed on the state by one of these treaties, or a right therein awarded, not only violates the country's obligations under international law, but is also unconstitutional.[34] Social rights considerations can accordingly not be ignored when the government enters into international agreements, when Parliament enacts legislation implementing the measures agreed therein, or when government formulates its economic and financial policy. Before looking at the specific relation between economic and social rights and the constitutionality of sovereign debt, some general issues need to be introduced.

At the international level, various documents postulate economic and social rights obligations of states. The UDHR, for example, grants the individual the right to social security and the realization of 'the economic, social and cultural rights indispensable for his dignity and the free development of his personality' (Article

---

33   World Bank, Economic Memorandum on Argentina (1985), at 17–19.
34   Abramovich and Courtis (2002), at 72.

22), the right to an adequate standard of living, 'including food, clothing, housing and medical care and necessary social services', as well as the right to social benefits in cases of need (Article 25), and the right to education (Article 26). Comparable rights can be found in the CRC.[35] The ICESCR guarantees the right to social security (Article 9), to social protection (Article 10), to an adequate standard of living and to food (Article 11); to the highest attainable standard of health (Article 12), and to education (Article 13).

While it already follows from the international economic and social rights obligations assumed by the country that governmental policies must respect economic and social rights, their constitutional status adds a crucial dimension, and that is that of constitutional review and justiciability. In Argentina, the acts of all organs of the state are subject to constitutional review by the courts.[36] Consequently, the courts have the role and the power to control the compatibility of all decisions of the executive and the legislative with the human rights guarantees contained in the National Constitution, and also in those international human rights documents that have been given constitutional status. This raises interesting legal questions in the context of the country's policies regarding its sovereign debt, as the constitutionality of any act in this context, from agreements with creditors or legislation regulating debt restructurings, refinancing or repayment, to the act of payment itself, can potentially be challenged in court. Also, to the limited extent that claims for debt repayment against Argentina might be heard by Argentinian courts, this could bear on the enforceability of such claims.

In the context of the debt taken up by the Argentinian military regime, it needs to be noted that Argentina became a member to the ICESCR only in 1986, that is after the return to democracy, and that international human rights treaties, including the ICESCR, only received constitutional status with the constitutional reform of 1994. However, while constitutional issues surrounding the link between debt and economic and social rights can then only to a limited extent influence the constitutionality of the original debt, they are nevertheless important in the context of an analysis of the debt inherited from the military regime, as they might have a part to play in the context of the recognition of that debt by the democratic follow up governments.

2.1 *Debt policies as violation of international economic and social rights obligations*[37]

In Chapter Two, it was demonstrated that there are various facets to the relationship between sovereign debt and the protection of economic and social rights in a debtor

---

35   For example the right to health (Article 24), the right to social security (Article 25), the right to an adequate standard of living (Article 27), and the right to education (Article 28).

36   Zarini (1999), at 87–93.

37   Given that the link between debt and economic and social rights is more obvious than that between debt and cultural rights, the following part will concentrate on economic and social rights, but this is not meant to imply that debt does not also have an impact on the protection of cultural rights.

state.[38] A legal analysis of the potential consequences of this relationship requires an examination of whether any of the effects of debt contracting or repayment amounts to an actual violation of economic and social rights. Here, it becomes necessary to take a brief look at how economic and social rights work, and under what circumstances it can be said that they are violated. Economic and social rights impose on states the duty to respect, protect and fulfil them. The duty to respect prevents the state from interfering with an economic or social right the rights holder already enjoys, so that it would, for example, be violated if a state expropriated land that provides the main source of alimentation for the landowners without providing an adequate alternative. The duty to protect requires that the state prevents third parties from interfering with social rights held by others, for example where, in the above example, persons other than the state were to interfere with the land and its use by the landowners. The most far-reaching duty is the duty to fulfil, as it imposes on the state an obligation 'to take appropriate legislative, administrative, budgetary, judicial and other measures towards the full realization of such rights. Thus, the failure of States to provide essential primary health care to those in need may amount to a violation.'[39]

Particularly with regard to the duty to fulfil which requires the provision of resources, it is difficult to define a standard according to which it can be judged whether or not the steps undertaken by a state were, in fact, sufficient to meet its economic and social rights obligations. In order to give economic and social rights, and the corresponding state obligations, a more specific content, the UN Committee on Economic, Social and Cultural Rights produces general comments in which the content of different rights is outlined.[40] When determining the content and scope of economic and social rights, it needs to be borne in mind that according to Article 2 of the ICESCR, each state 'undertakes to take steps ... to the maximum of its available resources, with a view of achieving progressively the full realization of the rights recognized in the present Covenant.' Given the huge inequality of resources among states, the content of the obligation varies according to the economic possibilities of each member state.[41] However, all social rights have a minimum core that binds all states, so that states that fall below this minimum standard would automatically be in violation of the relevant right.[42] In this respect, the UN Committee on Economic, Social and Cultural Rights declared that states in which an important number of individuals are deprived of essential food stuff, primary health care, shelter and basic housing, or the most basic forms of education, are *prima facie* not complying with their obligations under the Covenant.[43] Beyond the minimum standard, the assessment of whether or not a state is in violation of its economic and social rights

---

38   Chapter Two, 7, supra.
39   Maastricht Guidelines on Economic, Social and Cultural Rights (1997), para. 6. See also Hunt (1996), at 31–33; Abramovich and Courtis (2002), at 30.
40   Rosas and Scheinin (2001), at 427. See, for example, General Comment No. 15 (2002): The right to water, E/C.12/2002/11; General Comment No. 14 (2000): The right to the highest attainable standard of health, E/C12/2000/4. While the comments issued by the Committee are not binding, they are highly persuasive.
41   Eide (2001), at 27.
42   See, for example, Alston (1987), at 352–353.
43   General Observations No. 3, 1990; see also Maastricht Guidelines (1997), para. 9.

obligations would depend on the resources available to it[44] and on the requirement of non-regression below the protection already granted.[45] With regard to the latter, the Committee explained that every measure that is deliberatively regressive needs to be thoroughly justified with reference to the totality of rights protected by the ICESCR.[46]

Applying these principles, it can first of all be stated that in many debtor countries, indicators such as high poverty and destitution rates and the lack of access to basic health care, education etc. for significant parts of the population, point towards a *prima facie* violation of economic and social rights obligations by those states, as they seem to be falling even below the minimum standard of protection. However, important for present purposes is not the general question of whether or not debtor states are in violation of their economic and social rights obligations. Instead, what is at issue is the specific question of whether to indebt a country and/or to repay debts in cases in which either not even the core of economic and social rights is protected, or where, as in countries such as Argentina, in the course of an economic crisis the economic and social protection of the population decreases dramatically, would this amount to a violation of economic and social rights obligations? The Maastricht Guidelines on Economic, Social and Cultural Rights[47] suggest in this respect that:

> 13. In determining which actions or omissions amount to a violation of an economic, social or cultural right, it is important to distinguish the inability from the unwillingness of a State to comply with its treaty obligations. A State claiming that it is unable to carry out its obligation for reasons beyond its control has the burden of proving that this is the case. A temporary closure of an educational institution due to an earthquake, for instance, would be a circumstance beyond the control of the State, while the elimination of a social security scheme without an adequate replacement programme could be an example of unwillingness by the State to fulfil its obligations.

Debtor states could then try to argue that the reason for falling below the minimum protection of economic and social rights and/or regressing on their protection was economic inability to meet its obligations. However, it is submitted that to the extent that a country that falls foul of its economic and social rights obligations at the same time services its debts, this is based on a decision to prioritize contractual obligations over social rights, which is not a reason beyond the government's control. A possible counterargument could be that to fulfil contractual obligations is not a matter of choice, and that the resources that are necessary to service debt do not form part of the 'available resources', given that the state is under an obligation to dedicate them to debt repayment. However, this interpretation would overlook that being under a contractual obligation does not mean that the funds that need to be dedicated to the fulfilment of the obligation are therefore not at the free disposition of the debtor. Instead, while it might give rise to claims for breach of contract if a debtor does not

---

44   Skogly (2001), at 151.
45   See also Hunt (2002), at 115.
46   General Observation No. 3, point 9.
47   Again, this is not a binding document, but instead no more than a persuasive statement on how the ICESCR should be understood and implemented.

fulfil their contractual obligations, the debtor is nevertheless free to use the funds for whichever purpose they see fit. If funds owed as debts were not part of the available resources in the meaning of the ICESCR, then it would not even be necessary for the state to justify giving precedence to debt repayment over social programmes etc., and as a consequence, states could easily contract out of their social rights obligations by simply entering into financial transactions by which the country's resources would be bound. As a result, contractual obligations would be given a higher importance than economic and social rights, which is not in accordance with the supreme value of human rights protection in international law.[48]

As a temporary conclusion, it could be said that at least to the extent that debt related policies adversely affect the protection of the core of economic and social rights, or lead to a regression of the protection awarded, they are in violation of the relevant government's economic and social rights obligations under international law. Indeed, it could be argued that debt repayment made by a country which lacks sufficient funds to guarantee both the servicing of its sovereign debt and an adequate protection of the economic and social rights of the people always amounts to a violation of economic and social rights. The same conclusion would apply to the implementation of structural adjustment policies that result in a regression on economic and social rights protection. Indeed, as the UN High Commission on Human Rights rightly emphasized, the economic and social rights of the people of the debtor states 'cannot be subordinated to the implementation of structural adjustment policies and economic reforms arising from the debt.'[49] Countries are moreover under the obligation to assert and defend these rights in their negotiations with IFIs and other creditors.[50]

To summarize, if debtor states cannot meet in full both their debt servicing and their economic and social rights obligations, so that it needs to be decided how the state would have to set its policies in order to resolve the conflict between its contractual obligations towards the creditors to repay loans, on the one hand, and economic and social rights obligations towards the people of the country, on the other, at least with regard to the core of social rights and the prohibition of non-regression, a debtor state would, in principle, have to prioritize the protection of economic and social rights over other obligations in order to meet its obligations under international law.

---

48   See Friedman (2000), at 198, with reference to the UN Charter.

49   UN Commission on Human Rights, Resolution 1999/22, 23 April 1999.

50   See the observations made by Sadi in the 33rd meeting of the Committee for Economic, Social and Cultural Rights on 25 November 1999, E/C.12/1999/SR.33, at para. 13. See also para. 15(j) of the Maastricht Guidelines. See also Hunt (2003), at 146, who formulates this not as an obligation of the debtor state, but instead as a possible policy approach.

2.2 *Constitutional dimension of the relationship between sovereign debt and economic and social rights*

In the Argentinian domestic context, this suggestion received the support of Supreme Court judges, who stated in *Galli*[51] that while contractual debt repayment obligations usually have to be fulfilled,[52] this obligation finds its limits where the state would otherwise not be able to meet the essential needs of its citizens and minimum human rights standards the upholding of which is required by international treaties and the constitution itself.[53] Consequently, at the national level, not only can the state decide to prioritize the fulfilment of constitutional obligations over contractual obligations, but it is even under an obligation to do so where these minimum standards are at risk. One problem that might arise in this context is that of the extent to which the government could defend policies, such as measures implementing SAPs,[54] but also the repayment or restructuring of debts, even where this has the short-term effect of deteriorating the economic and social rights protection available to the citizens, on the basis that this is the only, the best or at least a reasonable measure to guarantee a medium or long-term improvement of the social and economic situation of the country. While governments usually have a broad leeway when formulating and determining their economic and social policies, it is submitted that in the light of the obligations imposed on states by the provisions of the ICESCR, the reasonableness assessment according to which judicial control of such policies can be exercised[55] needs to take place within the framework created by the ICESCR. This means that a measure cannot be regarded as reasonable merely on the grounds that it is plausible that it will be successful in achieving a long-term improvement of the country's economic and social situation. Instead, it needs to be taken into account whether the adverse short-term effects violate the minimum standards required.[56] If that is the case,

---

51　"Galli, Hugo y Otro c/ PEN – s/ Amparo Ley 25.561", 6 April 2005.

52　Indeed, in Argentina, it is well established that contractual rights are included in the constitutional protection awarded by Article 17 to property rights; see, for example, "Bourdieu, Pedro E. v Municipalidad de la Capital Federal", Supreme Court, 16 December 1925, Fallos 145:307, at 307–308; "Badaro, Adolfo Valentín c/ ANSeS s/ reajustes varios", Supreme Court, 8 August 2006, at paras 4 and 11; Sabsay and Onaindia (2004), at 69.

53　"Galli, Hugo y Otro c/ PEN – s/ Amparo Ley 25.561", 6 April 2005, per Justices Zaffaroni and Lorenzetti, at paras 12–14.

54　For a discussion of the relevance of economic and social rights in this context see, for example, Cheru (1999); Figueredo (2000); Morgan-Foster (2003); Anghie (2000). See also UN Commission on Human Rights Resolution 2002/29, 'Effects of structural adjustment policies and foreign debt on the full enjoyment of all human rights, particularly economic, social and cultural rights', at para. 9.

55　See, for example, "Peralta y otro v Nación Argentina (Ministerio de Economía – BCRA)", Fallos 313:1513 (1990), at para. 48; "Prodelco v Poder Ejecutivo Nacional", Fallos 321:1253 (1998), at para. 7. See also Bidart Campos (1996), at 92–94; Cabral and Maljar (2002), at 1540–1552.

56　See also Abramovich and Courtis (2002), at 72 and 96–97; Pazmiño Freire and Kumin (2001), at 154.

the relevant measure would violate the constitutional and international obligation to protect economic and social rights and therefore be unconstitutional. Thus, it can be said that measures that temporarily sacrifice the minimum core of economic and social rights obligations would not be in compliance with the international obligations under the ICESCR and must therefore be regarded as unreasonable, even if the measure was aimed at the medium or long-term improvement of this right. The state has more discretion, on the other hand, if policy measures temporarily restrict the enjoyment of economic and social rights beyond the core.[57]

In the Argentinian context, an allegation that debt repayment and debt restructurings violate social rights can moreover be based on the requirement of non-regression. As the UN Committee on Economic, Social and Cultural Rights explained, every measure that is deliberatively regressive needs to be thoroughly justified with reference to the totality of rights protected by the ICESCR.[58] It could then be argued that where an act or norm has a regressive effect on the protection of economic and social rights, there is a presumption of unreasonableness and therefore invalidity or unconstitutionality, which the state would have the burden to rebut.[59] What the state would need to show is the strict necessity of the measure, which requires its imperative need, the unavailability of less restrictive alternatives, and that it pursues a legitimate state goal.[60] The requirement that the justification must refer to other rights protected in the ICESCR means that considerations of general public policy, fiscal discipline or other financial or economic goals would not be admissible reasons for cutting down the protection of economic and social rights.[61]

Where the constitutionality of specific acts in the context of sovereign debt, for example a particular instance of debt repayment or debt restructuring, is at issue, the incompatibility of such an act with the economic and social rights obligations of the state would seem to depend on whether the specific act has an adverse impact on the constitutionally required protection of economic and social rights. It is submitted that it will only in rare cases be possible to demonstrate a direct link between a specific debt related act and the violation of the obligation to respect or protect economic and social rights. However, one example of such a case is the Argentinian Zero Deficit Act (Law 25.453), which was enacted in July 2001, that is before the Argentinian crisis exploded, but when the country was already in a very grave economic and social situation. This statute aimed to implement a policy according to which every month the effective tax income would first be used to service the interests of the debt, and the remaining balance would then be dedicated to other public expenditures.[62] It empowered the executive to reduce, *inter alia*, pensions and the salaries of public employees if public spending exceeded the State's activa. In August 2001, the executive made use of this empowerment and reduced, retrospectively as of 1 July

---

57   For a discussion see also Skogly (2001), at 152.
58   General Comments No. 3, point 9.
59   Abramovich and Courtis (2002), at 102.
60   Ibid., at 109. See also General Comments No. 3 point 9; No. 13 point 45; and No. 14 point 32.
61   Abramovich and Courtis (2001), at 110.
62   Kulfas and Schorr (2003), at 46; Kanenguiser (2003), at 173.

2001, both salaries and pensions by 13 per cent.[63] Here, we have a case in which a state decides to cut down on the protection of economic and social rights in order to meet debt repayment obligations and achieve a balanced budget. Thus, this is a clear case of a redistribution of funds for the purpose of debt repayment. It can then hardly be said that the regression of the economic and social rights protection took place for reasons beyond the control of the government. The statute was struck down as unconstitutional by the Supreme Court.[64] This was partly based on considerations that resemble those of economic and social rights protection, as the court relied on the fact that the statute adversely affected salaries and pensions which constituted income that guaranteed the subsistence of the individuals concerned.[65]

In most cases of policies or legislation in the context of sovereign debt, it will be more difficult to establish a link between the act or policy and a violation of economic and social rights. An attempt to achieve this was, however, for example made in a petition that challenged Argentina's debt restructurings in 2005 as unconstitutional. The petition, *inter alia*, relied on the argument that the measure would result in social rights violations. In this respect, it was submitted that: 'If according to statistics, there are more than 15 million poor and indigent people, and the unemployment rate fluctuates between 14 and 18 per cent, it is easy to demonstrate what it would mean if these sums could be used to improve the general situation of the community.'[66] It was further argued that by dedicating huge amounts of money to financing the debt swap, the government would be in violation of its international and constitutional obligations, as there was no possibility that social rights could be respected and fulfilled without these funds.[67] Similar arguments were made when questioning that the payment of the debt with the IMF was compatible with the state's social rights obligations.[68]

Even though it seems plausible that the Argentinian state is, in fact, in violation of its social rights obligations towards quite significant parts of the population, particularly in some of the poorer provinces, the statements in the petition with regard to the necessary link between the shortcomings in the social rights protection and the challenged acts are rather vague. While it seems logical that money that goes into debt repayment cannot at the same time be used for the protection and realization of social rights, this does not necessarily mean that there are no other funds that might instead be used or redistributed in order to achieve an adequate level of social rights protection. It is submitted that the argument in favour of unconstitutionality would be much stronger if it could be demonstrated that the funds in question form such a large part of the state budget that it is unlikely, if not impossible, that the social rights obligations of the state can be met with the remaining budget. In such a case,

---

63   Decreto 1.060/01.
64   "Tobar, Leonidas c Estado Nacional. M°Defensa – Contaduría General del Ejército – Ley 25.453 s/amparo"; La Ley, 2002-E, 428.
65   Ibid., at para. 16. See also Abramovich (2002).
66   Causa No. 42.170/2004, "Olmos, Alejandro E. Y otro c/Gobierno Nacional s/ amparo", Juzgado en lo ContenciosoAdministrativo Federal No 3, 28 December 2004, unpublished.
67   Ibid.
68   See www.enredando.org.ar/noticias_desarrollo.shtml?x=27265.

it seems justified to apply a presumption that the challenged act would, in fact, have a detrimental effect on the social rights protection, which the state could rebut by demonstrating which other funds are available and will be dedicated to giving social rights the necessary protection.

The problem here then is that the alleged unconstitutionality of the challenged acts is not based on a direct link between social rights protection and the acts that prioritize debt repayment, but that the argument is rather built on the fact that as long as social rights violations occur, it would not be constitutional to use funds for purposes that are of lesser constitutional importance, including debt repayment. But this would also apply to many other state expenditures, and it would have to be left to the legislature to decide which funds to redistribute in order to comply with the state's social rights obligations, as it is not the task of the courts to make specific policy decisions and tell the other constitutional organs how to allocate the budget. Indeed, courts should do no more than outline where the state falls short of the requirements of economic and social rights obligations, and which considerations need to be taken into account in order to redress this.[69]

Another important point that needs to be considered in this context is what the consequences would be if a petition for a declaration of unconstitutionality were to be successful. If, for example, the debt restructuring performed in 2005 had been declared unconstitutional, the situation that existed before would have been reinstated, that is the state would have faced the extensive debt repayment obligations on which it had defaulted and on which interest kept accruing. It is then submitted that a declaration of unconstitutionality of a particular act with regard to debt repayment would only have a very limited effect on the overall problem of the relationship between debt and economic and social rights, as the real problem goes deeper and affects more general issues: that of how to strike a balance between the conflicting interests with regard to all obligations the state faces, not just those that were part of the individual act to which the challenge refers; that of the extent to which contractual obligations need to be honoured where the economic and social rights situation of the country is far from ideal; and that of where to set the limit below which social rights protection cannot be compromised for the benefit of creditors. The debt restructuring of 2005 was an attempt to find such a balance, and the government perceived it as achieving an important reduction of the overall debt. While this is debated and debatable,[70] it is questionable whether a court is well placed to declare the unconstitutionality of such a political decision based on economic and social rights violations, given the extreme complexity of the assessment of what the impact of the particular measure on economic and social rights would really be.

It then seems that to challenge the constitutionality of particular acts or policies in the context of debt repayment based on economic and social rights arguments will only in very rare cases be successful, namely where either a measure directly violates the obligation to respect economic and social rights, as in the Zero Deficit Act scenario, or where it can exceptionally be demonstrated that a measure will violate the obligation to fulfil economic and social rights, given the impact of the

---

69   Abramovich and Courtis (2002), at 167 and 250.
70   See, for example, Giuliano (2006).

measure of debt repayment or restructuring on the overall budget and consequently the availability of funds for the protection of at least the minimum core of social rights.

3 Impact of substantive considerations on debt related acts and policies

In this chapter it could be seen that some constitutions not only set formal requirements with regard to the taking up of foreign debt, but also contain substantive provisions that have an impact on the policies that can be adopted in this context. These substantive provisions can become effective at different stages. First of all, they need to be taken into account when debt is taken up, so that in the case of Argentina, debt that is not contracted for purposes that comply with Article 4 of the Constitution, or that violates economic, social or other human rights obligations of the state, would be unconstitutional, even if the debt were incurred in compliance with the formal and procedural requirements of the Constitution. However, in the specific context of the Argentinian debt taken up by the military regime, this applies only to the prerequisites of Article 4. With regard to economic and social rights considerations, on the other hand, at least the main international treaty guaranteeing the protection of economic and social rights, that is the ICESCR, had not been ratified by Argentina at the relevant time, neither did it enjoy constitutional status.

In the context of the debt of the military regime, another stage at which substantive considerations that set limits to debt policies may become important is that of the acts of subsequent democratic governments with regard to this debt. Where acts or omissions are found to be unconstitutional and the unconstitutionality persists, this needs to be redressed and a constitutional situation restored. What that means in the context of Argentina's debt is not that easy to determine. In the light of the conclusion of the previous chapter, which is that so far the debt of the military regime has not been recognized in the constitutionally required form, an obvious answer is that as a first step, Congress would finally have to settle the payment of the debt, which would involve an auditing of the debt taken up by the military regime. Here, it needs to be borne in mind that settling the payment of the debt involves a qualitative aspect. While this does not mean that at the end of this auditing procedure the debt cannot be approved and accepted as binding, it is important to recognize that Congress is not entirely free in deciding whether or not to accept the debt and how to settle its payment. As the Argentinian Constitution demands substantive constitutionality of all state acts, the content of all decisions made by constitutional organs must be in accordance with constitutional principles. This is where the substantive considerations discussed earlier in this chapter come in.

Whether the powers of Congress retrospectively to settle the payment of the debt are as restricted as its powers of contracting it to begin with, is not entirely clear, and no authority on the issue exists. It is submitted that this should be the case, as otherwise the constitutional limits on the power to contract debt could be easily circumvented if debt that was contracted in violation of constitutional provisions could nevertheless be recognized by Congress. It would follow that when settling the payment of the debt according to Article 75(7), Congress could only accept a debt as valid and binding if, but for the fact that it was not agreed by the competent state organ, it was contracted in accordance with constitutional standards. The requirement of substantive constitutionality further supports the argument that to settle the payment of the debt according to Article 75(7) should require a careful audit, as it is otherwise impossible to know which parts of the debt were contracted in compliance with substantive constitutional principles.[71]

It was seen that under the Argentinian Constitution, debt can only be contracted for the purposes mentioned in Article 4, that is in cases of national emergencies or to finance enterprises of national interest. With regard to most of the debt taken up by the military regime, this was not the case, so that the debt was not contracted for constitutionally accepted purposes. It is then submitted that for this reason alone Congress could, in principle, not validly recognize this debt, as such a recognition would mean that the country would accept a debt the burdens of which cannot be justified on the basis of the only considerations which the Constitution accepts, that is the idea of solidarity in cases of emergencies, or that of future benefits in the context of enterprises of national interest.

In this context, economic and social rights considerations could also become significant. The considerations discussed above showed the difficulties with invoking economic and social rights to counter claims for debt repayment or to challenge the constitutionality of debt restructuring operations. However, in the particular situation of the recognition of the debt of the military regime these reservations might not apply to the same extent. This is because in this specific context, even if the auditing of the debt had taken place right at the end of the military regime, the debt burden was already so high[72] that it might have been possible to establish that to dedicate the required amounts of money to debt repayment would have impeded the country from living up to its social rights obligations, not under the ICESCR, as the country had not ratified it at that time, but under the UDHR. The case would be stronger today, were Congress ever to settle the payment of the original debt. First of all, since the constitutional reform of 1994, Article 75(22) awards the ICESCR constitutional rank. Second and more importantly, the servicing obligations related to the original debt have exploded, mainly because of the amount of interest that still needs to be repaid, and because of refinancing credits, so that the amount in question is now much higher than originally, while the social situation of the country has deteriorated dramatically.[73] However, social rights considerations seem less relevant with regard to the decision of whether or not to recognize as valid the rights of the creditors arising under the loans, and more so with regard to repayment decisions. With regard to the former, they might nevertheless be relied on to the extent that when exercising its discretion as to whether or not to recognize as valid the precarious rights the creditors obtained under the loan agreements with the military regime, the compatibility of that decision with economic and social rights considerations would have to be taken into account by Congress. The scale of the obligations in question might make it less difficult to establish a causal link between debt and social rights

---

71 See Chapter Five, 2.2, supra.
72 See Chapter Two, 1, supra.
73 See Chapter Two, 7, supra.

as is usually the case with regard to individual loan transactions or specific debt related policies. Thus, the context of settling the payment of the debt might be the most promising scenario for social rights based arguments to become effective and restrict Congress' power to prioritize the repayment of a debt taken up by a military regime over meeting its social rights obligations.

Furthermore, the conclusions reached in Chapter Four on odious debts could be made fruitful in the context of Argentinian constitutional law. If it were accepted that a loan that made a contribution to the *ius cogens* violations committed by the military government is void,[74] the democratic government would be prevented from validly recognizing these contracts. An essential part of the auditing process would then have to be an analysis of whether specific loans contributed to the violation of *ius cogens* norms, which, in turn, could assist in developing and delineating the criteria according to which such an assessment can be made. Such criteria would have to be refined first of all in the course of the congressional audit, and furthermore in potential proceedings in the national courts in which the relevant decisions of Congress could be questioned. Here, just as in the context of the social rights based arguments, the fact that the settling of the debt did not take place in the 1980s might benefit the situation of the country, in this particular context because the legal principles developed by the Supreme Court in recent decisions such as *Arancibia Clavel*[75] and *Simón*[76] with regard to crimes against humanity committed by the military regime could be used to support the argument. It of course needs to be borne in mind that the odious debts doctrine based on a violation of *ius cogens* norms cannot at present be regarded as a recognized principle of international law that would bind the state. However, even prior to its recognition as a doctrine of international law, a state would be free to adopt such a theory on the ground of its own understanding of its obligations under peremptory international law,[77] which could in turn influence the constitutionality analysis, given that the Argentinian Constitution needs to be interpreted in the light of international law obligations.[78]

Thus, to the extent that the original debt was not taken up in compliance with Article 4; the loan contributed to a violation of *ius cogens* norms; or the recognition or payment of the debt were to result in a violation of economic and social rights, an audit would presumably come to the conclusion that large parts of the original debt were unconstitutional.

---

74   See the analysis in Chapter Four.
75   "Arancibia Clavel, Enrique Lautaro s/homicidio calificado y asociación ilícita y otros –causa No.259", 24 August 2004.
76   "Simón, Julio Héctor y otros s/ privación ilegítima de la libertad, etc. –causa No. 17.768", 14 June 2005.
77   This is in line with the US approach where Restatement Third of Foreign Relations Law defines *ius cogens* for the purposes of national law (see § 102 and § 702), a definition which is widely used by courts in the context of ATCA litigation. See, for example, *Siderman de Blake v Republic of Argentina*, 965 F2d 699 (Cal 1992), at 714–718.
78   See, for example, "Arancibia Clavel, Enrique Lautaro s/homicidio calificado y asociación ilícita y otros –causa No.259", 24 August 2004, at para. 36.

In addition to the constitutional arguments developed so far, Congress' attitude towards the settling of the debt would be subject to the requirement of reasonableness.[79] While the state has a broad discretion in making policy decisions,[80] some possible grounds on which a finding of unreasonableness might be based should nevertheless be considered. As a very general consideration, it could be questioned whether it can be reasonable to restructure debts the legal validity of which was never determined. Here, even if one does not accept the constitutional argument that Congress has not yet validly settled the payment of that debt and that this would require an audit, the same issue, that is the need for an audit of the debt, can be brought up at a different level, that is in the context of an assessment of the reasonableness of the relevant acts. Indeed, given the many irregularities that took place in the context of the debt taken up by the military regime and which are evidenced in the decision of *Olmos*,[81] the reasonableness of repaying or restructuring this debt without examining its legality and legitimacy must be questioned. This shows, yet again, that a thorough auditing of the original debt would be essential, difficult as it might have become, given the lapse of time and the numerous restructuring operations, as this is the only way to separate valid loan contracts from those which were void and therefore did not create repayment obligations.

In the Argentinian context, a starting point could be an analysis of the relevance of the holdings in *Olmos* as to their impact on the validity of the loan contracts. The findings in *Olmos* highlight that many of the operations performed in the course of the original debt transactions showed irregularities, were fraudulent, or otherwise violated legal principles. A factual and legal analysis of these allegations in individual cases is beyond the scope of this book, but it is nevertheless important to emphasize that if it can be proved in individual cases that such irregularities which affected the validity of the original loan agreements existed, and in *Olmos* many such instances were, in fact, regarded as proved by the court, this has far-reaching consequences for the validity of the debt. Given that *Olmos* was a criminal case, the findings that parts of the debt had come about by fraud presumably refer to criminal offences that were committed in the context of the loan transactions.[82] What follows from such fraud for the validity of the loan contracts would need to be examined according to contract law principles. However, to the extent that the fraud affecting the loan transactions might invalidate the underlying loan agreements, it could be argued that a recognition of the resulting debt would be unreasonable. It should be added that if an original loan contract were to be invalid under such an analysis, the question mentioned in the context of odious debts,[83] that is the legal differences between later transactions regarding this debt that were performed by the way of assignment and

---

79 "Peralta y otro v Nación Argentina (Ministerio de Economía – BCRA)", Fallos 313:1513 (1990), at para. 48; "Prodelco v Poder Ejecutivo Nacional", Fallos 321:1253 (1998), at para. 7.

80 Ibid.

81 "Olmos, Alejandro S/denuncia", causa N°14.467, 13 July 2000, Juzg. Nac. Crim. y Corr. Fed., n. 2., JA 2001-I-514.

82 Although the decision is surprisingly general and does not provide a legal analysis which would determine with any clarity which offences were committed by whom.

83 See Chapter Three, 4, supra.

those that were carried out by the means of novation, does not have a significant impact. If a debt is transferred by assignment, the original flaws subsist,[84] so that in case of an original invalidity of the debt the assignment cannot have the effect of validating this debt. Where a debt is restructured in the form of a novation, under Argentinian law, a novation is itself void if the original obligation did not validly exist,[85] so that the original invalidity could equally not be healed.

Another argument on the basis of which the validity of the loan agreements is often questioned is that of usury.[86] The usury argument largely refers to the unilateral rise of the interest rates by the US Treasury,[87] which led to a rocketing of the interest obligations given that most loans at that time had stipulated floating interest rates.[88] However, while this is an interesting argument, it does not affect the validity of the original contracts as such, as it does not go as far as challenging the validity of floating interest rate clauses, but instead only objects to the effects of the unilateral rise of interest rates by the US Treasury. This argument then concerns the amount of interest that might be owed, not the validity of the contracts themselves, and it is sometimes linked to an argument of *rebus sic stantibus*.[89] However, the concern might be of relevance here to the extent that it could be argued that if the usury argument could be upheld, the debt should be reduced accordingly, something that arguably needs to be taken into account in the context of settling the payment of the debt.

---

84   This follows, for example, from the sample assignment clauses presented by Buckley (1999), at 237. See also Article 1434 of the Argentinian Civil Code.
85   Article 802 of the Argentinian Civil Code.
86   Lozada (2002), at 184.
87   For an interesting legal analysis of responsibility following from these policies see Gómez-Pinzón (1986).
88   See, for example, Espeche Gil (2004), at 8.
89   See, for example, Parlamento Latinoamericano (2001), at 7.

Chapter Seven

Impact of the Unconstitutionality of Loans on Creditor Rights

Over the last two chapters, it has been argued that Argentina's debt that was incurred by the latest military regime was not taken up according to the standards of the Constitution. Given the complexity and technicality of the legal analysis presented, it seems appropriate to start this chapter with a brief summary of the main legal arguments before examining the consequences of this unconstitutionality for Argentina's current debt repayment obligations. The arguments presented in Chapter Five are primarily based on the premise that the debt was taken up in disregard of formal/procedural constitutional principles, as Congress is the only organ that is empowered by the Constitution to take up foreign debt. However, Congress had been dissolved by the military regime and the debt was instead contracted by the executive. According to the *de facto* doctrine, upon return to democracy, the validity of the acts of the *de facto* regime depend on their recognition by Congress, and it was submitted that such a recognition needs to take place in compliance with constitutional principles. While this is controversial, it was further suggested that this would require that Congress settle the payment of the debt in the form of auditing it as to its origins, amount and lawfulness, taking into account the substantive criteria developed in Chapter Six. This means, in particular, that when deciding whether or not to recognize the debt, Congress would have to consider the constitutional limits following from Article 4 as to the purposes for which foreign debt can only be taken up. It was also argued that the repayment, refinancing and restructurings of the debt undertaken by the various democratic governments amounted to no more than a factual recognition, as the delegations which formed the legal basis of these acts were too broad to comply with constitutional principles. Moreover, the repayment and restructuring of a debt that was not first settled by Congress would, for that very reason, be unconstitutional.

Chapters Five and Six thus present, from a formal/procedural and a substantive perspective, respectively, an analysis of the Argentinian constitutional framework in the context of sovereign debt, and argue not only that the original debt was unconstitutional, but moreover that the original unconstitutionality has never been healed. For the purposes of this book, that is to provide a legal assessment of arguments against repayment of the debt originally incurred by the military regime, the analysis cannot end here. Given that sovereign debt obviously not only involves the rights and interests of the debtor country and its people, but also those of the creditors, it rather remains to be analysed to what extent creditor rights might influence the constitutional analysis, and how, on the other hand, the constitutional analysis impacts on the rights of the creditors.

When bringing the rights and interests of creditors into the equation, the issues that need to be addressed all touch upon the fundamental question of the relationship between domestic constitutional principles governing sovereign debt, on the one hand, and the rights and interests of creditors, on the other. In this respect, it needs to be decided whether or not unconstitutional state acts with regard to debt can nevertheless confer contractual rights on the creditors, or at least interests that the state cannot simply ignore. More importantly, it needs to be determined to what extent the state can rely on the unconstitutionality of the debt to avoid its repayment obligations. In the context of the legal argument that in order to redress the continuing unconstitutional situation with regard to this debt, Congress needs to settle its payment, it also has to be examined to what extent Congress' freedom to recognize or reject the debt might be limited by the rights of the creditors to have the loan agreements honoured.

The discussion of Argentina's debt by anti-debt campaigners is largely characterized by the assumption that the unconstitutionality of the debt automatically invalidates the relevant loan agreements.[1] However, it is submitted that such an outcome is not self-evident and rather needs to be justified based on a thorough legal analysis of the potential link between the unconstitutionality of the debt and the invalidity of repayment obligations. In the case of Argentina, such an analysis is complicated by the discrepancy between the legal status of the debt and political practice in this context. As was argued in the previous chapters, the unconstitutionality of Argentina's debt that dates back to the military regime still persists, so that all acts that are carried out with regard to this debt, including repaying, renegotiating and restructuring it, are also unconstitutional until Congress settles the payment of this debt in the constitutionally required way. However, Argentina's various democratic governments were and are completely unmoved by any arguments concerning the unconstitutionality of the debt, and instead consistently treated it as valid and binding.

The discussion will start from the premise that it is at least possible that the weight to be given to creditor rights and interests might depend on whether they were generated by a *de facto* or by a democratically legitimized government, a hypothesis which follows from the analysis in Chapter Five of the problem of rights acquired under the *de facto* doctrine.[2] A distinction will accordingly be made between the original debt incurred by the military regime, and the debt that was factually recognized by the democratic successor governments. The first part of this chapter provides an analysis of the consequences of unconstitutionality under domestic Argentinian law. In a second part, it will be analysed to what extent the conclusions reached according to Argentinian law are of practical significance given that, like in most cases of sovereign debt of developing countries, the relationship between Argentina and its creditors is largely not governed by Argentinian law, but instead by the law the parties to the relevant loan contracts agreed upon, which is usually the law of one of the world financial centres, that is US or English law, or that of the countries of those who hold Argentinian bonds, for example German or Italian law.

---

1   See, for example, Argentina's Odious Debts Bills 2004 and 2006.
2   See Chapter Five, 2.1, supra.

1 Effects of unconstitutionality under domestic Argentinian law

1.1 Original debt

A discussion of the consequences of the unconstitutionality of the original debt is mainly academic, given that debt repayment and the innumerable acts of debt restructuring carried out by the various democratic successor governments led to the consequence that the debt obligations incurred by the military regime no longer persist in their original form. However, an analysis of how this debt should have been dealt with upon return to democracy is nevertheless necessary as it helps to delineate the constitutional criteria according to which the interests of the creditors and of the state need to be balanced. This discussion must be seen in the light of the analysis presented in Chapter Five,[3] that is that the creditors of the original debt only acquired precarious rights which cannot be regarded as fully-fledged contractual rights, until they are ratified as such by a legitimate successor government. The origins of these 'rights', that is that they stem from a relationship with an unconstitutional government, thus influence the scope of their legal protection which is limited to a guarantee that they cannot be taken away arbitrarily.

The arguments developed in Chapter Six with regard to the substantive constitutionality of sovereign debt and debt related policies might be of some assistance when determining according to which criteria a democratic successor government can decide whether or not to recognize the binding nature of this debt. It is submitted that in respect of the debt of the military regime which was not affected by substantive unconstitutionality, or by flaws which would make its recognition unreasonable,[4] the democratic successor government would have had a lot of freedom to decide whether, on the balance, the relevant contracts should have been accepted as binding the Argentinian state. The outcome would have depended on a weighing of all the interests involved, but the weight given to the interests on both sides would have been affected by the origin of the debt, as the importance to be attached to the creditors' interests in the validity of the contract was diminished by the fact that the contracting partner was not a legitimate and constitutional government. The state, on the other hand, would have had an interest in retrospectively performing a critical evaluation of whether the deals struck by the military regime were compatible with the mandates of the Constitution, as well as in the interest of the country, given that such an assessment was not carried out at the time when the contracts were concluded. Where, on the basis of a balancing exercise, Congress would have come to the conclusion that the recognition of the debt was not desirable, it would have been free to decide not to assume it, with the effect that the creditors' interests would not have ripened into full contractual rights against the state. On the other hand, Congress could, of course, also have come to the opposite conclusion and decided to honour the contracts, for example on the basis that the loans had been beneficial to the country, or that to respect even precarious rights might benefit the credit rating and international standing of the state. Where the validity of the contract was not in

---

3   Ibid.
4   According to the criteria developed in the course of Chapter Six.

conflict with the rights of others or constitutional principles, Congress might even have had to recognize the debt as binding, as a decision not to honour the debt could then have been regarded as arbitrary.[5]

The situation is different where the original loan transaction was affected by a substantive constitutional flaw, for example where the original debt was not taken up in compliance with Article 4 of the Constitution. The democratic successor government cannot have the same discretion to recognize these loans as it does with regard to loans that were not affected by substantive unconstitutionality. The public interest in ending an unconstitutional situation in principle outweighs that of the creditors in the protection of the precarious rights which they obtained in the course of contractual relationships with a *de facto* regime.[6] With regard to those parts of the original debt that came about in violation of Article 4 or other substantive constitutional principles, these debts could thus usually not have been validly recognized by Congress. Given the requirement of reasonableness of all state acts,[7] where the recognition of a loan contract would not be reasonable based on the considerations introduced at the end of Chapter Six,[8] Congress would equally not have been free to assume such a debt as binding. Arguments based on economic and social rights could also have played an important role. As to favour precarious contractual rights over economic and social rights obligations would be unacceptable under both constitutional and international law,[9] Congress would have had to take this into account when deciding whether or not to accept the debt as binding.

To the extent that a democratic successor government decides not to assume a debt incurred by a *de facto* regime, the creditors do not have any contractual rights of debt repayment against the Argentinian state. However, this does not necessarily mean that the creditors lose all rights to debt repayment. Instead, just like in other cases in which a transaction was made in the absence of a valid legal relationship, the question of restitution would be dealt with by the principles of unjust enrichment.

1.2 The factually recognized debt

Given that not many, if any, of the obligations incurred by the military regime persist in their original form, the more relevant scenario that needs to be examined is that of the position of creditors whose rights arising out of the original contracts with the military government were later factually recognized by a democratic successor government, though not in a constitutionally valid manner, for example not in the constitutionally required form. In those cases which fall in a comparable category, new creditors obtained this debt in the context of unconstitutional operations performed

---

5   See Chapter Five, 2.1, supra. Also Nino (1983), at 945–946.
6   See the discussion in Chapter Five, ibid.
7   See, for example, "Peralta y otro v Nación Argentina (Ministerio de Economía – BCRA)", Fallos 313:1513 (1990), at para. 48; "Prodelco v Poder Ejecutivo Nacional", Fallos 321:1253 (1998), at para. 7. See also Bidart Campos (1996), at 92–94; Cabral and Maljar (2002), at 1540–1552.
8   See Chapter Six, 3, supra.
9   See Chapter Six, 2, supra.

by a democratic successor government, for example through debt restructurings that were carried out on the basis of unconstitutional delegations of power. Mainly two issues arise here. First of all, it needs to be examined whether this unconstitutionality has any consequences for the repayment obligations of the state. Secondly, if it is accepted that the factual but unconstitutional recognitions of the original debt do not amount to the constitutionally required settling of the payment of the debt by Congress, and that such settling in the form of an audit of the original debt is still outstanding, it needs to be resolved how Congress should approach this task. Thus, the subsequent analysis needs to address the issue of how the unconstitutionality of the debt affects the legal position of the creditors; and it must develop criteria according to which Congress can decide whether or not retrospectively to legitimize the debt that was already factually recognized by a democratic government.

1.2.1 Validity of the loan contracts

To determine the validity of the loan agreements is important with regard to both of these issues. First of all and most importantly, if the new loan contracts entered into by a democratic government with regard to the debt of the military regime were found to be valid, or the factual recognition of the original debt were to validate the originally precarious contracts, the creditors would have contractual rights to debt repayment against the Argentinian state. Secondly, in order to determine the weight to be given to the creditors' rights when deciding whether or not Congress could retrospectively reject to recognize (and repay) the debt of the military regime that was since restructured or otherwise factually recognized by a democratic regime, one issue to be examined is whether the factual recognition of the debt conferred valid contractual rights on the creditors. This is significant, as contractual rights receive special protection that can only be taken away under limited circumstances. Indeed, in the specific context of Argentinian constitutional law, it would have to be taken into account that contractual rights fall under the constitutional protection of property pursuant to Article 17.[10]

The answer to the question of the validity of the contracts depends on the relationship between the unconstitutionality of the relevant acts carried out by democratic governments[11] and the creation of contractual rights of the creditors, that is on whether unconstitutional acts can give rise to valid contractual rights. This approach makes it necessary to investigate the legal status of a contract that was concluded on the basis of an unconstitutional act of a state organ and presupposes that unconstitutionality does not automatically void the contract, but that it might under certain circumstances have an impact on its validity. With regard to the first point, it needs to be remembered that it is well accepted that unconstitutionality can have different consequences and does not in all cases automatically result in

---

10   See, for example, "Bourdieu, Pedro E. v Municipalidad de la Capital Federal", Supreme Court, 16 December 1925, Fallos 145:307, at 307–308; "Badaro, Adolfo Valentín c/ ANSeS s/ reajustes varios", Supreme Court, 8 August 2006, at paras 4 and 11; Sabsay and Onaindia (2004), at 69.

11   See the analysis provided in Chapter Five.

an invalidity *ab initio* of the unconstitutional act and all acts based upon it. While invalidity *ab initio* would be one possible consequence of unconstitutionality, courts could, for example, also declare an act to be unconstitutional but decide that this declaration does not have retroactive effect.[12] It follows that unconstitutionality is not synonymous with nullity; that it can instead have various consequences; and that the decision of which approach is preferable in a given case would depend on a careful weighing of all the interests involved.[13] The unconstitutionality of the debt, both with regard to its origins and because it was never recognized in the constitutionally required manner, does therefore not necessarily mean that the individual loan transactions carried out by the various democratic governments, though unconstitutional, did not result in valid contracts.

That unconstitutionality does not automatically invalidate the loan agreements does not mean that unconstitutionality cannot have an impact on their validity or at least on their enforceability. This could at first sight be questioned, as in most cases of loan agreements and debt restructurings, Argentina accepted that it was not acting *iure imperii*, but much rather *iure gestionis*, which means that the state is acting in the private domain and does not exercise sovereign powers.[14] While this distinction is mainly important in the context of state immunity,[15] some might want to infer that the state waived its rights to rely on its position as a sovereign in the context of the relevant acts, including the right to invoke the binding nature of constitutional principles.[16] However, from the fact that the state acts *iure gestionis* does not follow that the relevant activity is therefore exclusively governed by private law. Instead, even where the administration acts in the realm of private law, several issues arising in the context of these contracts, such as questions surrounding the authority to conclude the relevant contract, would nevertheless have to be determined according to public law.[17]

In Argentina, the provisions of the National Administrative Procedures Act (LNPA),[18] which govern the consequences of a lack of authority, illegality, defects of intention etc., apply not only to acts of the administration that take place strictly in the realm of public law, but equally to activities that could be regarded as *iure gestionis*.[19] Furthermore, general principles of public law, for example the principle of reasonableness, apply indiscriminately to all activities of the administration, be they administrative acts, administrative contracts, or contracts which are otherwise governed by private law.[20] As a consequence of the fact that one of the parties to

---

12   See, for example, Bidart Campos (1996), at 140.
13   Ibid., at 91.
14   See, for example, Brownlie (2003), at 328; Cassese (2005), at 109.
15   See, for example, *Republic of Argentina v Weltover, Inc.*, 504 U.S. 607 (USNY, 1992); also Valdez (2004), at 976–978.
16   For the discussion of this issue in German law see, for example, Peine (2006), at 46.
17   Gordillo (2000), at II-29; Mairal (1987), at 163. This is also accepted in the UK. See, for example, *Merrill Lynch Captial Services Inc. v Municipality of Piraeus* [1997] CLC 1214, at 1234 per Cresswell J.
18   Ley Nacional de Procedimientos Administrativos, Law 19.549.
19   Gordillo (2000), at II-31; Mairal (1988), at 77. See also Marienhoff (1997), at 123.
20   Gordillo (2000), at II-33.

the contract is the state, reasons for a potential illegality of the contract go therefore beyond those generally known in private law, and might include violations of the state's obligations under international law, in particular international human rights treaties,[21] under the national constitution, or under other domestic legislation.[22] It is accordingly frequently highlighted that in Argentina, to label activities of the state as private law activities or private law contracts would be inappropriate, as this would not sufficiently take account of the applicability of administrative law to the relevant acts of public officials.[23] Under Argentinian law there is thus ample room for the assumption that the unconstitutionality of loan agreements might influence their validity, regardless of *iure gestionis* clauses.

When examining how constitutional law might impact on the validity of loan agreements, one of the main issues arising in the context of Argentina's debt is that of a lack of authority of the acting state organ. In Argentinian law, authority is conferred upon a state organ by the Constitution or other legal provisions.[24] It was seen that the Constitution vests the authority to contract sovereign debt (Article 75(4)) and to settle its payment (Article 75(7)) in Congress. Where an organ other than Congress becomes active in these areas of exclusive congressional competence, the authority of that organ, even if granted by statute, would depend on the validity of the empowering provision by which Congress delegated the relevant powers. A delegation that exceeds the constraints of Article 76 would, for example, be invalid.[25] The nullity of executive regulations in the context of sovereign debt which were enacted without being based on a valid empowering statute,[26] or which exceed the authorization thereby conferred, follows directly from Article 99(3) which sets the principle that legislative acts performed by the executive are void. Such regulations cannot be ratified by Congress,[27] and the nullity extends to all acts undertaken on their basis.

Here, the previous analysis of the validity of the delegations on which the various debt restructurings carried out by democratic Argentinian governments were based becomes significant. It was demonstrated that these delegations were unconstitutional because they were too broad to conform with the requirements of

---

21   Ibid., at VIII-6.

22   See Comadira (2003), at 132–133. For contracts that violate ordinary domestic law, this follows from Article 14 of the LNPA, see Gordillo (2000), at VIII–7. At II-30, Gordillo moreover gives the example of Article 17 of the Ethics in the Exercise of Public Office Act (Law 25.188) which stipulates that acts that violate Articles 13 to 15 of that Act are null. According to him, the wording and context of this provision suggest that it applies to all acts, including contracts under private law.

23   Gordillo (2000), at II-34; Mairal (1987), at 164.

24   "Pastor, José M. Felipe v Reconstrucción de San Juan", Cámara Nacional de Apelaciones de Mendoza, 23 August 1957, J.A. 1957-III, 517, at 520; Mairal (1987), at 158.

25   Gordillo (2000), at VIII-27.

26   Unless in cases of valid regulations of necessity and emergency.

27   Gordillo (2000), at VIII-31; "Franco, Rubén Oscar y otros v Estado Nacional /Mrio. de Defensa s/personal militar y civil de las FF.AA. y de seguridad", 19 August 1999, Fallos 322:1868, at para. 14; "M. Langenauer e Hijos SA. y AG c Estado nacional" CNFed Contencioso administrativo, sala IV, 18 November 1999, LL 2000-D, 576, at 579.

Article 76 of the Constitution. Pursuant to Article 14 of the National Administrative Procedures Act administrative acts that are issued without authority with regard to subject matter, which includes lack of authority to legislate or issue regulations,[28] are void, and this nullity cannot be healed.[29] Applied to the debt restructurings at issue, all acts in respect thereof, including the resulting loan agreements themselves, are then void, and Congress could not heal this unconstitutionality by ratifying the relevant regulations or the acts based thereon. The state would also not be time-barred from invoking the absolute nullity of these loan contracts, as no limitation period applies.[30] Administrative law principles dictate in these cases that the nullity always take effect *ab initio*, as the seriousness of the defect does not allow for the act to stand. Thus, Argentinian law adopted the approach that the interest of society in avoiding that such acts have any legal effect outweighs that of the individual beneficiary of the act in its validity.[31] It would then follow that the loan contracts between the various democratic governments and Argentina's creditors are void, as they were entered into without authority, given the unconstitutionality of the delegations based on which the relevant acts were carried out.

A significant problem that arises here is that it has been (and still is) consistent practice in Argentina to regard the relevant delegations as constitutional, or at least not to attach any legal consequence to their unconstitutionality, and accordingly to accept that the organs representing the Argentinian state in the debt restructuring operations acted with legal authority. If the legal interpretation and practice in this respect were to change in accordance with the principles suggested here, it needs to be analysed whether this could be done with retroactive effect. What could be argued is that the consistent representations made by all democratic governments over many years created legitimate expectations in the creditors. Moreover, it might be possible that the creditors could successfully rely on ostensible or apparent authority, which means that the principal, in this case Congress, made a representation that the agent, in this case the executive, was duly authorized to perform the transaction in question.[32]

Here, the Supreme Court decision in *YPF*[33] becomes relevant. The case arose out of a controversy about the term of bonds that had been issued by the then state owned petrol company YPF. The prospectus circulated by the director of the company resolved the question of how to determine the amount for which YPF would recover the bonds differently from the legislation that empowered YPF to issue the bonds. When the moment of recovery of the bonds arrived, YPF calculated the amount based on the terms laid down in the delegating provision, as they were more favourable to the company. In this respect, the company suggested that the prospectus had no legal value, but was instead strictly informational. The terms of

---

28   Gordillo (2000), at VIII-30–31.
29   See also Comadira (2003), at 77.
30   Ibid., at 71; Cassagne (2006), at 494.
31   Comadira (2000), at 72.
32   See Craig (2003), at 155.
33   "SA Consolidación IIC y F v Yacimientos Petrolíferos Fiscales", Fallos 302:1065 (1980).

the empowering statute had to be decisive, YPF argued, as the company would not have had the power validly to change these terms in its prospectus. The bondholder, on the other hand, asserted that the more beneficial terms of the prospectus should apply. The lower courts accepted YPF's argument concerning the legal status of the prospectus and moreover regarded the prospectus as invalid, as within the company the director was not the competent organ to issue this document. The Supreme Court reversed, suggesting that:

> If in the opinion of the issuing entity there was a mistake or a discrepancy between the dates fixed in the 'Prospectus' and the norms regulating this matter … which caused [YPF] to change the date of recovery 15 years after the issuing of the 'Prospectus' … it cannot be claimed that this situation internal to the issuing entity could be used against third parties who in good faith relied on the information of a 'Prospectus' that … did not appear to contradict the legal norms regulating the loan.[34]

This argument seems to rest on considerations resembling those underlying the concept of legitimate expectations. The Court then based its conclusion decisively on a balancing of interests which was summarized in another Supreme Court decision, *Caja de Valores*.[35] The state had to be held to the contract, because of:

> the behaviour to be expected from the entities in question and the trust that the guarantees given by the state [with regard to the bonds] need to inspire in the citizen. It would be improper to lose sight of the fact that the interest that a public and voluntary loan awakens in the population is based, on the one hand, on the favourable and particular conditions under which it is offered, and, on the other hand, on the trust, seriousness and responsibility of the issuing entity and of the state that guarantees them.[36]

In *YPF*, the Court accordingly attached legal value to the specifications contained in the prospectus, even though they deviated from those of the empowering statute, as it was the content of the prospectus that formed the basis on which the public was invited to obtain the bonds.[37] The decision thus seems to stand for the principle that where, in the context of public debt, the state creates an expectation with regard to the validity and the terms of the operation, it cannot later free itself from the resulting obligation owed to a third party that had acted in good faith, by relying on legal defects of the operation that lie in the state's own sphere.

A lot can be said in favour of the view that the public must be able to rely on representations made by the state, in general,[38] and on those that induced individuals to buy bonds issued by the state, in particular. Indeed, if the state could easily negate its obligations under loan contracts because of irregularities the state itself is responsible for, this would not only affect the interests of the creditors, but the

---

34 Ibid., at 1077.
35 "Caja de Valores S.A. v Provincia de Buenos Aires y otra" Fallos 318:1322 (1995).
36 Ibid. at para. 20; see also "S.A. Consolidación IIC y F V Yacimientos Petrolíferos Fiscales" Fallos 302:1065 (1980), at para. 8.
37 See also "S.A. Consolidación IIC y F V Yacimientos Petrolíferos Fiscales" Fallos 302:1065 (1980), at para. 8.
38 See, for example, Bidart Campos (1987), at 172–173; Borda (2000), at para. 123–3.

consequences of such a principle might moreover be disastrous for the state and its credit rating.[39] However, to derive from this a general principle that in all cases of public debt a potential conflict between the legality of the operation and the trust in public securities should be resolved in favour of trust, unless the defect was either obvious for the common creditor, or particular diligence could have been expected given their professional status,[40] is a step too far. First of all, such an outcome would go against Article 66 of the already mentioned Act 24.156 (Financial Administration and the Control Systems of the National Public Sector Act), which states that:

> Operations of public credit that violate the norms laid down in the present statute are null and without effect, regardless of the personal responsibility of those who performed them.

> Neither the central administration nor any other entity of the national public sector shall be liable for any obligations arising from them.[41]

And Act 24.629, usually known as 'Second Reform of the State', stipulates in Article 5 that:

> Any act or contract issued by any entity, even if it had authority, that was not preceded by a fulfilment of the norms prescribed in Act 24.156; in the regulation [on which the act or contract is based]; and in the present statute, shall be null if it results in the obligation of the national Treasury to pay sums of money. The official who authorizes and issues acts that are null and prohibited under this provision, shall be personally liable to third parties.

These provisions seem to confirm the view expressed more generally in the LNPA, that under certain circumstances the state interest in compliance with the norms which govern public debt operations outweighs that of the creditors in the validity of the relevant contracts. A consideration which the Court did not take into account in *YPF* was that when balancing the interests at stake when public debt operations are affected by irregularities that shed doubts on the validity of the underlying contracts, not only the already mentioned interests of the bondholders in the validity of the agreement, and those of the state in its credibility are at stake. Instead, another interest that also needs to be taken into consideration is the interest of society that acts that are affected by particularly serious legal defects will not have any effect and need to be annulled.[42] Indeed, the legislature decided that the existence of such acts could not be tolerated and that they would be null and could not be ratified (Article 14 of the LNPA). Thus, while one might at first sight be tempted to say that the state should be bound by its own precedents, and that a consistent state practice should give rise to legitimate expectations, a view that seems to gain more and

---

39   For a discussion see, for example, Valdez (2004), at 988–991.
40   Ibid., at 990–991. For a discussion of comparable issues in the context of English cases of loans to local authorities see Cane (1994), in particular at 517.
41   But see Valdez (2004), who seems to argue at 988–991 that this provision is unconstitutional.
42   Gordillo (2000), at XI–8.

more prominence in general Argentinian administrative law,[43] this would not apply to unlawful or void acts, as the administration can plead its own turpitude.[44] This argument is supported by Article 17 of the LNPA[45] which regulates the revocation of acts affected by absolute nullity even if they created subjective rights.[46] Thus, a return to a legal and/or constitutional situation cannot be prevented by the concept of legitimate expectations.

It is submitted that the consequences for the debt of the military regime that was factually recognized by democratic successor governments are as follows: Given the lack of authority of the acting state organ to conclude the relevant loan agreements, they would be void according to Article 14 of the LNPA and could be revoked in judicial proceedings. The fact that the state consistently made representations to the effect that it regarded its debt operations as binding and would meet the resulting obligations, did not create legitimate expectations in the creditors that would preclude the state from invoking the unconstitutionality of its representations.

Moving from the question of legitimate expectations to the other issue alluded to in *YPF*, that is the question of ostensible authority, in this respect the Court argued that even if the director of YPF had not had the necessary authority to issue the prospectus, this was irrelevant because a lack of internal authority could not be invoked against third parties who had in good faith relied on it. In this context, the Court attached particular importance to the fact that the prospectus had been published, upon the request of YPF, in the *Journal of the Commercial Stock Exchange* after having been presented to the Securities Commission.[47] Given that the decision does not provide an analysis of the issue, and that the published facts do not indicate in what the alleged defect of authority consisted, it is difficult to draw any conclusions from this for the way in which the problem of the factually recognized debt should be dealt with. It is, however, submitted that the approach that lack of authority is an internal issue that does not have any external effect on the contracting parties cannot be generalized. Otherwise, Article 14 of the LNPA which regards as absolutely null all acts that were performed without subject matter authority, territorial authority or temporal authority, would be obsolete. Indeed, in the light of this provision, it seems as if

---

43   Ibid., at VIII–9.
44   "Pastor, José M. Felipe v Reconstrucción de San Juan", Cámara Nacional de Apelaciones de Mendoza, 23 August 1957, JA 1957-III, 517, at 521; Mairal (1987), at 161; Borda (2000), at para. 79; Genera (1994), at 702; Alterini and López Cabana (1984), at 879. But see Coviello (1998), who, based on a comparative legal analysis, seems to argue at 921 that legitimate expectations should in certain situations outweigh the interest in the legality of state acts.
45   Article 17: An administrative act that is affected by absolute nullity is irregular and needs to be revoked or replaced on the grounds of its illegitimacy by the administrative body itself. However, if the act was firm and consented and generated subjective rights which are being fulfilled, its continued existence and that of its effects that are still outstanding can only be prevented by a judicial declaration of nullity.
46   Although according to Article 17, such acts can only be revoked by a court, not by the administration itself.
47   "SA Consolidación IIC y F v Yacimientos Petrolíferos Fiscales" Fallos 302:1065 (1980), at para. 5.

the principle of ostensible authority cannot form part of Argentinian administrative law,[48] as the statute does not contain any exception for such a scenario.

Consequently, all debt operations of the democratic governments which were based on unconstitutional delegations were performed without the necessary authority to conclude a valid contract, so that the resulting loan agreements are void. However, while these void contracts cannot be ratified, Congress might have the possibility to heal the particular flaw of lack of authority with effect for the future. Indeed, Congress would be free to issue new delegations for new debt restructurings, which would, in principle, be valid if Congress avoided the flaws of the existing unconstitutional delegations by setting a clear policy framework. Alternatively, Congress could itself take the decision to restructure the debt. A result similar to that of the void debt operations could then be achieved with effect for the future simply by restructuring the same debt on the same terms as foreseen in the debt restructurings that were void because of a lack of authority. However, in the light of the arguments presented in Chapter Five, it needs to be taken into account that before Congress settles the payment of the debt in the form of auditing it as to its amount and validity, any delegation would be invalid, as it would refer to debts the existence and validity of which have not yet been determined in the constitutionally required way. Thus, it is submitted that until Congress performs its task of settling the payment of the debt, it cannot validly delegate the power to restructure the debt, not even if it were to enact a clear and narrowly framed empowering provision.[49] Instead, all new delegations issued prior to this would be void and could not result in valid loan agreements.

To summarize the conclusions so far, in the particular context of the operations performed by the democratic governments in respect of the debt inherited by the military dictators, it would follow that loan agreements based on these acts are void according to Article 14 of the LNPA because of a lack of authority, a defect which could not be healed by ratification. Thus, the creditors did not acquire valid contractual rights on which the claims for debt repayment could be based. Nor did the consistent representations made by democratic governments with regard to the validity of these unconstitutional and void operations give rise to legitimate expectations on the basis of which the state would be precluded from invoking this invalidity.

1.2.2 Criteria for retrospectively recognizing or rejecting the debt

It remains to be seen whether the factual relationship between the state and the creditors of the democratic governments should be dealt with according to the same principles that apply to the relationship between the state and the original creditors of the *de facto* regime. In the light of the outcome of the preceding discussion of the validity of the loan contracts and of legitimate expectations of the creditors, one might at first sight be tempted to conclude that the creditors of the democratic successor governments are not in any better position than those of the *de facto*

---

48   See also Mairal (1987), at 161. For a similar conclusion under English law see, for example, Cane (1994), at 519.

49   See Chapter Five, 4, supra.

regime, that is that they have no more than precarious rights the legal fate of which depends on Congress' decision regarding its recognition or rejection. Indeed, both scenarios have in common that the operations were affected by constitutional flaws that prevented the creditors from obtaining full contractual rights.

However, there are also some fundamental differences between the two situations. The creditors who made loans to the *de facto* regime knew that they were not dealing with a constitutional regime, whereas the creditors of the democratic state will in most cases not have been aware of the reasons for which they could not acquire full contractual rights, particularly bearing in mind the consistent representations of the various democratic governments as to the validity and binding nature of the debt they acquired. Moreover, the main reason why the subsequent debt related acts of the democratic governments were regarded as invalid is that Congress never performed its constitutional task of settling the payment of the debt of the military regime, so that the debt transactions related to a debt that had never been assumed by the state in a constitutionally and legally valid manner. In addition, the debt transactions were not based on delegations that complied with constitutional principles. Thus, while the unconstitutionality of the debt taken up by the *de facto* regime is directly related to the origin of the debt, the reasons for which the unconstitutionality and consequent invalidity of this debt persist are only indirectly linked to the *de facto* origins of the debt, and lie instead mainly in the sphere of the democratic successor governments. This might have an impact on the amount of discretion Congress has with regard to settling and thereby recognizing or rejecting the already factually recognized debt.

Admittedly, Congress could in both cases (*de facto* and factually recognized debt) not validly recognize the debt if the auditing showed that the debt was not only unconstitutional because it originated from a *de facto* regime, but that it was moreover affected by substantive unconstitutionality, as Congress could then never have contracted this debt in compliance with the Constitution, and Congress' powers to recognize a debt do not exceed those of contracting it to begin with. In all cases in which the original debt was not affected by substantive unconstitutionality, on the other hand, upon return to democracy, Congress would have been free to refuse the recognition of the rights of the creditors of the *de facto* regime short of arbitrariness, that is Congress would have had great leeway when deciding which state interests to favour over those of the creditors. That this should also be the case in the context of settling the payment of the factually recognized debt is not so clear. As the state was not constitutionally represented during the *de facto* period, upon return to democracy, the incoming constitutional government had the constitutional task of controlling the constitutionality, lawfulness and beneficial nature of this debt retrospectively (Article 75(7) of the Constitution). However, the principles derived from the *de facto* doctrine do not apply to debt transactions that were entered into and performed by representatives of the democratic state, even if these acts are unconstitutional and void. Indeed, with regard to the factually recognized debt, the democratic governments expressed the view that a recognition of the debt of the military regime in the different forms that it took over the years, was beneficial for the country, and the main reason why these decisions are unconstitutional and void is that they took place before the debt was audited and assumed in the constitutionally required way.

An argument could then be made that while Congress, prior to the factual recognition of the debt by the democratic regimes, would have had a far-reaching discretion with regard to the acceptance or rejection of the debt, short of arbitrarily taking away the precarious rights which the creditors acquired under the *de facto* regime, this discretion might be limited by the fact that Congress factually assumed this debt and thereby created expectations in the creditors that should only be taken away if this is necessary in order to redress a situation of substantive unconstitutionality or illegality, or if the creditor was not in good faith. This result would be fair, because it would prioritize the state interest only to the extent that past unconstitutionalities and illegalities would otherwise persist. In such cases, it is justified to give precedence to the interests of the state on the basis that if the country were bound to assume and repay a debt that had come about by unconstitutional means and that was then recognized in an unconstitutional way, this would deprive the state of any possibility to redress the unconstitutionality and to return to a situation that is in line with constitutional principles and mandates. As a consequence, a government would have the power validly to contract out of its constitutional obligations, and contractual obligations would be regarded as of higher rank than the Constitution.[50] However, based on the expectations caused by the representations made by a democratic regime, the creditors' interests would be paramount in all other cases, that is where the debt does not violate constitutional or other legal principles.

To bring a principle close to that of legitimate expectations back into the debate does not contradict the conclusions reached with regard to the validity of the contract. The reason why legitimate expectations could not preclude the state from relying on the invalidity of the loan agreements was that society's interest in not being bound by a transaction entered into by a state official without authority outweighs the creditors' interest in its validity. The loan transactions violated fundamental legal principles, and this violation could not be healed by representations made by the state to the effect that it regarded the relevant acts as valid. However, this does not mean that Congress' discretion when retrospectively settling the payment of this debt and deciding whether or not to recognize it as binding might not be reduced by these representations. This differentiation between the two scenarios can be justified on the grounds that the creation of legitimate expectations is only excluded to the extent that the underlying acts were unlawful.[51] With regard to lawful activities of the executive, on the other hand, the doctrine of *venire contra factum propium* is applicable, that is that no one can go against their own representations in the validity of which others trusted.[52] In *Balanceadores,*[53] it was argued in this respect that a consistent lawful state practice would have a self-binding effect, in that the executive would lose its

---

50   See also Mairal (1988), at 78.

51   "Pastor, José M. Felipe v Reconstrucción de San Juan", Cámara Nacional de Apelaciones de Mendoza, 23 August 1957, JA 1957-III, 517, at 521; Mairal (1987), at 161; Borda (2000), at para. 79; Genera (1994), at 702; Alterini and López Cabana (1984), at 879. But see Coviello (1998), at 921

52   Bidart Campos (1987), at 170–173; Broda (2000), at para. 123–3.

53   "Asociación de Balanceadores, corredores y mart. Pub. C. Est. Nac. (M° de Just. De la Nación – Dir. Nac. Reg. Oficial) s/juicios de conocimientos", 2 August 1994, as quoted in Coviello (1998), at 914–915.

freedom to choose between various lawful options that would otherwise have been open to it. A change of such a practice would require thorough justification.[54]

Thus, while prior to the settling of the payment of the debt the creditors cannot obtain valid contractual rights, the consistent representations of the democratic governments with regard to the validity of the previous debt operations have the effect of limiting Congress' discretion of rejecting the recognition of the debt to cases of substantive unconstitutionality or unlawfulness. In all other cases, the debt needs to be retrospectively recognized as valid. Once such a recognition has taken place, valid future transactions with regard to this debt could be made in the course of which the creditors could obtain full contractual rights.

1.3 Summary

The preceding legal analysis resulted in the conclusion that neither the creditors of the *de facto* regime, nor those who made transactions with the various democratic successor governments with regard to this debt, obtained valid contractual rights on which a claim for debt repayment could be based. Neither did the representations of the democratic governments create legitimate expectations in the creditors which preclude the state from raising the unconstitutionality of the debt. As the invalid contracts cannot be ratified, the only possibility to confer valid contractual rights would be for Congress to settle the payment of the debt and assume as valid those parts of the factually recognized debt that were not affected by unconstitutionality or other illegality, and then for the competent state organs to make valid operations concerning this debt. With regard to the remainder of the debt, the invalidity of the contracts cannot be healed and contractual claims for debt repayment therefore not arise.

1.4 Non-contractual claims for debt repayment

In the light of the conclusion that neither the creditors of the *de facto* regime, nor those of the democratic governments obtained valid contractual rights on which a claim for debt repayment could be based, a situation that could only be rectified in the future, based on the outcome of Congress' audit of the debt, for that part of the debt that was not affected by substantive unconstitutionality or illegality, the question arises of where this leaves the creditors with regard to the loans they paid out under invalid contracts. Could they base a claim for repayment of the capital and possibly also for payment of interest, on other legal grounds? Mainly two legal concepts on which such claims could be based come to mind: unjust enrichment and state responsibility. The concept of state responsibility in this context is rather ill-defined. However, in Argentina it is sometimes put forward that if the state decides to plead its own turpitude and rely on the unconstitutionality of its own acts, or their nullity on other grounds, it can revoke these acts but cannot avoid responsibility towards third parties that in good faith relied on their validity.[55] The exact elements

---

54 Ibid.
55 See, for example, Barra (1984a), at 591; Bidart Campos (1987), at 170–173.

of such an action against the state are not very clear, but it has been suggested that the other party should be able to recover expenses incurred in reliance on the validity of the contract.[56] Given the tentative nature of the suggestions made in this context it is difficult to know with any certainty what the creditors would be able to recover on this basis.

With regard to claims for restitution based on unjust enrichment, it is largely accepted that the relevant legal principles apply not only to the legal relations between private parties, but also to those between individuals and the state.[57] The prerequisites of a successful unjust enrichment claim are that the state is enriched;[58] that the other party suffered a correlative loss; and that the enrichment is unjust and without legal cause.[59] The enrichment aspect of the claim is usually said to depend on whether the state actually obtained a benefit. To the extent that the state no longer holds that which it unjustly obtained, all rests upon whether the state's assets increased overall.[60] In the specific context of loans, it was suggested that the state will usually at least be enriched by the principal of the loan, so that, as a minimum, the capital of the debt would have to be returned.[61]

No Argentinian authority exists on unjust enrichment claims in the context of loan transactions that were *ultra vires* and therefore void. However, case law in other contexts, in particular that of contracts entered into by the state without following the procedure of public bidding required by law, gives an indication of how Argentinian courts might approach claims for unjust enrichment against the state. In a case where a company had been contracted for public works without following the relevant procedure,[62] for example, the court rejected the claim for restitution in the form of payment for the work that had already been carried out. This was based on the argument that otherwise the contractor would, by the means of restitution, obtain the same they would have received had the contract been valid. Restitution would then lead to enforcing the terms of an unlawful contract through the back door, and the legal principles according to which such contracts are void would lose their force if they could be easily circumvented by relying on the principles of unjust enrichment to achieve the purpose of the contract.[63] In a case with a comparable factual situation but concerning a contract of sale, however, the Supreme Court decided differently

---

56   Marial (1988), at 146–147; Monti (2001).

57   See, for example, "Asociación Escuela Popular Germana Argentina Belgrano v Nación Argentina", 7 November 1957, Fallos 245:146, at 159; "Pfizer Argentina SAC e I c/ Santiago del Estero, la Provincia de s/ cobro de m$n. 115.678,40", 15 March 1967, Fallos 267:162, at 163–164; "Empresa Constructora Obras Civiles e Industriales, SRL c Administración General de Puertos", 1ª Instancia Cont.-adm. Fed. (Juzgado N° 1), 30 August 1983, ED-109, 390, at 401; Monti (2001); Barra (1984b), at 395.

58   Monti (2001).

59   "Pastor, José M. Felipe v Reconstrucción de San Juan", Cámara Nacional de Apelaciones de Mendoza, 23 August 1957, JA 1957-III, 517, at 530.

60   Monti (2001).

61   Marial (1988), at 146–147.

62   See, for example, "Pastor, José M. Felipe v Reconstrucción de San Juan", Cámara Nacional de Apelaciones de Mendoza, 23 August 1957, JA 1957-III, 517.

63   Ibid., at 530.

and ordered restitution of the value of drugs the state had received and was unable to return because they had been used.[64]

It remains to be assessed how these considerations can be related to the case of debt repayment. In the absence of Argentinian case law on and legal analysis of this point, it might be useful to have a look at some of the legal arguments that dominated the English discussion of borrowing contracts that were *ultra vires*.[65] An argument similar to that endorsed by the Argentinian courts in respect of public works was sometimes put forward against recovery of such loans according to unjust enrichment principles, that is that this would allow the creditor to obtain what they would have received had the contract been valid.[66] However, it is submitted that Lord Goff was right when pointing out in his dissenting opinion in *Westdeutsche Landesbank* that 'a personal claim in restitution would not indirectly enforce the *ultra vires* contract, for such an action would be unaffected by any of the contractual terms governing the borrowing, and moreover would be subject (where appropriate) to any available restitutionary defences.'[67] Indeed, for example, the contractually agreed interest rates cannot apply to unjust enrichment claims, as the relevant contract is void and its terms are therefore irrelevant for the restitutionary claim. This is particularly important in the context of the debt of Argentina's military regime, as most of the relevant loan agreements stipulated floating interest rates, which was an important factor in triggering the debt crisis when the interest rates were later raised drastically.[68]

In respect of the recovery of interest, one suggestion in England has been that:

> The ban on restitution of payments made under a void borrowing contract might be challenged by arguing, as a matter of policy, that so long as the restitutionary remedy was limited to the capital of the loan and did not extend to interest, such a remedy would strike a suitable compromise between the conflicting interests of the public and the bank.[69]

---

64 "Pfizer Argentina SAC e I c/ Santiago del Estero, la Provincia de s/ cobro de m$n. 115.678,40", 15 March 1967, Fallos 267:162, at 163–164.

65 Mainly in the context of interest rate swap agreements entered into by local authorities.

66 *Sinclair v Brougham* [1914] AC 398 (HL), at 418 per Viscount Haldane LJ; *Westdeutsche Landesbank Girozentrale v Islington London Borough Council* [1994] 1 WLR 938, per Leggatt LJ at 952; overruled by *Westdeutsche Landesbank Girozentrale v Islington London Borough Council* [1996] AC 669 (HL).

67 *Westdeutsche Landesbank Girozentrale v Islington London Borough Council* [1996] AC 669 (HL), at 688.

68 See Chapter Two, 1, supra. Another effect of the invalidity of the loan contracts worth considering might be that the provisions regarding the repayment in instalments which are a common feature of loan agreements would be ineffective, with the consequence that, in principle, the loan would have to be repaid immediately. This outcome would cause highly indebted states considerable problems. In German law, the courts overcome this problem in the context of unjust enrichment claims for restitution of immoral loans by allowing the debtor to keep the borrowed money during the contractually agreed period without having to pay interest, but imposing the obligation to repay the capital of the debt in full at the end of this period, see BGH NJW 1995, 1152, 1153.

69 Cane (1994), at 521. But see Davies (2006), who argues at 114–115 that it would not be in the interest of the state to deprive the other party of its profits this way.

While this statement was made with the aim of avoiding the harsh consequences of the House of Lords' decision in *Sinclair v Brougham*[70] which excluded all recovery, it is submitted that it provides an interesting approach to the issue of restitution of interests.[71]

Coming back to Argentina, the debt incurred by the military regime raises some doubts about the appropriateness of restitution even with regard to the capital of the debt, as this remedy is only available where there was an actual enrichment of the state. This brings an important point into the debate, which is that of how and by whom it is to be decided to what extent the state was enriched by a loan. It is submitted that in the particular context of the debt of the military regime, the question of whether or not the loan benefited and enriched the country is one of the issues that needs to be addressed by Congress in the context of settling the payment of this debt. The decision of whether or not to recognize it if it was not affected by substantive unconstitutionality to some extent depends on whether or not this debt is beneficial to the state, so that in that particular context considerations similar to those that arise with regard to restitution in the case of an invalid loan already influence the decision about the validity of the loan itself.

Nevertheless, as a matter of principle, the questions of whether a state should be held to a contract and whether it should return money it received in the context of an invalid loan contract, require different considerations. Indeed, the issue of the extent to which the country owes the creditors restitution only arises once the contracts are regarded as invalid, and Congress has, with regard to a specific loan agreement, come to the conclusion that it should not be recognized as binding the state. With regard to the validity of loan contracts, the Constitution and other legal provisions set requirements that need to be complied with in order for such contracts to be valid and binding. If any fundamental constitutional or other legal principles are violated by the contract, it is null and the state does not have to perform it. But while it is justified that the state can annul such a contract and return to a constitutional and lawful situation, it is not so clear that this necessarily means that the state does not have to return that which it obtained in the context of the void relationship. Indeed, the reason why claims for unjust enrichment can be raised against the state are that the state has no right, and no reason, to keep what it received from the creditors in the belief that a valid contract existed. This principle is particularly important bearing in mind that the state can plead its own turpitude and void the contract in reliance on its own unconstitutional behaviour. The general principle is thus that the creditors would have a claim for restitution of that which was delivered to the state without a valid legal ground, unless exceptional circumstances justify a different conclusion in an individual case.

It then needs to be examined whether the situation of Argentina's debt contracted by the military regime might give rise to such an exception. Some uncertainty has been expressed in this regard as to whether the recovery of the principal of the debt would be legally enforceable in the case of loans made to *de facto* regimes which were

---

70   [1914] AC 398 (HL).

71   This also seems to be in line with the German approach, see BGH NJW 1995, 1152, 1153.

later regarded by the incoming democratic government as 'extravagant or odious'.[72] In respect of the debt that was affected by substantive unconstitutionality and could therefore not be validly recognized by Congress, the case against restitution might at first sight seem to be rather strong, as the main reason for which the debt could have violated substantive constitutional principles was a disregard of Article 4 of the Constitution which restricts the purposes for which debt can only validly be contracted. It might be argued that Article 4 at the same time sets the framework for an assessment of whether or not foreign debt can legitimately be regarded as beneficial. However, it is submitted that to conclude that whenever a loan was contracted in violation of Article 4 the state can keep the borrowed money seems unfair on the creditors. Instead, it might be more appropriate to apply a broader benefits test. Even if loans fall outside of the narrow limits of Article 4, restitution should only be excluded where they were not made for legitimate government purposes. Another criterion to take into account when assessing to what extent restitution can be regarded as fair and desirable might be the good faith of the creditor.[73]

It can be seen that the criteria according to which extra-contractual claims for repayment of the loans made to Argentina under invalid contracts are rudimentary and would need further refinement in order to overcome the many legal problems that might arise in the context of such claims.

2 International dimension[74]

Given that the relevant loan agreements usually contain foreign jurisdiction clauses and waivers of sovereign immunity, an international dimension needs to be brought into the discussion. In particular, it needs to be examined what effect, if any, the unconstitutionality and invalidity of the debt transactions under domestic Argentinian law might have on the claims of the country's foreign creditors that will mostly be brought in foreign courts according to the law of countries other than Argentina. Looking at litigation for debt repayment against Argentina in foreign courts,[75] it seems as if the unconstitutionality or other potential invalidity of the Argentinian debt is not at all an issue before these courts, which might be partly explained by the fact that the Argentinian Government does not raise the issue, so that there is then no apparent reason for the court to analyse it. While it is not likely that this situation is going to change, in the context of assessing how objections to debt repayment might influence the legal position of both debtor countries and creditors, it is nevertheless

---

72   Mairal (1988), at 146–147.
73   Ibid. See also Monti (2001); and "Pastor, José M. Felipe v Reconstrucción de San Juan", Cámara Nacional de Apelaciones de Mendoza, 23 August 1957, J.A. 1957-III, 517, at 523.
74   This part relies heavily on Michalowski (2006), at 318–323.
75   See, for example, the many cases brought against Argentina in federal courts in New York, for example *NML Capital Ltd. v Argentina*, WL 743086 (SDNY 2006); *EM Ltd. v Argentina*, 382 F3d 291 (2nd Cir 2004); *Lightwater v Argentina*, 2003 WL 1878420 (SDNY 2003). See also Elespe (2005b).

important to examine what effect, if any, the invalidity of the debt according to domestic law could have in the context of such litigation.

In the context of Argentina's sovereign debt, the loan contracts mostly determine that the national courts of a chosen country, not international courts or tribunals, are competent to decide disputes arising from these agreements, and they usually contain a choice of law clause that stipulates which law governs the contracts (usually not the law of the debtor state). This means that questions with regard to the validity of the contract will have to be decided according to the chosen national law. However, the issue of determining the authority of the state party is usually regarded as governed by the domestic law of the debtor country,[76] which in the case of Argentina's debt implies a referral to the country's Constitution. The constitutional provisions on authority were not complied with, so that the executive acted without authority and the loan contracts are accordingly void. Even in cases in which foreign law applies to the loans contracted by Argentina, the considerations mentioned above could then potentially have a far-reaching effect, as it would be possible to raise the argument of lack of authority according to Argentinian constitutional law in the national courts of the countries in which the claims are brought. Moreover, contracts that violate the constitution of a debtor state will not be enforced by its local courts, so that the constitutional law of the debtor state might become relevant at the execution stage.[77]

The argument that courts outside of the debtor state should regard loan agreements as void if a debt was not taken up in compliance with the domestic constitutional law of the debtor state finds support in some international arbitration cases that discuss the validity of obligations that were incurred by state organs acting *ultra vires*.[78] In one case, for example, the President of Venezuela had authorized the Venezuelan consul in New York to enter into certain contracts. The consul exceeded his authority, but the authorization issued by the President contained an 'anticipatory all powers clause', approving all future acts of the consul with regard to those contracts. The tribunal held that the validity of the contracts depended on whether the President himself had the power to enter into such contracts. Given that under the Venezuelan Constitution the legislature had the exclusive competence to conclude contracts in the particular subject matter, the contract was found to be *ultra vires* and the claim against Venezuela was rejected.[79] Similarly, in the *Tinoco* case,[80] a cabinet member of the Tinoco Government of Costa Rica had entered into a concessionary contract with a foreign corporation. The contract was then authorized

---

76   Stone (2006), at 299–300; Dicey, Morris and Collins (2006), Rule 162. This also seems to have been assumed by the English Court of Appeal in *Marubeni v Mongolian Government* [2005] EWCA Civ 395, [2005] 1 WLR 2497, at 2508–2509 per Carnwath LJ with regard to state representatives; equally *Merrill Lynch Capital Services Inc. v Municipality of Piraeus* [1997] CLC 1214, at 1234 per Cresswell J.

77   See Carrillo-Batalla Lucas (1995), at 474, n. 143.

78   For a discussion of these cases see Meron (1957), at 274–275.

79   *Beales, Nobles and Garrison (US v Venezuela)*, as summarized in Meron (1957), at 279–280.

80   *Great Britain v Costa Rica* (1923), Reports of International Arbitral Awards, Vol. 1, 371. For a discussion of the other part of the claim in *Tinoco* see Chapter Three, 1.2, supra.

by the President and approved by the Chamber of Deputies. Taft, the US Chief Justice who was the arbitrator in that case, argued that the validity of the contract had to be determined according to the law of Costa Rica in existence at the time of its making. The contract contained provisions concerning taxes, so that, according to the Costa Rican Constitution, the approval of both Houses of Congress, not just that of the Lower Chamber, was required. As Senate had not approved (or disapproved) the contract, it was invalid, and Taft took it for granted that the nullity of the contract based on domestic constitutional law had the effect of invalidating the contractual claim of the international concessionary.[81] Based on these cases, it would then seem as if Argentina could invoke the lack of authority based on its own constitutional law to counter the claims of its creditors in courts outside of Argentina.

However, other cases make the prospect of successfully relying on the unconstitutionality of a contract according to national constitutional law rather unlikely. In some cases, for example, international tribunals held that the conduct of a state subsequent to the conclusion of a contract must be taken into account when deciding whether or not contracts are valid even though they were entered into *ultra vires*. In a case involving Mexico,[82] for example, a contract for legal services was concluded between a US lawyer and an official acting for the Provisional Mexican Government. After having made several payments under the contract, the incoming Mexican government refused to pay the remaining sum on the basis that the contract was *ultra vires* and thus void under Mexican law. The Commission held that it was unwarranted to pronounce the nullity of the contract in the light of the fact that the new Mexican government had recognized the validity of the contract by making several payments under it.[83] In a comparable case in which a US Consul in India had appointed a lawyer to render legal services to the US, and in which the US Government refused to pay the fees on the grounds that the Consul had not been authorized to employ the lawyer on behalf of the Government, the tribunal decided that:

> Whatever at the outset was the authority of the United States Consul to employ an attorney at the expense of the United States Government, it is plain from the correspondence referred to above that that government was perfectly aware … of Hemming's employment in a prosecution initiated solely for its benefit, that it did not object in any way whatever during the progress of the case to the steps taken by its Consul but appeared implicitly at all events to approve of those steps and of Hemming's employment. This Tribunal is, therefore, of the opinion that the United States is bound by the contract entered into, rightly or wrongly, by its Consul for its benefit and ratified by it.[84]

---

81   Ibid., at 397–398.
82   *Davies (USA) v Mexico* (1927), Reports of International Arbitral Awards, Vol. 4, 139.
83   Ibid., at 141. For a related argument in a different factual situation, see *Z v ABC* (1983) 8 YCA 94, at 104.
84   *Hemming (GB) v US* (1920), Reports of International Arbitral Awards, Vol. 6, 51, at 53. See also *Shufeldt (US v Guatemala)*, Annual Digest and Reports of Public International Law Cases, 1929–1930, Case No.110, 180.

In the case of Argentina, it could then easily be argued that the consistent acts of the various democratic governments to repay and restructure the country's foreign debt might be regarded as a subsequent ratification of the originally void loan agreements concluded by the military regime. Given that in Argentina, a ratification of debt transactions that are void because of a lack of authority is not possible, not even where this is done explicitly, the outcome of the same case would then differ depending on whether or not it was decided according to Argentinian law.

The enforceability of the contract could also follow from a good faith argument,[85] on the grounds that the representations made by the debtor state create the appearance of the validity of the transaction on which the creditor can rely, or a legitimate expectation that the country will not turn round and repudiate the contract at some later point. In *Aboilard*,[86] for example, a concessionary contract entered into between a French company and several Haitian Secretaries of State in the name of the Haitian government was later repudiated by that government on the grounds that it had not been submitted to the legislature and was therefore void under domestic law. The tribunal accepted the invalidity of the contract under domestic Haitian law. However, it held that while the contract itself could therefore not produce any legal effects, Haiti was internationally liable for the repudiation of the contract, because the government was responsible for the legitimate expectations created by government officials in the validity of the contract. The government was accordingly liable for the damage suffered by the concessionary. In another case in which the Venezuelan government declared a contract to be void on the grounds that it had not been submitted by the executive for legislative approval as required by the country's Constitution, it was held that this omission should not be ascribed to the other party to the contract, but rather to the Venezuelan executive to whom the compliance with said formality corresponded.[87] These decisions seem to be based on concepts of legitimate expectations and good faith with regard to the fact that the state organ that originally entered into the obligation acted within its authorities. Thus, based on cases such as *Aboilard*, it could be argued that the reasons for the invalidity of the obligations lie with the Argentinian Government, not with the foreign creditors, and that the Argentinian state through its acts created legitimate expectations in its creditors and can accordingly not escape liability, even if the loan agreements were to be regarded as invalid under domestic law.

According to the majority of the arbitration cases, in respect of apparent ratification of an invalid contract, or apparent authority, it seems to be decisive whether the other party was in good faith with regard to the representations made by the state. In order to be able to rely on good faith, the other party must have trusted in the appearance of original authority or of ratification. It must further have applied reasonable care in order to ascertain the authority of the state official, and the amount of care required seems to depend on the expertise of the creditor and the importance and the subject

---

85   Meron (1957), at 286.

86   *Aboilard (France v Haiti)*, (1905) 1 Revue de Droit International Privé et de Droit Pénal International, at 893.

87   *Rudloff (US v Venezuela)* (1903), as summarized by Meron (1957), at 285.

matter of the contract.[88] The outcome of Argentinian challenges of the validity of the loan agreements based on unconstitutionality would then depend on the good faith of the country's creditors. While with regard to the original debt contracted by the military regime, an argument can be made that the unconstitutionality should have been obvious to foreign lenders,[89] it is more difficult to sustain a similar argument with regard to the acts of subsequent democratic governments. Even to the extent that the relevant acts of the democratic successor governments are unconstitutional under the Argentinian Constitution, it could be argued that through the continuous practice of debt repayment, renegotiation and restructuring, the Argentinian state created a legitimate expectation at the international level that it would honour its obligations. If, based on this line of reasoning, the state were barred from relying on the domestic invalidity of the contract, the good faith of the creditor could give effect to an unconstitutional state act, an outcome which differs from the conclusion reached under Argentinian law, where the good faith of the creditor in representations only prevails with regard to acts that could have been performed lawfully.

The example of debt repayment in Argentina demonstrates clearly the problems of an approach that would separate the domestic constitutionality of a contract from its validity under international[90] or foreign law. If acts related to debt repayment either by the Argentinian executive, or by Congress before settling the payment of the debt, were to be regarded as valid, or as potentially giving rise to legitimate expectations in the country's creditors without any regard to domestic constitutional principles, this would have far-reaching consequences. It would mean no less than that the repayment of a debt taken up by a military regime and factually accepted by a democratic government, in the case of Argentina under a lot of international pressure,[91] develops its own dynamics. If the unconstitutionality cannot be invoked to counter the claims of the creditors, this cycle can never be broken, no matter what the audit required by the Argentinian Constitution were to find with regard to the legitimacy of this debt and the compatibility of its servicing with constitutional principles and human rights protection. A country's constitution which is supposed to be the supreme expression of a nation's governing principles, as well as superior to the acts of the government of the day, would lose this very characteristic if the unconstitutionality of an act can be disregarded in the international context. Governments or government officials could then bind nations even if their acts violate constitutional principles, and could effectively contract out of their constitutional obligations.[92] This diminishes the value of the constitution, at least in the context of international transactions. If representative democracy is a valid principle, it is difficult to sustain that the people can be bound by *ultra vires* acts of state organs that did not have the authority to

---

88   Meron (1957), at 288–289.

89   See also the arguments advanced by Taft in the *Tinoco* case, *Great Britain v Costa Rica* (1923), Reports of International Arbitral Awards, Vol. 1, 371, at 394.

90   For a detailed argument against the internationalization of contracts, though in the specific context of foreign direct investment see, for example, Sornarajah (2004), at 85–104 and 223–278.

91   See Chapter Two, 2, supra.

92   For a comparable point in the context of investment contracts see Leader (2006), at 683, who warns that contracts might turn into unofficial constitutions.

represent them. Indeed, to disregard constitutional principles in the context of the contractual relationship between Argentina and its creditors would result in the situation that the Argentinian government would be more accountable to its 'external creditors (the IMF and the World Bank in particular) than to [its] own citizens.'[93]

It is accordingly submitted that the unconstitutionality of an act, at least where it is regarded as so fundamental that it results in nullity, should not be ignored in the context of the legal relationship between debtor countries and their international creditors. This means in respect of Argentina's debt that the state interest in not being bound by representations with regard to unconstitutional debt transactions should outweigh the creditors' interest in the validity of the loan contracts. With regard to the question of ratification, the issues of original authority and ratification should not be separated, but instead both be decided according to the law of the debtor state the acts of whose representatives are at issue. Only if the organ that ratifies the situation has the authority to do so, and if the ratification complies with constitutional and other legal principles, can this ratification be any more valid than the act thereby ratified.[94] In respect of the consequences of this invalidity, a decisive issue would be which law applies to the question of ostensible authority and legitimate expectations. If the law of the debtor state applied, then according to the analysis of Argentinian law presented above there was no ostensible authority that could validate the contract. If, on the other hand, the law governing the contract applies,[95] all depends on how that law approaches the issue, and whether it takes into account the relevant principles of the law of the debtor state.

The domestic Argentinian approach to the conflict between the interests of the creditors and those of the state does not appear to be entirely unusual. In fact, it is very similar to that adopted in England where, just as in Argentina, the doctrine of estoppel or legitimate expectations[96] applies to the administration, but cannot legitimize an act that was *ultra vires*, that is give a state official powers they do not have.[97] Again

---

93   See Cheru (1999), who made this statement with reference to all debtor states, not just Argentina.
94   In the UK, a comparable point was made by Lord Templeman in *Hazell v Hammersmith and Fulham LBC* [1992] 2 AC 1 (HL), at 39, though in a rather different context. However, see Stone (2006), at 301; and *Merrill Lynch Capital Services Inc. v Municipality of Piraeus* [1997] CLC 1214, at 1231 per Cresswell J, where it is argued that the issue of ratification should be governed by the proper law of the contract.
95   This is the English approach to this matter, see, for example, *Merrill Lynch Capital Services Inc. v Municipality of Piraeus* [1997] CLC 1214, at 1231 per Cresswell J; Dicey, Morris and Collins (2006), at 33–434; but see Stone (2006), who argues at 300 that whether or not to hold the principal liable for an act they did not authorize should be governed by the law closest to the principal, which in this case would be Argentinian law.
96   For an overview of the courts' almost identical use of the concepts of estoppel and legitimate expectations see Craig (2003), at 670–671. But see *R (Reprotech (Pebsham) Ltd) v East Sussex County Council* [2003] 1 WLR 348, at 358 per Lord Hoffmann, who distinguishes between the two concepts.
97   Wade and Forsyth (2004), at 237. *R v North and East Devon Health Authority, Ex p Coughlan* [2001] QB 213, at 247–248 per Lord Woolf CJ; *Rowland v Environment*

as in Argentina, in England 'ostensible authority cannot validate a transaction that is *ultra vires* the public body itself'.[98] The only remedies potentially open to the individual who legitimately relied on such a representation would be restitution or compensation.[99] The considerations on which the relevant rules of English law are based very closely resemble those discussed above in the context of the Argentinian approach.[100] It thus seems as if English and Argentinian administrative law reach a similar conclusion with regard to the prevalence of the state interest in redressing an unconstitutional or unlawful situation over the creditor's interest in its perpetuation. The Argentinian approach can accordingly not be regarded as unique, or easily disqualified as a debtor state's attempt to disregard the interests of its creditors.

Of course, it might be argued that an approach that gives precedence to the interests of the debtor country and allows the state to go back on its own promises in order to preserve constitutional principles does not give sufficient weight to the interests of the creditors. Indeed, it has been suggested that the good faith approach adopted by some of the arbitral tribunals strikes a better balance between the interests of the debtor nations and those of the creditors who relied in good faith on representations made by officials of the debtor state.[101] This assessment is presumably in part based on the idea that the defect of the contract emanates from the sphere of the debtor state, not the creditor. Moreover, it could be argued that it might not necessarily be in the interest of the state to be allowed to raise the invalidity of its own actions in order to invalidate a contract. This is because creditors will be reluctant to enter into contracts with the state, or only do so on conditions that take into account the risk of invalidity of the contract, thus making the transactions more costly for the state.[102] However, the suggested consequence is usually not to extend the principle of estoppel or legitimate expectations to unlawful representations of the state, but

---

Agency [2005] Ch 1, at 28 per Peter Gibson LJ, and at 55–56 per May LJ.

98   Craig (2003), at 155, and also at 524 and 668–669; and *Rowland v Environment Agency* [2005] Ch 1, at 28 per Peter Gibson LJ.

99   *Rowland v Environment Agency* [2005] Ch 1, at 55–56 per May LJ. See also the discussion in Craig (2003), at 678–680 with regard to the general principle and some exceptions to the rule.

100 See, for example, *Hazell v Hammersmith and Fulham LBC* [1992] 2 AC 1 (HL), at 36 per Lord Templeman; *Western Fish Products Ltd. v Penwith District Council and Another* [1981] 2 All ER 204, at 219–222, per Megaw LJ; *South Bucks District Council v Flanagan and another* [2002] 1 WLR 2601, at 2607 per Keene LJ. Also Wade and Forsyth (2004), at 340.

101 For a discussion of these issues from an international perspective see Meron (1957), at 274–275.

102 See, for example, Cane (1994), at 517; Davies (2006), at 99 and 114–115. See also *Hazell v Hammersmith and Fulham LBC* [1992] 2 AC 1 (HL), and for the debate triggered by this decision, for example Loughlin (1991).

instead to allow for compensation or restitution,[103] an outcome which also seems to be in line with the holding in *Aboilard*.[104]

Most of the arbitration decisions did not specify on the basis of which law the conclusion in favour of good faith was reached. In *Davies*, the General Claims Commission addressed the issue in passing and argued that it was irrelevant whether the national law of the US or of Mexico applied to the contract, as the Mexican government had clearly ratified the contract. However, it was not explained from which law the principles of ratification were derived. In *Shufeldt*, the arbitrator based the conclusion that the Guatemalan government could not have relied on the invalidity of a concession under Guatemalan national law after having recognized it over a 6-year period on the conviction that this was 'in keeping with the principles of international law'.[105] It seems as if these cases expressly or impliedly rely on general principles of international law in order to justify the conclusion that the invalidity of a contract under national law might not be decisive with regard to the issues of legitimate expectations and implied ratification.

However, it is at least questionable that international law recognizes a principle according to which good faith creditors can rely on legitimate expectations created by officials of debtor states even if their representations are *ultra vires* and violate constitutional principles. It is difficult to determine the exact content of the principle of estoppel in international law, and it has, in fact, been argued that 'the "principle" has no particular coherence in international law, its incidence and effects not being uniform'.[106] Even to the extent that estoppel is accepted as a general principle of international law,[107] however, it presupposes an authorized representation,[108] which makes it comparable to the concept of legitimate expectations and estoppel in Argentinian and English law. Admittedly, the provisions of the Vienna Convention on the Law of Treaties might lend some support to the view endorsed by those arbitral decisions that adopted a good faith approach based on principles of international law. According to Article 46(1), a state can only rely on the invalidity of a treaty under its own national law if the national law violation was manifest and concerned

---

103   For Argentina, see the discussion supra under 1.4. For the UK, see, for example, *Rowland v Environment Agency* [2005] Ch 1, at 55–56 per May LJ; Cane (1994), at 518. But see the provisions of the Local Governments (Contracts) Act 1997, which was enacted as a consequence of the ruling in *Crédit Suisse v Allerdale Borough Council* [1996] 3 WLR 894, where a guarantee given by a local authority to a bank was regarded as *ultra vires* and void. See also the Memorandum of the Bank of England. "Local Authority Swaps" in *Second Report of the Treasury and Civil Service Committee* (1990–91), The 1991 Budget, Minutes of Evidence, at 15, as quoted in Loughlin (1991), at 574, according to which restitution is an inadequate remedy in such cases.

104   *Aboilard (France v Haiti)*, (1905) 1 Revue de Droit International Privé et de Droit Pénal International, at 893.

105   *Shufeldt (US v Guatemala)*, Annual Digest and Reports of Public International Law Cases, 1929–1930, Case No.110, at 180.

106   Brownlie (2003), at 616.

107   See, for example, *Case Concerning the Temple of Preah Vihear (Cambodia v Thailand)* 1962 ICJ 6, at 39–51 per Vice-President Alfaro, and at 52–61 per Justice Fitzmaurice.

108   Brownlie (2003), at 615; see also Bowett (1957), at 192 and 202.

a rule of fundamental importance. Even then, a state is precluded from invoking this invalidity 'if, after becoming aware of the facts … it must by reason of its conduct be considered as having acquiesced in the validity of the treaty or in its maintenance in force or in operation …' (Article 45(b)). Moreover: 'A party may not invoke the provisions of its internal law as justification for its failure to perform a treaty. This rule is without prejudice to article 46' (Article 27). However, these provisions would only directly apply to the relationship between the debtor state and private creditors if, and to the extent that, bonds were protected by Bilateral Investment Treaties, which is uncertain.[109]

Even if international law principles existed that required to disregard national constitutional principles in favour of creditor rights and expectations, such principles would only have to be taken into account to the extent that they form part of the *ordre public* of the country whose law applies,[110] constitute general principles of international law that need to be taken into account by the courts,[111] or are directly applicable to these contracts, none of which can easily be argued. However, if the approach that favours the interests of creditors in the validity of contracts that are invalid under the domestic constitutional law of the debtor country were really derived from generally accepted principles of international law, it needs to be borne in mind that at least with regard to agreements that might violate a state's obligations under international treaties, such as the ICESCR, the potential conflict to be resolved can then not be reduced to one between domestic law and international law, but turns into a conflict between conflicting principles of international law.

If all of the problems raised so far could be overcome and a foreign court hearing a case for debt repayment would accept the arguments suggested here, the legal fate of the creditors' claims for debt repayment would stand and fall with the Argentinian Congress performing its task of settling the payment of the debt, and on the outcomes of the inherent audit. The foreign court would then be faced with the problem that it could not decide on the validity of the claim before the Argentinian Congress settles the payment of the debt, which is something the court can neither require nor even influence. Before this has taken place, it is difficult to see how the Argentinian state could rely on the invalidity arguments presented above, as it could be regarded as unconscionable to invoke the invalidity of the contracts before fulfilling its own task which forms the prerequisite of determining whether the debt in question was invalid or not. It then seems as if before such a settling of the debt takes place, foreign courts would not be able to take the considerations suggested above into account. In particular, it would neither be possible nor appropriate for a foreign court to analyse itself to what extent the debt was unconstitutional according to the law of the debtor state, or whether its recognition would be unreasonable.

---

109 See, for example, Wälde (2005). In the context of Argentinian sovereign debt, this might soon be tested, as a group of holdout creditors resorted to ICSID for claims under their bonds, see *Clarín*, 19 September 2006.

110 See Herdegen (2005), at 26.

111 For example, in Germany according to Article 25 of the Basic Law.

3 Conclusion

Given the many difficult and complex legal arguments that were necessary in order to reach the conclusion that the debt is unconstitutional and the loan contracts void, the practical use of the preceding analysis could be seriously questioned. However, it is submitted that even though it is obvious that the chances that these arguments will make a difference in practice in that they might convince Congress to settle the payment of the debt, and the Argentinian state to invoke these arguments against debt repayment claims, are very slim indeed, a thorough legal analysis nevertheless serves important purposes. First of all, the analysis demonstrates that constitutional law could have played an important part in dramatically reducing the problem of the debt burden. Indeed, if constitutional principles had been complied with, large parts of Argentina's debt might not have been incurred, and the debt crisis would accordingly have been avoided.[112] It also shows that the claims of the creditors are far less clear-cut than they want to make believe, and that in fact good legal arguments exist for limiting them to restitutionary rights, if the political will were there to make use of them. This is essential in order to grasp the complexities of the conflict between the interests of the creditors and those of the Argentinian people.

While the preceding legal analysis shows a way of how to redress the current unconstitutional situation, mainly by retrospectively auditing the debt according to the criteria developed over the last three chapters, this argument can be no more than a starting point for future research into many of the complex issues that would arise if it were to be implemented in practice. In particular, a lot more work would need to be done in order to address convincingly the complex practical problems Congress would face if it were to attempt to audit a debt that was taken up many years ago without proper documentation, and has since been restructured several times, and to separate between originally unconstitutional debt, originally illegal debt, and debt that would have been constitutional and lawful, had it not been taken up by a *de facto* regime. Another important issue to be addressed would be that of refining the criteria according to which restitutionary claims of the creditors could be approached.

While to apply and implement the criteria suggested here in order to return to a constitutional situation would have far-reaching consequences and would require the unravelling of innumerable past debt transactions, this is not a good reason to shy away from the task and eternally to perpetuate an unconstitutional and also deeply unjust situation. It might be useful to remember Lord Templeman's words in *Hazell v Hammersmith*,[113] which sum up quite well some of the considerations that equally apply to unconstitutional sovereign debt transactions:

> Counsel for the banks contended that the application of the *ultra vires* doctrine in the present circumstances is so harsh that if swap transactions entered into by local authorities are unlawful, the swap market and the banks and other parties to swap transactions will be involved in great difficulties, the creditworthiness of local authorities would be impaired and there would be an increase in taxation. The major problem concerns the activities of the council which indulged in speculation on a vast and admittedly unlawful scale.

---

112   Conesa (2004), at 1007.
113   *Hazell v Hammersmith and Fulham LBC* [1992] 2 AC 1 (HL).

It may not follow that, as between the council and the banks, payments made by the council before or after the period of the interim strategy can be recovered by the council. Nor does it follow that payments received by the council before or after the period of interim strategy cannot be recovered by the banks. The consequences of any *ultra vires* transaction may depend on the facts of each case.[114]

---

114   Ibid., at 36.

Chapter Eight

Conclusion

This book's primary purpose was to examine whether one of the main arguments on which the campaigns for debt cancellation rely, that is that parts of the debt of developing countries do not need to be repaid because of their origin, can be given a clear and convincing legal basis. The preceding analysis accordingly concentrated on one particular issue arising in the context of the debt crisis that affects many developing countries, namely that the people of debtor countries are to a large extent obliged to repay a debt the taking up of which was out of their control. In order to assess the legal validity of potential arguments against the repayment of such debt, it was necessary to carry out a detailed and in large parts rather complicated legal analysis of the underlying issues. The complexity and technicality of the legal discussion has several drawbacks, one being that the arguments developed and the conclusions presented are not easily accessible to non-lawyers. Moreover, complicated arguments usually have a lesser chance of being invoked successfully, at least where they are needed in order to counter allegedly clear-cut claims under seemingly valid contracts. Indeed, the creditors rely on *pacta sunt servanda* which is an almost universally accepted principle, both of international law and the national law of most countries, while legal arguments challenging the validity of certain sovereign debts, or justifying their repudiation, are complex, controversial and underdeveloped. Nevertheless, the preceding analysis demonstrates that in addition to the recent focus on developing defences against the creditors' contractual claims based on the economic impossibility to repay all loans in full,[1] a more radical challenge to the validity of the loan agreements as such can be made.

Chapter Two demonstrates that in the case of Argentina, and it is submitted that this applies similarly, and in some cases even more strongly,[2] to many other developing countries, a debt crisis was created by transactions between dictatorial

---

1   For a discussion of a defence of economic necessity see, for example, OLG Frankfurt NJW 2003, 268; Reinisch (2003); Pfeiffer (2003); Bothe and Hafner (2003); Tietje (2005); Baars and Böckel (2004), at 460–461. This defence was also accepted by an ICSID arbitral tribunal in *LG & E v Argentina*, Case ARB/02/1, 3 October 2006, at paras 226–266. The discussions of sovereign insolvency (see for example, Raffer (2005), and of debt restructurings involving haircuts for the creditors (see, for example, Reinisch (1995), provide other ways to address problems of the economic impossibility of repaying sovereign debt in full.

2   The cases of the Congo under Mobutu, Indonesia under Suharto, and the Philippines under Marcos are among the most prominent examples of qualifying regimes. See, for example, Hanlon (2006), at 123–125.

and/or corrupt governments and irresponsible international lenders.[3] The majority of the people who are still paying the bill, and large parts of whom live in extreme poverty, usually had no input in these operations, which brings up the question of whether it is then legally justifiable to impose the obligation to repay this debt on the people of the debtor country, rather than on those who were responsible for and benefited from the loans. The legal analysis of international law and of national Argentinian law showed that there are different ways of approaching and conceptualizing the underlying issue of a potential lack of representation of the people of the debtor countries. As a matter of principle, under international law, the state and with it the people are usually responsible for the acts of their rulers, and bound by transactions entered into by them.[4] This extends to governments who take over a country by force, without the people having any say in the matter, at least if the regime exercises *de facto* power over the country.[5] Even the doctrine of odious debts, the main international law doctrine usually referred to in order to question the validity or enforceability of debt that was taken up by the dictatorships of the 1970s and 1980s, does not seem to question the principal assumption that the people of a country are bound by the acts of their governments, regardless of whether they came into power and govern the country in accordance with its constitutional rules. In its traditional form, the doctrine of odious debts allows for the repudiation of certain debts on moral grounds. To the extent that it considers debts that qualify as odious as personal debts of the regime, and not as debts of the people,[6] the odious debts doctrine could be regarded as providing a theoretical framework for deciding under which circumstances a regime does not represent its people. However, according to the doctrine, even in the absence of actual representation, the debt is that of the people, not the regime, unless the people did not derive any benefits from it, and the creditors knew this.[7] Given that the assessment of the beneficial nature of the loan is to be performed by an international tribunal according to objective criteria,[8] this approach is obviously not concerned with retrospectively healing the lack of representation. Otherwise, this evaluation would have to be left to the people, or their newly instated representatives. Taken together, the criteria of the odious debts doctrine demonstrate that the main focus of the doctrine is not to address a lack of representation, but to find a balance between the interests of the creditors and those of the debtor state, in the context of which the fact that the people of the debtor state were not properly represented by their government is only one, but not the decisive factor. Thus the doctrine of odious debts regards the people in principle as bound by loans entered into by governments that rule the country *de facto* even if the people of the country have no means to participate in the governing process.[9]

---

3   For Argentina see, for example, the finding in "Olmos, Alejandro S/denuncia", causa
     N°14.467, 13 July 2000, Juzg. Nac. Crim. y Corr. Fed., n. 2., JA 2001-I-514.
4   Buchheit, Gulati and Thompson (2006), at 3.
5   See, for example, Warbrick (2003), at 226–227.
6   See, for example, Sack (1927), at 157.
7   Ibid.
8   Ibid., at 162.
9   But see Nitti (1931), at 754–755 and the discussion in Chapter Three, 7, supra.

Possibilities to address the problem of lack of representation in international law might be found in the right to self-determination, the concept of democratic entitlement, or the growing law on the obligation of non-recognition. The obligation of non-recognition is an obligation of states not to recognize a situation that comes about by or constitutes a blatant violation of international law, in particular obligations *erga omnes* or norms of *ius cogens*, and not to assist other states in creating or perpetuating such a situation.[10] To extend this principle to the situation that a regime denies its people active participation in government would require that such a form of government could be regarded not just as a violation of the internal law of that country, but also as a serious violation of international law. However, it is controversial whether the right to self-determination protects the people not only from outside interference, but also internally against the infringement of participation rights of the people by their own government.[11] It is equally controversial whether international law recognizes a democratic entitlement,[12] and of what this might consist. Until it is settled that international law requires a form of government which guarantees internal participation, military or other dictatorial regimes usually cannot be said to violate international law simply by taking over a country by the means of a coup. An obligation of non-recognition of such a regime could then only be justified if in addition to the means by which it came into government, the regime commits serious violations of international law. Before international law can effectively address the issues raised, international agreement on fundamental theoretical and ideological questions of the meaning of democracy and participation would have to be reached. As things are, outside of the narrow limits of the traditional odious debts doctrine, international law does not seem to provide a promising starting point for challenging, based on lack of representation, that a debt taken up by a *de facto* regime binds the state. To the extent that international law recognizes, or will recognize, a principle of democratic entitlement and internal self-determination, it is not clear what the consequences of a violation of the people's democratic entitlement or their right to internal self-determination, and of the resulting non-recognition of the regime would be in general,[13] and for the validity of loans contracted by such a regime, in particular. However, it could be argued that this creates a general assumption that certain regimes are not entitled to represent their country, which could be an important factor in evaluating the validity of transactions entered into by regimes.

As Chapters Five to Seven show, the constitutional law of debtor countries might go further and not only require that the government that represents the country in international relations, including loan transactions, possesses constitutional legitimacy, but moreover set a more detailed framework for valid representation in

---

10   *Wall in the Occupied Palestinian Territory* (2004) ICJ 136, at 159. For a discussion see also Talmon (2006); Murphy (2000).

11   The idea of an international law principle of internal self-determination finds more and more supporters. See, for example, Cassese (1995), 101–140; Shaw (2003), at 272–273; *Loizidou v Turkey* (1997) 23 EHRR 513, at 535 per Judge Wildhaber, concurring.

12   In favour see, for example, Shaw (2003), Franck (2000), Fox (2000), critical for example Roth (2000); Marks (2000).

13   See Talmon (2006), at 104–106.

particular transactions, which can reach from the question of which organ within a government has the power to represent the state, to the procedure that needs to be complied with, and substantive considerations that govern the relevant transaction. As could equally be seen in Chapters Five and Seven, unlike in international law, for the outcome of the analysis of Argentinian constitutional law the lack of representation of the people was determinative. Indeed, the debt taken up by the *de facto* regime was unconstitutional precisely because it was not contracted by the organ that the Argentinian Constitution entrusted with the task of representing the people in loan transactions. In the Argentinian case, the result that the loans contracted by the military regime violated the constitutional provisions on representation could easily be reached because the *de facto* regime had dissolved Congress, the organ responsible for contracting public loans. However, had the Constitution allocated this role to the executive, reliance on a technical/procedural argument would not have been sufficient for a finding that the people were not properly represented. It would instead have been necessary to bring in considerations such as whether a regime that takes power in disregard of constitutional provisions can be regarded as validly representing the country if it then governs in compliance with formal constitutional prerequisites. It is submitted that this question would usually have to be answered in the negative, as a government that came into power in disregard of the fundamental constitutional provisions on representation cannot be regarded as representing the people of the country.

However, this raises several issues. First of all, not all debtor states might have a constitutional framework that requires at least indirect representation of the people in the form of democratically elected governments. Indeed, where a country is ruled by a regime whose coming into power and/or methods of governing raise serious doubts as to the extent to which it actually represents the people, but where no violation of national constitutional or other legal principles occurs, reliance on national law would not provide a way to invalidate the acts of this government. These are the cases where the absence of a principle of international law according to which the validity of the acts of such regimes, including debt transactions, could be questioned, is most strongly felt. Another scenario that could cause difficulties would be that of a regime that came into force in violation of the existing constitution of the relevant country and which then changed the constitution before entering into loan agreements that are valid according to the new, but not under the abolished, constitution. One issue to be taken into account might be whether the old constitution contained a provision to the effect that if the previous constitutional order were to be restored, the acts and transactions of the *de facto* government might not be recognized as valid.[14] However, this still leaves the question of how to deal with the situation that no such provision was in place when the unconstitutional government took power.

---

14   See Pogge (2005), at 154. See also Article 36 of the Argentinian Constitution that was introduced in the context of the constitutional reform of 1994 and states that: 'This Constitution shall rule even when its observance is interrupted by acts of force against the institutional order and the democratic system. These acts shall be irreparably null…'

In Argentinian law, the *de facto* doctrine developed by the Argentinian Supreme Court would become relevant here. While the applicable case law is contradictory, it was suggested in Chapter Five that the more convincing approach is that acts of *de facto* regimes only continue to be legally valid upon return to democracy if they were ratified by the competent organ of the constitutional successor government.[15] To some extent, the outcomes of the *de facto* doctrine of Argentinian constitutional law could also be explained with reference to agency law principles. If a government is understood to act as an agent of the people, the principal,[16] then 'if the circumstances of the transaction raise reasonable doubts about whether the agent is faithfully representing the interests of his principal, these principles [of agency] suggest that the third party is under a duty to investigate.'[17] It could then be argued that the principal can only be bound by these transactions by the means of ratification. However, it would have to be considered whether there comes a point, and if so how exactly this point could be determined, at which a new government might be regarded as sufficiently consolidated that its constitution can safely be treated by lenders as the legitimate constitution of the country.

The legal analysis in Chapters Five, Six and Seven of the constitutionality of Argentina's debt that was taken up by the military regime stands and falls with the acceptance of the argument that the Argentinian Constitution requires that the constitutional successor government audit debts taken up by unconstitutional regimes before recognizing them as binding the state. This is a crucial point at least for each legal system that has a constitution in place which sets a framework of fundamental rules which cannot be changed by the government of the day. From the domestic point of view, it would be unacceptable that a constitution can be circumvented by the means of force, that is where a regime, instead of complying with constitutional requirements, overthrows a constitutional government and then governs the country without constitutional legitimization and control. If such a regime could validly bind the country, including in long-term debt transactions, without at least a retrospective constitutional control of the underlying policies, incoming constitutional governments might be faced with highly detrimental legacies that limit their own policy choices for many years to come.[18] In order to avoid this, and to guarantee constitutionality at least retrospectively, a debt that was taken up outside of the usual constitutional control mechanisms that aim to ensure that the people of a country are duly represented in loan transactions, and that the transactions are entered into responsibly and within the constraints of the country's constitution, needs to be audited by an incoming constitutional regime as to its constitutionality, lawfulness and its compatibility with the interests of the country. While the legal arguments presented in Chapter Five in favour of this interpretation of the Argentinian Constitution are not only complicated, but moreover highly controversial, and while it is moreover unlikely that many

---

15   Chapter Five, 2, supra.

16   In favour of such a conceptualization of the government-people relationship with further references to US law and political philosophy see Buchheit, Gulati and Thompson (2006), at 36–37.

17   Ibid., at 41.

18   For an interesting analysis of related issues see Jain (1993).

countries have constitutional provisions that can be interpreted so as to require such an audit, it is submitted that the underlying principle is sufficiently convincing to be suggested for general adoption: a constitutional government succeeding an unconstitutional regime should audit transactions undertaken by that regime in the name of the country and only ratify those that do not violate constitutional principles or the interests of the country.[19]

If this were accepted, then two more problems need to be addressed: what are the legal consequences for the relationship between the country and the creditor if an incoming government rejects all or part of the debt taken up by its unconstitutional predecessor based on an audit, and what follows for the constitutionality and validity of the debt if it is assumed by the successor government without carrying out such an audit? With regard to the first question, it was argued both in Chapters Six and Seven that the incoming democratic government would have to reject the recognition of a debt that was taken up in violation of substantive constitutional principles, such as norms that limit the amount of sovereign debt or the purposes for which it can be taken up, or where the loans violate other legal principles, as it would neither be constitutional nor reasonable to accept such debt.[20] In all other cases the incoming government would have great leeway to decide whether or not to assume the debt. In Chapter Seven it was further argued that as a consequence of the refusal to recognize the debt as valid, the loan contracts would be void.[21] Whether and to what extent the creditors could recover the money lent would have to be decided according to the rules of unjust enrichment. This strikes a fair balance between the interests of the creditors and those of the debtor state, as the country should not be bound by the terms of contracts which were concluded without authority of the acting agent, but it cannot have a legitimate interest in keeping borrowed money that increased the assets of the state.[22] However, while this result can be easily reached under the national law of Argentina, and probably also that of many other countries, its usefulness in the sovereign debt context largely depends on the extent to which the law that is applicable to the loan, which is in many cases not that of the debtor state, will accept this outcome. As explained in Chapter Seven, whether or not a state was validly represented in a transaction, including transactions *iure gestionis*, is usually determined by the national law of that state, which generally means by national constitutional and administrative law principles.[23] It could then be argued that at least those states in which the military or other dictatorial regimes contracted loans without authority under national law would not be bound by those contracts.

However, in the Argentinian context and that of many other debtor countries, one of the most difficult legal questions that needs to be addressed is whether the original

19   See also Ruiz Díaz and Toussaint (2004).
20   See Chapter Six, 3, and Chapter Seven, 1.1, supra.
21   Chapter Seven, 1.1 and 1.2.1, supra.
22   Chapter Seven, 1.4, supra.
23   See, for example, Stone (2006), at 299–300; Dicey, Morris and Collins, Rule 162. This also seems to have been assumed by the English Court of Appeal in *Marubeni v Mongolian Government* [2005] EWCA Civ 395, [2005] 1 WLR 2497, at 2508–2509 per Carnwath LJ with regard to state representatives; equally *Merrill Lynch Capital Services Inc. v Municipality of Piraeus* [1997] CLC 1214, at 1234 per Cresswell J.

unconstitutionality of the debt that was taken up by the military regime was healed by the consistent approach of all of the governments that ruled the country since the return to democracy to recognize this debt as binding. Looked at from the point of view of representation, it could be argued that if a constitutional government, which the democratic governments in Argentina that succeeded the military regime clearly were, recognizes a debt as valid that was contracted by a ruler who did not have the constitutional authority validly to represent the country, the original lack of representation is cured, and the binding nature of the debt can no longer be questioned on this basis. The main problem here would be to what extent this result might be questioned where the recognition itself did not comply with constitutional principles, for example because, as in Argentina, it was not performed by the constitutionally authorized organ, Congress, and took place even though the debt was never audited as to its constitutionality and lawfulness.

In Chapters Five and Seven it was argued that the recognition of a debt in violation of constitutional principles cannot amount to more than a factual recognition which would not validate the loan transactions under national Argentinian law.[24] However, this is not the predominant view. To the contrary, it is widely assumed that such acts of factual recognition have the effect of writing the debtor's obligations in stone, and of taking away every right to redress the persisting unconstitutionality in the future. The argument is that if not by the contracts concluded by the military regime, then at least by the democratic governments' factual recognition thereof, inalienable rights of the creditors were created. Indeed, it seems as if the factual recognition of the debt of the military regime by acts of repayment, debt restructurings etc. before the debt was audited is regarded as a valid ratification of this debt by the democratic successor governments, the potential unconstitutionally of this ratification notwithstanding. This approach finds support in the provisions of the Vienna Convention on the Law of Treaties. Even though they are not directly applicable, they nevertheless provide authority for the view that in international relations a state cannot rely on invalidity under its own law, and that it is moreover precluded from invoking the invalidity of a treaty if its conduct must be regarded as a ratification (Article 45).

However, while such rules might have an important role to play in the context of treaties between states, it is not so clear that this approach to legal certainty is appropriate in the context of contracts between a state and a private lender.[25] As long as the principle of legal certainty is applied unilaterally to the financial interests of the creditors, the law adopts a biased and limited approach towards this concept. For the people of the debtor countries, legal certainty would mean that their affairs are primarily governed in accordance with their constitutions, and that violations of national constitutional law can be reversed, even where an incoming democratic regime accepted, in disregard of constitutional principles, the validity of contracts entered into by their unconstitutional predecessor with parties who happen to be foreign nationals. In Chapter Seven, it was argued that under Argentinian law, a ratification of an act that was carried out without authority is not possible

---

24   See Chapter Five, 4, and Chapter Seven, 1.2, supra.
25   Wälde (1987), at 127.

under administrative law.[26] This principle serves the purpose of preventing that a circumvention of constitutional and other fundamental norms can have the effect of creating inalienable rights that cannot be revoked. Otherwise, contractual rights would stand above all other values.

This consideration is particularly important in the dealings of developing countries with international lenders. Looking at the history of Argentina's sovereign debt, when the first democratic government took over from the military regime, it was determined to do exactly what the constitution demanded, which is to audit the inherited debt as to its validity before repaying it. An important reason why it did not follow this through was the pressure exercised by the creditors, and in particular the IMF, although internal factors, such as the precarious situation of the government which significantly limited its political leeway, also played a significant role.[27] Here, one of the real problems not only of the sovereign debt of developing countries, but more generally of the relationship between developing countries and IFIs, other creditors, and the governments representing their interests, comes into the equation. The reality of the international power structure, and with it that of international politics as well as international economic law, is such that even in states which have legal mechanisms in place according to which the legitimacy of acts of unconstitutional governments can be questioned, it was and is[28] made difficult, if not impossible for the countries to use them effectively. It is submitted that to the extent that the international community is now said to be more and more concerned with protecting democracy and self-determination,[29] a simple way to accomplish this in the context of debt that originated from an unconstitutional regime would be not to ignore the constitutional law of the debtor state when it comes to determining the validity of the loan agreements. Where foreign law governs the loan contract, this could easily be achieved if not only the issue of actual authority, but also the questions of ostensible authority and ratification were determined according to the law of the debtor state. Otherwise, a country that is struggling to make the difficult transition from an unconstitutional to a constitutional regime would be forever precluded from complying with constitutional mandates if the incoming regime gives in to international or internal pressure and recognizes loans in disregard of the constitution.

An alternative to the approach suggested here would be not to focus on the domestic law of the debtor country, but instead on the law that governs the loan contract, and to develop legal arguments against the validity of the contract on the basis of the provisions of that law.[30] This could, for example, be achieved by

---

26   Chapter Seven, 1.2.1, supra.

27   See Chapter Two, 2, supra.

28   See, for example, the constant pressure of the IMF that the Argentinian executive constrain Congress and the courts and change legislation according to the wishes of the creditors, explained in Chapter Five, 3.2.6, supra.

29   See Cassese (2005), at 395; *Loizidou v Turkey* (1997) 23 EHRR 513, at 535 per Judge Wildhaber, concurring; Ipsen (2004), at 428–430.

30   See Buchheit, Gulati and Thompson (2006). For interesting approaches see also Lothian (1995); and Diez-Picazo, Ponce de León (1995).

extending private law principles to states by way of analogy.[31] While the possibilities of such an approach are worth exploring, it is submitted that an approach that refers the questions of actual and ostensible authority and ratification to the law of the debtor state is, in principle, preferable, as it allows to take into account the specific situation of a state as sovereign and the constitutional limitations imposed on state organs, instead of artificially treating the state as if it was in the same position as a private actor.

Moving on to the question of how the arguments discussed in this book might be put into practice, mainly two strategies can be applied: debt repudiation or invoking the invalidity of the loan. Both strategies would require a political decision of the debtor country to reject the debt as binding, but depending on the chosen approach, the decision would be based on different grounds. Repudiation could mainly be based on the international law doctrine of odious debts and would require an active step of the debtor country to reject the repayment of the loans based on their illegitimacy. As the main purpose of the doctrine is to challenge the legal enforceability of certain debts on moral grounds, and to allow for their repudiation on the basis of a decision by an international tribunal, it is not meant to provide debtor states with a defence against repayment claims in court proceedings. Nor would it be appropriate for courts to apply the odious debts doctrine in the context of contractual claims for debt repayment, as the criteria are so broad and politically charged that such a use of the doctrine would be questionable and could give rise to arbitrary results.[32] Instead, its applicability would depend on the implementation of an international mechanism according to which the doctrine could be invoked and enforced. Even if a government were to repudiate all or parts of its sovereign debt, this would not necessarily prevent the creditors from seeking debt repayment in court proceedings, so that the lawfulness of the repudiation would then have to be scrutinized by the court hearing the claim, unless the consequence of a successful repudiation before an international tribunal would be to exclude such claims.

The redefined odious debts doctrine discussed in Chapter Four according to which loans that are made to regimes that commit *ius cogens* violations would be void might be more promising when it comes to its potential use in court proceedings. If it were to be accepted as a doctrine of international law, it could be invoked before national courts that hear claims for debt repayment, to the extent that the relevant legal system within which the court operates requires the national courts to take principles of international law into account. As the courts would then be prevented from handing down decisions that violate international law principles, the creditors' contractual claims could be countered by relying on the invalidity of the loans because of their violation of *ius cogens* norms.[33] Moreover, an argument could be made that the reasons that militate in favour of the recognition of such a doctrine as part of international law also favour integrating the doctrine into the national *ordre public* of countries.

---

31   See also Wälde (1987), at 127.
32   But see Khalfan (2003), at 71 and 80–81.
33   See Chapter Four, 2.3, supra.

To rely on the invalidity of loans under the national law of the debtor state or that of the law that applies to the proper contract would mean using invalidity as a legal defence against the creditors' claims. However, it needs to be borne in mind that proceedings for debt repayment will only be initiated once the debtor state defaulted on its debt servicing obligations. If the default is caused by a political decision to challenge the legal validity of the debt, rather than by the impossibility to repay, a better strategy than defaulting and then raising the invalidity as a defence against the creditor's claim might be to seek a court declaration on the question of invalidity before defaulting on debt servicing. Otherwise, the debtor state risks the adverse consequences of a default in case the court does not accept the argument.

This book was concerned with providing a legal analysis of some of the issues on the basis of which the validity of parts of the debt of developing countries could be challenged. Many of the arguments could appear to be unnecessarily complex, and their application completely impractical. It is true that an implementation of the principles suggested in this book would require a lot of effort in order to make the concepts workable in practice, but this does not discredit the arguments as such. Nevertheless, a lot of additional academic work would still need to be carried out, in particular with regard to the application of the principle of unjust enrichment to the situations in which a loan can be regarded as void, as this would be the primary legal tool to achieve a fair balancing of the interests of the debtor states and those of the creditors. While it is undoubtedly true that legal arguments in themselves will not resolve the debt problem and that the debt crisis rather needs a political solution, it is essential that lawyers make their contribution to the discussion,[34] and challenges to the legal validity of the debt to counter the legal claims of the creditors are one possible line to pursue. Indeed, the main purpose of the analysis was to provide an intellectual framework according to which the logic of *pacta sunt servanda* that predominates the legal approach to the debt taken up by unconstitutional regimes can be challenged, and it is submitted that this logic loses a lot of force when realizing that the contracts which receive the protection of this principle are not necessarily legally valid.

---

34   See also Toussaint (1999), at 35; Carty (1986), at 419; MacLean (1989), at 43.

Bibliography

Abrahams, C. P. 'The doctrine of "odious debts"' (LLM thesis: Leiden, NL, 2000), www.odiousdebts.org/odiousdebts/publications/ApartheidDebtThesis.pdf.

Abramovich, V. 'Equilibrio fiscal al margen de la legalidad', *Clarín*, 9 August 2002.

Abramovich, V. and Courtis, C. *Los Derechos Sociales como Derechos Exigibles* (Editorial Trotta: Madrid 2002).

Acquaviva, G. 'The dissolution of Yugoslavia and the fate of its financial obligations' (2002) 30 *Denver Journal International Law & Policy* 173–216.

Adams, P. 'Iraq's odious debts' (2004) 526 *Policy Analysis*, www.cato.org/pub_display.php?pub_id=2465.

Adams, P. *Odious Debts* (Earthscan: London, Toronto 1991).

Akacem, M. and Miller, D.D. 'The odious debt principle: the case of Iraq', Paper presented at the Thirty First Annual Conference of the Association of Private Enterprise Education Las Vegas, (April 2006), unpublished.

Albanese, S., Dalla Vía, A., Gargarella, R., Hernández, A. and Sabsay, D. *Derecho Constitucional* (Editorial Universidad: Buenos Aires 2004).

Alexander, J. 'Baker the bailiff? Assessing US policy on Saddam's debt', Middle East Report Online, 2 March 2004, www.odiousdebts.org/odiousdebts/index.cfm?DSP=content&ContentID=9637.

Alston, P. 'Out of the abyss: the challenges confronting the new UN Committee on Economic, Social and Cultural Rights' (1987) 9 *Human Rights Quarterly* 332–381.

Alterini, A. A. and López Cabana, R.M. 'La virtualidad de los actos propios en el derecho argentino', *La Ley* 1984-A, 877–880.

Amadeo, E. *La Salida del Abismo* (Planeta: Buenos Aires 2003).

Ambrose, S. 'Social movements and the politics of debt cancellation' (2005) 6 *Chicago Journal of International Law* 267–285.

Anderson, K.H. 'International law and state succession: a solution to the Iraqi debt crisis?' (2005) *Utah Law Review* 401–441.

Anghie, A. 'Time present and time past: globalization, international financial institutions, and the third world' (2000) 32 *NYU Journal of International Law & Politics* 243–290.

Arndt, H-W. 'Staatshaushalt und Verfassungsrecht' (1990) *Juristische Schulung* 343–347.

Arora, A. and Olivares-Caminal, R. 'Rethinking the sovereign debt restructuring approach' (2003) 9 *Law and Business Review of the Americas* 629–666.

Asp, D. 'Argentina's mystery of capital: why the International Monetary Fund needs Hernando de Soto' (2003) 12 *Minnesota Journal of Global Trade* 383–415.

Baars, A. and Böckel, M. 'Argentinische Auslandsanleihen vor deutschen und argentinischen Gerichten' *Juristenzeitung* 2004, 445–464.

Badeni, G. 'Límites de la delegación legislativa' *La Ley* 2001-E, 913-924.

Barra, R.C. 'La nulidad del acto administrativo y los efectos de su declaración', *El Derecho* 108, 587–591 (1984a).

Barra, R.C. 'Enriquecimiento sin causa y contrato administrativo', *El Derecho* 109, 390–395 (1984b).

Basualdo, E. *Estudios de Historia Económica Argentina*, (Siglo Veintiuno Editores: Buenos Aires 2006).

Bazán Lazcano, M. '¿Es constitucional la gestión de la deuda pública externa?', *El Derecho* 117, 963–976 (1986).

Bedjaoui, M. *Ninth Report on Succession of States in respect of matters other than Treaties*, A/CN.4/301, (1977) 2 *Yearbook International Law Commission* 1.

Beemelmans, H. 'State succession in international law', (1997) 15 *Boston University International Law Journal* 71–123.

Bianchi, A.B. 'Constitucionales e inconstitucionales', *La Nueva Provincia*, Bahía Blanca, 13 July 1984.

Bianchi, A.B. 'La delegación legislativa luego de la reforma constitucional de 1994', *Jurisprudencia Argentina* 1996-IV, 764–773.

Bidart Campos, G. 'La Derogación de la Ley de Amnistía 22.924' *El Derecho* 110, 340–347 (1985).

Bidart Campos, G.J. *La Interpretación y el Control Constitutionales en la Jurisdicción Constitucional* (Ediar: Buenos Aires 1987).

Bidart Campos, G. *Tratado Elemental de Derecho Constitucional Argentino*, Volume 2, (Ediar: Buenos Aires 1992).

Bidart Campos, G.J. *La Interpretación y el Control Constitucionales en la Jurisdicción Constitucional* (Ediar: Buenos Aires 1996).

Bidart Campos, G.J. 'Arreglar el pago de la deuda externa (¿?)' *La Ley* 2001-E, 1280.

Birk, D. 'Die finanzverfassungsrechtlichen Vorgaben und Begrenzungen der Staatsverschuldung', *Deutsches Verwaltungsblatt* 1984, 745–749.

Blustein, P. *And the Money Kept Rolling in (and out)*, (Public Affairs: New York 2005).

Bohoslavsky, J.P. (2006a), *Consecuencias jurídicas y económicas del crédito abusivo (especial referencia al endeudamiento soberano)*, (PhD thesis, University of Salamanca, Spain, October 2006), unpublished.

Bohoslavsky, J.P. (2006b), 'Matices y derivaciones jurídicas del pago al FMI', *Suplemento Constitucional de La Ley*, 10 March 2006, 4–10.

Bonelli, M. *Un País en Deuda*, (Planeta: Buenos Aires, 2nd ed. 2005).

Bonner Kommentar, *Kommentar zum Bonner Grundgesetz* (Rudolf Dolzer, Klaus Vogel, eds), (C.F. Müller: Heidelberg 2003).

Borda, A. *La Teoría de los Actos Propios* (LexisNexis Abeledo Perrot: Buenos Aires 2000).

Bothe, M., Brink, J., Kirchner, C. and Stockmayer, A. *Rechtsfragen der internationalen Verschuldungskrise* (Peter Lang: Frankfurt am Main, Bern, New York, Paris 1988)

Bothe, M. and Hafner, G.. 'Die völkerrechtliche Begründung staatlicher Leistungsverweigerungsrechte aus dem Gesichtspunkt des Notstands', Rechtsgutachten (2003), unpublished.

Bowett, D.W. 'Estoppel before international tribunals and its relation to acquiescence' (1957) 33 *British Yearbook of International Law* 176–202.

Bradford, S. and Kucinski, B. *The Debt Squad* (Zed Books: London 1988).

Brock, W.E. 'Trade and debt: the vital link' (1984) *Foreign Affairs* 1037–1057.

Brownlie, I. *Principles of Public International Law* (Oxford University Press: Oxford, 6th ed. 2003).

Buchheit, L.C., Gulati, G.M. and Thompson, R.B. 'The dilemma of odious debts' *Duke Law School Legal Studies Research Paper Series*, Research Paper No.127 (September 2006), ssrn.com/abstract=932916.

Buckley, R. 'A tale of two crises: the search for the enduring reforms of the international financial system' (2001) 6 *UCLA Journal of International Law & Foreign Affairs* 1–43.

Buckley, R. 'Why are developing nations so slow to play the default card in renegotiating their sovereign indebtedness?' (2005) 6 *Chicago Journal of International Law* 345–359.

Buckley, R. *Emerging Markets Debt* (Kluwer Law International: The Hague, London, Boston 1999).

Burgers, J.H. and Danelius, H. *The United Nations Convention against Torture: A Handbook on the Convention on Torture and Other Cruel, Inhuman or Degrading Treatment or Punishment* (M. Nijhoff: Dordrecht 1988).

Cabral, P.O. and Maljar, D.E. 'Herramientas para el control de la arbitrariedad de los poderes públicos en el orden nacional y bonaerense. Su antecedente español' *Jurisprudencia Argentina* 2002-III, 1524–1567.

Cafiero, M. 'El FMI y la debacle argentina 1976–2003' (2005), www1.hcdn.gov.ar/dependencias/Mario_Cafiero.

Cafiero, M. and Llorens, J. *La Argentina Robada* (Ediciones Macchi: Buenos Aires 2002).

Calcagno, A. E. and Calcagno, E. *La Deuda Externa Explicada a Todos (los que tienen que pagarla)*, (Catálogos: Buenos Aires 1999).

Cane, P. 'Do banks dare lend to local authorities?' (1994) 110 *LQR* 514–521.

Carrillo-Batalla Lucas, V. 'Conflicts of laws in international lending transactions – governing law and choice of forum', in: Carreau, D. and Shaw, M.N. (eds), *La Dette Exterieure, The External Debt*, (Martinus Nijhoff Publishers: Dordrecht, Boston, London 1995), 409–484.

Carty, A. 'The Third World debt crisis: towards new international standards for contraction of public debt' (1986) 19 *Verfassung und Recht in Übersee*, 401–419.

Cassagne, J.C. *Derecho Administrativo*, Volume 1, (Abeledo Perrot: Buenos Aires, 8th ed. 2006).

Cassese, A. *Self-determination of peoples: a legal reappraisal* (Cambridge University Press: Cambridge, New York 1995).

Cassese, A. *International Law* (Oxford University Press: Oxford, 2nd ed. 2005).

Chander, A. 'Odious securitization' (2004) 53 *Emory Law Journal* 923–927.

Cheru, F. *Independent Expert Report to the Economic and Social Council* 'Effects of structural adjustment policies on the full enjoyment of human rights', E/CN.4/1999/50.

Cheru, F. 'Playing games with African lives: the G7 debt relief strategy and the politics of indifference', in: Jochnik, C. and Fraser, A.P. (eds), *Sovereign Debt at the Crossroads* (Oxford University Press: Oxford 2006), 35–54.

Chowdhury, S.R. and De Waart, P. J.I.M. 'Significance of the right to development: an introductory view' in: Chowdhury, S. R., Denters, E.M.G. and de Waart, P.J.I.M. (eds), *The Right to Development in International Law* (Martinus Nijhoff Publishers: Dordrecht, Boston, London 1992), 7–23.

Colautti, C.E. 'La delegación de facultades legislativas y la reforma constitucional', *La Ley* 1996-B, 856–861.

Comadira, J.R. *Derecho Administrativo* (Abeledo Perrot: Buenos Aires 2003).

CONADEP *Nunca Más* (1984), http://www.nuncamas.org/investig/articulo/nuncamas/nmas0001.htm.

Conesa, E. 'Argentina: como convivir con el default', *La Ley* 2004-A, 993–1012.

Congdon, T. *The Debt Threat* (Basil Blackwell: Oxford 1988).

Corti, A.H.M. 'Algunas reflexiones sobre leyes de facto y derechos adquiridos', *La Ley* 1984-B, 970–973.

Corti, H.G. 'La ley de presupuesto ante la Constitución', Facultad de Derecho Universidad de Buenos Aires, *Lecciones y Ensayos 2002–77*, 35–84.

Coviello, P.J.J. 'La confianza legítima', *El Derecho* 177, 894–922 (1998).

Craig, P.P. *Administrative Law* (Thomson Sweet & Maxwell: London 5th ed. 2003).

Crawford, J. and Olleson, S. 'The nature and forms of international responsibility', in: Malcolm D. Evans (ed.), *International Law* (Oxford University Press: Oxford 2003), 445–472.

Czapliński, W. '*Jus cogens* and the Law of Treaties', in: Tomuschat, C. and Thouvenin, J.-M. (eds.), *The Fundamental Rules of the International Legal Order* (Martinus Nijhoff Publishers: Leiden/Boston 2006), 83–97.

Dalla Vía, A.R. 'El tratamiento constitucional de la deuda externa', *El Derecho Constitucional 2001/2002*, 547–556.

Dalla Vía, A.R. 'Los principios económicos y el crédito público', in: Albanese, S., Dalla Vía, A., Gargarella, R., Hernández, A. and Sabsay, D. *Derecho Constitucional* (Editorial Universidad: Buenos Aires 2004), 269–318.

Davies, A.C.L. '*Ultra vires* problems in government contracts' (2006) 122 *LQR* 96–123.

De Luna, A. 'Remarks', in: Summary Records of the 17th Session, 828th Meeting, [1966] 1 *Yearbook International Law Commission* 39, para. 31.

De Wet, E. 'The prohibition of torture as an international norm of *ius cogens* and its implications for national and customary law', (2004) 15 *EJIL* 97–121.

Delaume, G.R. *Legal Aspects of International Lending and Economic Development* (Oceana Publications: Dobbs Ferry 1967).

Diamond, M. and Naszewski, D. 'Argentina's foreign debt: its origin and consequences', in: Wionczek, M. (ed.), *Politics and Economics of External Debt Crisis. The Latin American Experience* (Westview Press: Boulder and London 1985), 231–276.

Dicey, A.V., et al. *Dicey, Morris and Collins on the Conflict of Laws* (Sweet & Maxwell: London, 14th ed. 2006).

Diez-Picazo, L. and Ponce de León. 'Libertad, responsabilidad contractuales e intereses vitales del deudor', in: Schipani, S. (ed.), *Debito Internazionale. Principi Generali del Diritto,* (Cedam: Padova 1995), 195–201.

Dornbusch, R. and de Pablo, J.C. 'Chapter 1: Argentina', in: Sachs, J.D. (ed.), *Developing Country Debt and Economic Performance, Volume 2: Country Studies – Argentina, Bolivia, Brazil, Mexico* (University of Chicago Press: Chicago and London 1989), 41–155.

Dreyfus, G. 'Me equivoqué al aplaudir el golpe', *Clarín,* 14 March 2006.

Eide, A. 'Economic, social and cultural rights as human rights', in: Eide, A., Krause, C. and Rosas, A. (eds), *Economic, Social and Cultural Rights* (Martinus Nijhoff Publishers: Dordrecht, Boston, London, 2nd ed. 2001), 9–28.

Ekmekdjian, M. A. *Tratado de Derecho Constitucional,* Volume 1 (Depalma: Buenos Aires 1993); Volume 2 (Depalma: Buenos Aires 1994); Volume 3 (Depalma: Buenos Aires 1995); Volume 4 (Depalma: Buenos Aires 1997).

Elespe, D.R. 'Post default. Análisis general de ciertas consecuencias y reflexiones post canje de la deuda pública', in: Elespe, D.R. (ed.), *El Canje de la Deuda,* (2005a) *La Ley* 2005, 3–26.

Elespe, D.R. 'Reestructuración de la deuda argentina', (2005b) *La Ley* 2005, 8 June 2005, 7–8.

Elsner, A. 'US considering "odious debt" doctrine for Iraq', *Reuters,* 29 April 2003, lists.mutualaid.org/pipermail/mgj-discuss/2003-April/002081.html.

Espeche Gil, M.A. 'La *Doctrina Espeche*. Ilicitud del alza unilateral de los intereses de la deuda externa' (2004), www.derecho.uba.ar/institucional/proyectos/dext_espeche.pdf.

Feilchenfeld, E.H. *Public Debts and State Succession* (The Macmillan Company: New York 1931).

Feinmann, J.P. *La Sangre Derramada* (Booket: Buenos Aires 2006).

Ferrer, A. *¿Puede Argentina pagar su deuda externa?* (El Cid Editor: Buenos Aires 1982).

Ferrer, A. *La Argentina y el Orden Mundial* (Fondo de Cultura Económica: Buenos Aires 2003).

Figueredo, R. *UN-ESC Human Rights Commission, Report of Special Rapporteur* E/CN.4/2000/51.

Fischer-Lescano, A. 'Odious debts und das Weltrecht', *Kritische Justiz* 2003, 225–239.

Fitzmaurice, G.G. 'Third Report on the Law of Treaties, March 18, 1953', Documents of the 10th Session (1958) 2 *Yearbook International Law Commission* 20, U.N. Doc. A/CN.4/115.

Flauss, J.-F. 'Compétence civile universelle et droit international général', in: Tomuschat, C. and Thouvenin, J.-M. (eds.), *The Fundamental Rules of the International Legal Order* (Martinus Nijhoff Publishers: Leiden, Boston 2006), 385–415.

Folz, H.-E. 'State Debts', in: *EPIL,* Volume 4 (North-Holland Elsevier: Amsterdam, London, New York, Oxford, Paris, Shannon, Tokyo 2000), 608-613.

Foorman, J.L. and Jehle, M.E. 'Effects of state and government succession on commercial bank loans to foreign sovereign borrowers' (1982) *University of Illinois Law Review* 9–38.

Ford, C.A. 'Adjudicating *ius cogens*' (1994) 13 *Wisconsin International Law Journal* 145–181.

Fox, G.H. 'The right to political participation in international law', in: Fox, G.H. and Roth, B.R. (eds), *Democratic Governance and International Law*, (Cambridge University Press: Cambridge 2000), 48–90.

Franck, T.M. 'The emerging right to democratic governance' (1992) 86 *AJIL* 46–91.

Franck, T.M. 'Legitimacy and the democratic entitlement', in: Fox, G.H. and Roth, B.R. (eds), *Democratic Governance and International Law* (Cambridge University Press: Cambridge 2000), 25–47.

Frankenberg, G. and Knieper, R. 'Legal problems of the overindebtedness of developing countries: the current relevance of the doctrine of odious debts', (1984) 12 *International Journal of the Sociology of Law* 415–438.

Friedman, E.A. 'Debt Relief in 1999: Only One Step on a Long Journey' (2000) 3 *Yale Human Rights & Development Law Journal* 191–220.

Galasso, N. *De la Banca Baring al FMI. Historia de la Deuda Externa Argentina* (Editorial Colihue: Buenos Aires 2003).

García Lema, A. 'Bases constitucionales y legales del proceso de reestructuración de la deuda pública', *La Ley* 2004-A, 956–971.

García Lema, A. 'Defensas jurídicas contra los bonistas no ingresantes al canje de la deuda externa', in: Elespe, D.R. (ed.), *El Canje de la Deuda* (La Ley Buenos Aires 2005), 36–44.

García-Hamilton Jr., J., Olivares-Caminal, R. and Zenarruza, O.M. 'The required threshold to restructure sovereign debt' (2005) 27 *Loyola L.A. International & Comparative Law Review*, 249–274.

Geiger, R. *Grundgesetz und Völkerrecht* (C.H. Beck: München, 3rd ed. 2002).

Gelli, M.A. 'Cuestiones de la Delegación Legislativa', *El Derecho* 182, 1277–1284 (1999).

Gelli, M.A. 'La convalidación del canje de la deuda pública regida por ley argentina en el caso "Galli"', *La Ley* 2005-C, 27–32.

Gelli, M.A. *Constitución de la Nación Argentina Comentada y Concordada* (La Ley: Buenos Aires, 2nd ed. 2003).

Gelpern, A. 'What Iraq and Argentina might learn from each other' (2005) 6 *Chicago Journal of International Law* 391–414.

Genera, F. 'La doctrina de los propios actos de la administración y sus facultades discrecionales', *Jurisprudencia Argentina* 1994-III-702.

General Assembly Resolution, *Policies of Apartheid of the Government of South Africa: Economic Collaboration with South Africa*, A/RES/31/6.H, 9 November 1976.

General Assembly Resolution, *Policies of Apartheid of the Government of South Africa: Comprehensive and Mandatory Sanctions Against the Racist Regime of South Africa and Imposition, Co-ordination and Strict Monitoring of Measures Against Racist South Africa*, A/RES/44/27 C & D, 22 November 1989.

Gialdino, R.E. 'Derechos humanos y deuda externa', *La Ley* 2003-E, 1468–1481.

Giuliani Fonrouge, C.M. *Derecho Financiero*, Volume 2 (La Ley: Buenos Aires, 9th ed. 2004).

Giuliano, H. 'El magacanje Kirchner, balance y perspectivas', 14 February 2006, http://64.233.187.104/search?q=cache:z1IERoDUZkcJ:www.lafogata.org/06arg/arg2/arg_23-1.htm+giuliano+megacanje+kirchner&hl=es&gl=ar&ct=clnk&cd=5.

Godio, J. *Argentina: En la Crisis está la Solución* (Biblos: Buenos Aires 2002).

Goldschmidt, W. 'La Procuración del Tesoro de la Nación y los préstamos y garantías internacionales', *El Derecho* 96, 845–852 (1982).

Gómez-Pinzón, E. 'State responsibility for external consequences of domestic economic-related acts' (1986) 16 *California Western International Law Journal* 52–89.

González, J.V. *Manual de la Constitución Argentina* (Angel Estrada y Cía: Buenos Aires 1959).

Gordillo, A. *Tratado de Derecho Administrativo*, Volume 3 (Fundación de Derecho Administrativo: Buenos Aires, 5th ed. 2000).

Grammer, C. *Der Tatbestand des Verschwindenlassens einer Person* (Duncker & Humblot: Berlin 2005).

Gros Espiell, H. *Report on the Right to Self-Determination*, E/CN.4/Sub.2/405/rev.1 (1980)

Hagan, S. 'Designing a legal framework to restructure sovereign debt' (2005) 36 *Georgetown Journal of International Law* 299–402.

Hanlon, J. 'Defining "illegitimate debt": when creditors should be liable for improper loans', in: Jochnik, C. and Preston, F.A. (eds), *Sovereign Debt at the Crossroads* (Oxford University Press: Oxford 2006), 109–131.

Harris, D.J. *Cases and Materials on International Law* (Sweet & Maxwell: London, 6th Edition 2004).

Hemmer, H.-R. 'The international debt crisis, its causes and possible solutions', in: Brochert, M. and Schinke, R. (eds), *International Indebtedness* (Routledge: London 1990), 76–85.

Herdegen, M. *Internationales Wirtschaftsrecht* (Verlag C.H. Beck: München, 5th ed. 2005).

Hernández, A. 'Las emergencias y la afectación del orden constitucional y de los derechos', in: Albanese, S., Dalla Vía, A, Gargarella, R., Hernández, A.and Sabsay, D. *Derecho Constitucional*, (Editorial Universidad: Buenos Aires 2004), 319–406.

Heun, W. 'Staatsverschuldung und Grundgesetz', *Die Verwaltung* 1985, 1–28.

Hocsman, H.S. 'El postcanje y la salida del default', in: Elespe, D.R. (ed.), *El Canje de la Deuda* (La Ley: Buenos Aires 2005), 59–60.

Hoeflich, M.H. 'Through a glass darkly: reflections upon the history of the international law of public debt in connection with state succession' (1982) *University of Illinois Law Review* 39–70.

Höfling, W. *Staatsschuldenrecht* (C.F. Müller: Heidelberg 1998).

Hunt, P. 'Relations Between the UN Committee on Economic, Social and Cultural Rights and International Financial Institutions', in: Genugten, W. van, Hunt, P.

and Mathews, S. *World Bank, IMF and Human Rights,* (Wolf Legal Publishers: Nijmegen 2003).

Hunt, P. 'Using rights as a shield' (2002) 6 *Human Rights Law and Practice* 111–116.

Hunt, P. *Reclaiming Social Rights* (Ashgate: Aldershot 1996).

Hyde, C.C. *International Law* Chiefly *as Interpreted and Applied by the United States* (Little, Brown and Company: Boston 1947).

Iguíñiz Echeverría, J. 'La deuda social de los acreedores: aproximaciones a su responsbilidad social', in: Jochnik, C. and Pazmiño Freire, P. (eds.), *Otras caras de la deuda* (Nueva Sociedad: Caracas 2001), 191–215.

IMF Independent Evaluation Office, *Evaluation Report: The IMF and Argentina 1991–2001* (2004), www.imf.org.

Inter-American Commission on Human Rights, *Annual Report 1978*, Part II.

Inter-American Commission on Human Rights, *Report on the Human Rights Situation in Argentina*, OEA/Ser.L/V/II.49, Doc. 19 corr.1, 11 April 1980.

International Law Commission, *Report of the International Law Commission on the work of its thirty-third session* (4 May–24 July 1980, Document A/36/10, (1981) 2 *YB ILC*, part 2.

International Law Commission, *Report of the International Law Commission*, GA 56th Session, Supp 10 (A/56/10) (2001).

Ipsen, K. *Völkerrecht* (C.H. Beck: München, 5th ed. 2004).

Jain, A.K. 'Dictatorships, democracy and the debt crisis' (1993), www.odiousdebts.org/odiousdebts/index.cfm?DSP=content&ContentID=10354.

Janson, B. 'Begrenzung der Staatsverschuldung durch Art. 115 GG – Wende in der Haushaltspolitik durch das BverfG?' *Zeitschrift für Rechtspolitik* 1983, 139–146.

Janssen, A. 'Anmerkung zu BVerfGE DVB1 1989, 610', *Deutsches Verwaltungsblatt* (1989), 618–619.

Jèze, G.P. A. *Cours de science des finances et de législation financière française* (M. Giard: Paris 1922).

Jochnik, C. 'Nuevos caminos legales para enfrentar la deuda: una petición a la Corte Mundial', in: Varios Autores, *Un Continente contra la Deuda: Perspectivas y Enfoques para la Acción* (Ediciones ABYA-YALA: Quito 1999), 127–155.

Joseph, S. *Corporations and Transnational Human Rights Litigation* (Hart Publishing: Oxford 2004).

Juliá, C. *La Memoria de la Deuda* (Biblos: Buenos Aires 2002).

Kadelbach, S. '*Jus cogens*, obligations *erga omnes* and other rules – the identification of fundamental norms', in: Tomuschat, C. and Thouvenin, J.-M. (eds.), *The Fundamental Rules of the International Legal Order*, (Martinus Nijhoff Publishers: Leiden, Boston 2006), 21–40.

Kadelbach, S. *Zwingendes Völkerrecht* (Duncker & Humblot: Berlin 1992).

Kaiser, J. and Queck, A. 'Verabscheuungswürdige Schulden – verabscheuungswürdige Gläubiger – Die deutschen Forderungen an den Irak nach Saddam Hussein' (2004), www.erlassjahr.de/content/publikationen/dokumente/is_200402_irakstudie.doc.

Kanenguiser, M. *La Maldita Herencia* (Editorial Sudamericana: Buenos Aires 2003).

Khalfan, A. 'Sites and strategic legal options for addressing illegitimate debt', in: CISDL Working Paper: *Advancing the Odious Debt Doctrine*, Montreal (2003), www.cisdl.org/pdf/debtentire.pdf.

King, J. 'The doctrine of odious debt under international law: definition, evidence and issues concerning application', in: CISDL Working Paper: *Advancing the Odious Debt Doctrine*, Montreal (2003), www.cisdl.org/pdf/debtentire.pdf.

Kirchhof, F. 'Der notwendige Ausstieg aus der Staatsverschuldung', *Deutsches Verwaltungsblatt* 2002, 1569–1578.

Kirchhof, P. 'The public debt, democratic principles and the rule of law', in: Dicke, D.C. (ed.), *Foreign Debts in the Present and a New International Economic Order*, (University Press: Fribourg Switzerland, 1986), 339–360.

Knieper, R. 'Transfer juristischer Techniken in die Diskussion um die Verschuldung der Dritten Welt', *Verfassung und Recht in Übersee 1988*, 448–454.

Kremer, M. and Jayachandran, S. 'Odious Debt' (2002), www.imf.org/external/np/res/seminars/2002/poverty/mksj.pdf.

Krueger, A. 'Crisis prevention and resolution: lessons from Argentina,' Paper at Conference on "The Argentina Crisis", Cambridge, 17 July (2002a), www.imf.org/external/np/speeches/2002/071702.htm.

Krueger, A. 'Sovereign debt restructuring and dispute resolution', www.imf.org/external/np/speeches/2002/060602.htm, 6 June (2002b).

Krugman, P. 'Private capital flows to problem debtors', in: Sachs, J.D. (ed.), *Developing Country Debt and Economic Performance*, Volume 1: *The International Financial System*, (University of Chicago Press: Chicago and London 1989), 299–330.

Kulfas, M. and Schorr, M. *La deuda externa argentina* (Fundación OSDE-CIEPP: Buenos Aires 2003).

Lappin, R. *Kreditäre Finanzierung des Staates unter dem Grundgesetz* (Duncker & Humblot: Berlin 1994).

Leader, S. 'Human rights, risks, and new strategies for global investment' (2006) 9 *Journal of International Economic Law* 657–705.

Leyendecker, L. *Auslandsverschuldung und Völkerrecht* (Peter Lang: Frankfurt am Main, Bern, New York, Paris 1988).

Lichtenstein, C.C. 'The U.S. response to the international debt crisis: The International Lending Supervision Act of 1983' (1985) 25 *Virginia Journal of International Law* 401–435.

Lischinsky, B. 'The puzzle of Argentina's debt problem: virtual dollar creation?' in: FONDAD, *The Crisis that was not Prevented: Argentina, the IMF and Globalisation* (2003), 81–100, www.fondad.org.

Lothian, T. 'The criticism of the Third-World debt and the revision of legal doctrine' (1995) 13 *Wisconsin International Law Journal* 421-470.

Loughlin, M. 'Innovative financing in local government: the limits of legal instrumentalism. Part 2', (1991) *PL* 568–599.

Lozada, S.M. *La Deuda Externa y el Desguace del Estado Nacional* (Ediciones Jurídicas Cuyo: Mendoza 2002).

Maastricht Guidelines on Violations of Economic, Social and Cultural Rights, Maastricht, January 22–26 1997, wwwescr-net.org/resources_more/resources_show.htm?doc_id=245803.

208 *Unconstitutional Regimes and the Validity of Sovereign Debt*

MacLean, R.G. 'Legal aspects of the external debt' (1989-II) 214 *Recueil des cours* 43.

Machinea, J.L. and Sommers, J.F. 'El manejo de la deuda externa en condiciones de crisis de balanza de pagos: La moratoria argentina de 1988–89', Documento CEDES/59 (1990), www.cedes.org.

Mairal, H.A. 'Issues arising from the legal and constitutional validity of the debt under the debtor's own law', in: Sassoon, D.M. and Bradlow, D.D. (eds), *Judicial Enforcement of International Debt Obligations* (International Law Institute: Washington 1987), 147–173.

Mairal, H.A. *La Doctrina de los Propios Actos y la Administración Pública* (Depalma: Buenos Aires 1988).

Mancina, E.F. 'Sinners in the hands of an angry God: resurrecting the odious debt doctrine in international law' (2004) 36 *George Washington International Law Review* 1239–1262.

Marienhoff, M.S. *Tratado de Derecho Administrativo*, Volume III-A (Abeledo-Perrot: Buenos Aires, 6th ed. 1997).

Marks, S. 'International law, democracy and the end of history', in: Fox, G.H. and Roth, B.R. (eds), *Democratic Governance and International Law* (Cambridge University Press: Cambridge 2000), 532–566.

Martínez-Alier, J. 'Deuda ecológica vs deuda externa: una perspectiva latinoamericana', in: Jochnik, C. and Pazmiño Freire, P. (eds.), *Otras caras de la deuda* (Nueva Sociedad: Caracas 2001), 163–180.

Mastrorilli, C. 'Atribuciones del Congreso en materia de deuda externa', *La Ley* 1984-C, 831–836.

Maunz, D. *Grundgesetz Kommentar*, Band V, Artikel 70–99 (C.H. Beck: München 2005).

McBeth, A. 'Holding the purse strings: the continuing evolution of human rights law and the potential liability of the finance industry for human rights abuses' (2005) 23 *Netherlands Quarterly of Human Rights* 7–34.

Menon, P.K. *The Succession of States in Respect to Treaties, State Property, Archives and Debts* (The Edwin Mellen Press: Lewiston, Queenstown, Lampeter 1992).

Meron, T. 'Repudiation of *ultra vires* state contracts and the international responsibility of states', (1957) 6 *ICLQ* 273–289.

Michalowski, S. 'Human rights in times of economic crises: the example of Argentina', in: Brownsword, R. (ed.) *Global Governance and the Search for Justice, Volume 4: Human Rights* (Hart Publishing: Oxford 2004), 33–51.

Michalowski, S. 'Repayment of sovereign debts from a legal perspective – the example of Argentina', in: Dine, J. and Fagan, A. (eds.) *Human Rights and Capitalism*, (Edward Elgar Publishing: Cheltenham, Northampton 2006), 303–329.

Mitchell, S. 'The charade of unaffordable debt cancellation', www.jubilee2000uk. org, (2004).

Montes de Oca, M.A. *Lecciones de Derecho Constitucional*, Volume 2, (Menéndez: Buenos Aires 1927).

Monti, L.M. 'Los contratos administrativos y el enriquecimiento sin causa', *Revista de Derecho Administrativo* (2001), 345.

Moore, J.B. *A Digest of International Law*, Volume 1 (Government Printing Office: Washington 1906).

Morello, A.M. 'Suspensión del pago de la deuda pública. Fundamentos jurídicos', *El Derecho* 196, 839–846 (2002).

Morgan-Foster, J. 'The relationship of IMF structural adjustment programs to economic, social and cultural rights, the Argentine case revisited' (2003) 24 *Michigan Journal of International Law* 577–646.

Morrison, F.L. and Hudec, R.E. 'Judicial protection of individual rights under the Foreign Trade Laws of the United States', in: Hilf, M. and Petersmann, E.-U. (eds.), *National Constitutions and International Economic Law* (Kluwer: Deventer, Boston 1993).

Mudho, B. *Report on Effects of structural adjustment policies and foreign debt on the full enjoyment of human rights, particularly economic, social and cultural rights*, E/CN.4/2003/10.

Murphy, S.D. 'Democratic legitimacy and the recognition of states and governments', in: Fox, H. and Roth, B.R. (eds), *Democratic Governance and International Law* (Cambridge University Press: Cambridge 2000) 123–154.

Mussa, M. *Argentina y el FMI: del Triunfo a la Tragedia* (Planeta: Buenos Aires 2002).

Natanson, José. 'Superpoderes y decretos en América Latina', *Página 12*, 9 July 2006, 8.

Naylor, R.T. *Hot Money and the Politics of Debt* (Black Rose Books: Montreal, London, New York 1994)

Negretto, G.L. 'Un criterio muy particular: la doctrina de facto de la Corte Suprema de Justicia', *El Derecho* 144, 833–842 (1991).

Nino, C. S. 'Una nueva estrategia para el tratamiento de las normas "de facto"', *La Ley* 1983-D, 935–946.

Nino, C.S. *Un país al margen de la ley* (Ariel: Buenos Aires, 3rd ed. 2005).

Nitti, F. *Principios de la Ciencia de las Finanzas* (Talleres Gráficos Argentinos: Buenos Aires 1931).

Norwegian Ministry of Foreign Affairs, 'Debt relief for development. A plan of action', www.regjeringen.no/upload/kilde/ud/rap/2004/0225/ddd/pdfv/217380-debtplan. pdf (June 2004).

O'Connell, D.P. 'Secured and unsecured debts in the law of state succession' (1951) 28 *British Yearbook of International Law* 204–219.

O'Connell, D.P. *The Law of State Succession* (Cambridge University Press: Cambridge 1956).

Okeke, C.N. 'The debt burden: an African perspective' (2001) 35 *International Lawyer* 1489–1505.

Olmos Gaona, A. *La Deuda Odiosa* (Ediciones Continente: Buenos Aires 2005)

Olmos, A. *Todo Lo Que Usted Quiso Saber Sobre La Deuda Externa Y Siempre Se Lo Ocultaron* (Ediciones Continente: Buenos Aires, 4th ed. 2004).

Oloka-Onyango, J. 'Beyond the rhetoric: reinvigorating the struggle for economic and social rights in Africa' (1995) 26 *California Western International Law Journal* 1–71.

Oschmann, F. *Calvo-Doktrin und Calvo-Klauseln* (Verlag Recht und Wirtschaft: Heidelberg 1993).

Padilla, M. 'Un mecanismo de control parlamentario: el examen y aprobación de la cuenta de inversión', *La Ley* 1985-A, 826–836.

Palazzo, E.L. 'Caducidad de las delegaciones legislativas', *El Derecho* 182, 1263–1271 (1999).

Parker, K. and Neylon, L.B. '*Ius cogens*: compelling the law of human rights', (1989) 12 *Hastings International and Comparative Law Review* 411–463.

Parlamento Latinoamericano, Consejo Consultivo, Report Version VII, November 2001, www.bacyam.com.ar/contribuciones/espeche_gil1.doc.

Paulus, A.L. '*Ius cogens* in a time of hegemony and fragmentation' (2005) 74 *Nordic Journal of International Law* 297–334.

Paulus, C. '"Odious Debts" vs. Debt Trap: A Realistic Help?' (2005) 31 *Brooklyn Journal of International Law* 83–102 (2005a).

Paulus, C. 'Stellen "odious debts" eine Rechtsfigur dar?' *Wertpapiermitteilungen* (2005), 53–60 (2005b).

Payer, C. *Lent and Lost – Foreign Credit and Third World Development* (Zed Books Ltd: London, New Jersey 1991).

Pazmiño Freire, P. and Kumin, A. 'Deuda externa: un desafío para los derechos humanos', in: Jochnik, C. and Pazmiño Freire, P. (eds.), *Otras caras de la deuda* (Nueva Sociedad: Caracas 2001), 143–161.

Peine, F.-J. *Allgemeines Verwaltungsrecht* (C.F. Müller: Heidelberg, München, Landsberg, Berlin, 8th ed. 2006).

Pfeiffer, T. 'Zahlungskrisen ausländischer Staaten im deutschen und internationalen Rechtsverkehr', *Zeitschrift für vergleichende Rechtswissenschaft* 102 (2003), 141–194.

Plan Fénix, 'La Argentina y su deuda externa: Enfrentar las presiones para atender la deuda social' (2004), www.econ.uba.ar/planfenix/index2.htm.

Pogge, T. *World Poverty and Human Rights* (Polity Press: Cambridge 2005).

Queck, A. *Die Auslandsverschuldung des Irak und die "Doctrine of Odious Debts"*, MA dissertation (Leipzig 2004), unpublished.

Quiroga Lavié, H. *Constitución de la Nación Argentina Comentada* (Zavalia: Buenos Aires, 3rd ed. 2000).

Raffer, K. 'Internationalizing US municipal insolvency: a fair, equitable, and efficient way to overcome a debt overhang' (2005) 6 *Chicago Journal of International Law* 361–378.

Ramasastry, A. 'Secrets and lies? Swiss banks and international human rights', (1998) 31 *Vanderbilt Journal of Transnational Law* 325–456.

Ramos, L.I. '¿Cómo es posible que uno de los países mas ricos del mundo esté al borde de la quiebra?' (2002), www.observatoriodeuda.org.

Randall, K.C. 'Universal jurisdiction under international law' (1988) 66 *Texas Law Review* 785–841.

Rapoport, M. *Historia Económica, Política y Social de la Argentina (1880–2000)*, (Ediciones Macchi: Buenos Aires 2000).

Rapoport, M. and Musacchio, A. 'La deuda externa argentina en el largo plazo', *El Correo de Económicas – No 1 No.2 – Revista de Economía*, Universidad y Ciencias Sociales, (2005) 37–61.

Rapoport, M. *Tiempos de Crisis, Vientos de Cambio* (Grupo Editorial Norma: Buenos Aires 2002).

Rassmussen, R.K. 'Integrating a theory of the state into sovereign debt restructuring' (2004) 53 *Emory Law Journal* 1159–1187.

Reina, V. 'Iraq's delictual and contractual liabilities: would politics or international law provide for better resolution of successor state responsibility?' (2004) 22 *Berkeley Journal of International Law* 583–614.

Reinisch, A. 'Anmerkung zu LG Frankfurt a.M.', *Juristenzeitung* (2003), 1013–1016.

Reinisch, A. 'Debt restructuring and state responsibility issues', in: Carreau, D. and Shaw, M.N. (eds), *La Dette Exterieure, The External Debt* (Martinus Nijhoff Publishers: Dordrecht, Boston, London 1995).

Richard, E.H. 'Problemática de la deuda externa y la mundalización financiera', paper given at the Congreso Iberoamericano de Academias de Derecho, Zaragoza 2005.

Rivera, J.C. 'Como debe ejercerse el control de razonabilidad de leyes que incursionan en materia socio-económica', *La Ley* 2002-D, 1116–1137.

Rodríguez Galán, A. and Girardi Gutiérrez, E.M. 'Operaciones de crédito público externo atribución presidencial', *La Ley* 1997-C, 1268–1279.

Rosas, A. and Scheinin, M. 'Implementation mechanisms and remedies', in: Eide, A., Krause, C. and Rosas, A. (eds), *Economic, Social and Cultural Rights* (Martinus Nijhoff Publishers: Dordrecht, Boston, London, 2nd ed. 2001), 425–453.

Rossi, M. 'Verschuldung in extremer Haushaltsnotlage', *Deutsches Verwaltungsblatt* 2005, 269–276.

Roth, B.R. 'Evaluating democratic progress', in: Fox, G.H. and Roth, B.R. (eds), *Democratic Governance and International Law* (Cambridge University Press: Cambridge 2000), 493–516.

Rozakis, C.L. *The Concept of* Jus Cogens *in the Law of Treaties* (North-Holland Publishing Company: Amsterdam, New York, Oxford 1976).

Ruffert, M. 'Special jurisdiction of the ICJ in the case of infringements of fundamental rules of the international legal order?' in: Tomuschat, C. and Thouvenin, J.-M. (eds.), *The Fundamental Rules of the International Legal Order* (Martinus Nijhoff Publishers: Leiden, Boston 2006), 295–310.

Ruiz Díaz, H. and Toussaint, E. 'Deuda externa y auditoría' (2004), www.cadtm.org/IMG/pdf/CEDESauditoria.pdf.

Sabsay, D.A. and Onaindia, J.M. *La Constitución de los Argentinos* (Errepar: Buenos Aires, 6th ed. 2004).

Sabsay, D. 'El poder ejecutivo', in: Albanese, S., Dalla Vía, A., Gargarella, R., Hernández, A. and Sabsay, D. *Derecho Constitucional*, (Editorial Universidad: Buenos Aires 2004), 589–631.

Sachs, J.D. 'Introduction', in: Sachs, J.D. (ed.), *Developing Country Debt and Economic Performance, Volume 1: The International Financial System* (University of Chicago Press: Chicago and London 1989), 1–35.

Sack, A.N. *Les Effets des Transformations des États sur leurs Dettes Publiques et autres Obligations Financières* (Receuil Sirey: Paris 1927).

Sadi. 33rd meeting of the Committee for Economic, Social and Cultural Rights on 25 November 1999, E/C.12/1999/SR.33.

Sarcevic, P. 'Two approaches to the debt problem: A) Adjustment of loan agreements (de lege lata), B) Strengthening of international monetary soft law (de lege ferenda)', in: Dicke, D.C. (ed.), *Foreign Debts in the Present and a New International Economic Order* (University Press: Fribourg Switzerland, 1986), 130–156.

Schvarzer, J. *Argentina 1976–81: El endeudamiento externo como pivote de la especulación financiera* (Cuadernos del Bimestre: Buenos Aires 1983).

SEC (Security and Exchange Commission) prospectus, 'Amendment No.3 to Registration Statement under Schedule B under the Securities Act of 1983, The Republic of Argentina (registrant)', (September 2004)

Security Council Resolution, *The Question of South Africa*, S/RES/418, 4 November 1977.

Shaw, M.N. *International Law* (Cambridge University Press: Cambridge, 5th ed. 2003).

Silva (h.), R.E. 'El Plan Brady para la República Argentina', *El Derecho* 148, 837–848 (1992).

Simms, A. 'Ecological debt – the economic possibilities for our grandchildren', in: C. Jochnik and F.A. Preston (eds), *Sovereign Debt at the Crossroads* (Oxford University Press: Oxford 2006), 83–108.

Sinclair, I. *The Vienna Convention on the Law of Treaties* (Manchester University Press: Manchester, 2nd ed. 1984).

Skogly, S. *The Human Rights Obligations of the World Bank and the International Monetary Fund* (Cavendish: London, Sydney 2001).

Sola, Juan Vicente. 'La Constitución y la renegociación de la deuda pública', in: Elespe, D.R. (ed.), *El Canje de la Deuda* (La Ley: Buenos Aires 2005), 32–35.

Sornarajah, M. *The International Law on Foreign Investment*, (Cambridge University Press: Cambridge, 2nd ed. 2004).

Steffan, H.-D. 'Perspectivas de desendeudamiento externo desde el derecho internacional', in: Jochnik, C. and Pazmiño Freire, P. (eds.), *Otras caras de la deuda* (Nueva Sociedad: Caracas 2001), 117–130.

Steiner, H. and Alston, P. *International Human Rights in Context*, (Oxford University Press: Oxford, 2nd ed. 2000).

Stiglitz, Joseph. 'Ethics, market and government failure, and globalization: perspectives on debt and finance', in: Jochnik, C. and Preston, F.A. (eds), *Sovereign Debt at the Crossroads* (Oxford University Press: Oxford 2006), 158–173.

Stiglitz, J. *Globalisation and its Discontents* (Allen Lane: London 2002).

Stone, P. *EU Private International Law*, (Edward Elgar: Cheltenham, Northampton 2006).

Talmon, S. 'The duty not to "recognize as lawful" a situation created by illegal use of force or other serious breaches of a *jus cogens* obligation: an obligation without real substance?' in: Tomuschat, C. and Thouvenin, J.-M. (eds.), *The Fundamental Rules of the International Legal Order* (Martinus Nijhoff Publishers: Leiden, Boston 2006), 99–125.

Tams, C.J. *Enforcing Obligations* Erga Omnes *in International Law* (Cambridge University Press: Cambridge 2005).

Tavernier, P. 'L'identification des règles fondamentales, un problème résolu?' in: Tomuschat, C. and Thouvenin, J.-M. (eds.), *The Fundamental Rules of the International Legal Order* (Martinus Nijhoff Publishers: Leiden, Boston 2006), 1–20

Thomas, B. 'The doctrine of odious debts and international public policy: assessing the options', in: CISDL Working Paper: *Advancing the Odious Debt Doctrine*, Montreal (2003), www.cisdl.org/pdf/debtentire.pdf.

Thompson, M. 'Finders weepers losers keepers: *United States of America v Steinmetz*, the doctrine of state succession, maritime finds, and the bell of the C.S.S. Alabama' (1996) 28 *Connecticut Law Review* 479–554.

Thompson, R. 'El presupuesto y su control de constitucionalidad', *El Derecho* 110, 937–942 (1985).

Tietje, C. 'Die Argentinien-Anleihen aus rechtlicher Sicht: Staatsanleihen und Staateninsolvenz', *Beiträge zum transnationalen Wirtschaftsrech*t 37 (2005), 5–23.

Tomuschat, C. 'Reconceptualizing the debate on *jus cogens* and obligations *erga omnes* – concluding observations', in: Tomuschat, C. and Thouvenin, J.-M. (eds.), *The Fundamental Rules of the International Legal Order* (Martinus Nijhoff Publishers: Leiden, Boston 2006), 425–436.

Toussaint, E. 'Impagable, incobrable, injusta: quebrar el círculo infernal de la deuda', in: Jochnik, C. and Pazmiño Freire, P. (eds.), *Otras caras de la deuda* (Nueva Sociedad: Caracas 2001), 191–215.

Toussaint, E. 'La dette odieuse de l'Irak', 16 May 2006, www.cadtm.org/article. php3?id_article=1884.

Toussaint, E. *Your Money or Your Life! The Tyranny of Global Finance* (Pluto Press: London 1999).

Udombana, N.J. 'The summer has ended and we are not saved: Towards a transformative agenda for Africa's development' (2005) 7 *San Diego International Law Journal* 5–60.

UN Commission on Human Rights, Resolution 1999/22, 23 April 1999.

UN Committee on Economic, Social and Cultural Rights, Concluding Observations: Argentina 08/12/99, E/C.12/1/Add.38.

UN Committee on Economic, Social and Cultural Rights, Country Report Argentina, E/C.12/1999/11.

UN Committee on Economic, Social and Cultural Rights, General Comment No.3 (1990): The nature of state parties' obligations, E/1999/23.

UN Committee on Economic, Social and Cultural Rights, General Comment No.14 (2000): The right to the highest attainable standard of health, E/C.12/2000/4.

UN Committee on Economic, Social and Cultural Rights, General Comment No. 15 (2002): The right to water, E/C.12/2002/11.

Valdés, S.P. 'Orígenes de la crisis de la deuda: ¿Nos sobreendeudamos o nos prestaron en exceso?', *Revista de Estudios Públicos*, N° 33 (1989), 135–174.

Valdez, O.A. 'Responsabilidad del estado por su actividad financiera', *La Ley* 2004-A, 972–992.

Van Schaack, B. 'With all deliberate speed: civil human rights litigation as a tool for change' (2004) 57 *Vanderbilt Law Review* 2305–2348.

Vanossi. 'La gestión constitucional de la deuda pública externa II', *La Nación*, 27 May 1985, 7.

Verdross, A. and Simma, B. *Universelles Völkerrecht* (Duncker & Humblot: Berlin 3rd ed. 1984).

Villegas, H.B. *Curso de finanzas, derecho financiero y tributario* (Astrea: Buenos Aires 2002).

Villegas, M., Bruno, E. and Piaggio, L. 'Los derechos de los inversores argentinos frente a la propuesta de reestructuración', *La Ley* 2004-A, 1025–1046.

von Münch, I. and Kunig-Rojahn, P. (eds), *Grundgesetz-Kommentar*, Band 2, Artikel 20–69 (C.H. Beck Verlag: München, 5th ed. 2001).

Vreedenburgh, S.T. 'The Saddam oil contracts and what can be done' (2004) 2 *DePaul Business & Commercial Law Journal* 559–592.

Wabnitz, H.-W. 'Islamic Banking und Entwicklungskredite: Lösung der Schuldenkrise?' *Kreditwesen* 1986, 662–664.

Wade, Sir W. and Forsyth, C. *Administrative Law* (Oxford University Press: Oxford, 9th ed. 2004).

Wälde, T. 'The sanctity of debt and insolvent countries: defences of debtors' in: Sassoon, D.M. and Bradlow, D.D. (eds), *Judicial Enforcement of International Debt Obligations* (International Law Institute: Washington 1987), 119–145.

Wälde, T. 'The Serbian Loans Cases – a precedent for investment treaty protection of foreign debt?', in: Weiler,T. (ed.), *International Investment Law and Arbitration: Leading Cases from the ICSID, NAFTA, Bilateral Treaties and Customary International Law* (Cameron May: London 2005), 383–424.

Walsh, R. 'Open Letter to the Military Junta', in: Link, D. (ed.), *El Violento Oficio de Escribir* (Planeta: Buenos Aires 1995).

Warbrick, C. 'States and recognition in international law', in: Evans, M.D. (ed.), *International Law* (Oxford University Press: Oxford 2003), 205–267.

Wendt, R. and Elicker, M. 'Staatsverschuldung und intertemporäre Lastengerechtigkeit', *Deutsches Verwaltungsblatt* 2001, 497–504.

Wetzel, R.G. and Rauschning, D. *The Vienna Convention on the Law of Treaties* (Alfred Metzner Verlag: Frankfurt am Main 1978).

Williams, P. and Harris, J. 'State succession to debts and assets: the modern law and policy' (2001) *Harvard International Law Journal* 355–417.

Wood, P. *Law and Practice of International Finance* (Clark Boardman Company Ltd.: New York 1986).

Woodward, D. *Debt, Adjustment and Poverty in Developing Countries*, 2 volumes (Pinter Publishers: London 1992).

World Bank, 'A World Bank Country Study: Economic Memorandum on Argentina', Washington 1985).

Zafra Espinosa de los Monteros, R. *La Deuda Externa – Aspectos Jurídicos del Endeudamiento Internacional* (Secretariado de Publicaciones Universidad de Sevilla: Sevilla 2001).

Zarini, H.J. *Derecho Constitucional* (Editorial Astrea: Buenos Aires, 2nd ed. 1999).

Index

For Product Safety Concerns and Information please contact our EU
representative GPSR@taylorandfrancis.com
Taylor & Francis Verlag GmbH, Kaufingerstraße 24, 80331 München, Germany

www.ingramcontent.com/pod-product-compliance
Lightning Source LLC
Chambersburg PA
CBHW070408270326
41926CB00014B/2749

9 781138 264564